Baseball and the Bottom Line
in World War II

WITHDRAWN

D0881498

Baseball and the Bottom Line in World War II

Gunning for Profits on the Home Front

JEFF OBERMEYER

Foreword by Michael S. Neiberg

McFarland & Company, Inc., Publishers

Jefferson, North Carolina, and London

LIBRARY OF CONGRESS CATALOGUING-IN-PUBLICATION DATA

Obermeyer, Jeff.
    Baseball and the bottom line in World War II : gunning
for profits on the home front / Jeff Obermeyer ; foreword
by Michael S. Neiberg.
        p.   cm.
    Includes bibliographical references and index.

    ISBN 978-0-7864-7043-3
    softcover : acid free paper ∞

    1. Baseball — United States — History — 20th century.
2. Baseball — United States — Management.   3. World War,
1939–1945 — United States.   4. United States — Social life and
customs — 20th century.   I. Title.
GV863.A1O25 2013
796.357′64097309044 — dc23   2013024267

BRITISH LIBRARY CATALOGUING DATA ARE AVAILABLE

© 2013 Jeff Obermeyer. All rights reserved

*No part of this book may be reproduced or transmitted in any form
or by any means, electronic or mechanical, including photocopying
or recording, or by any information storage and retrieval system,
without permission in writing from the publisher.*

Cover illustration by Ronald Norman McLeod (Pictures Now)

Manufactured in the United States of America

*McFarland & Company, Inc., Publishers
    Box 611, Jefferson, North Carolina 28640
    www.mcfarlandpub.com*

For all those who heed the call to service

Table of Contents

Foreword by
Michael S. Neiberg

Taking aim at sacred cows is never easy, especially when those cows are as sacred to Americans as baseball and the nobility of our nation's collective effort in World War II. We tend to think of Bob Feller, who asked to be sent into combat, and Ted Williams, who fought not only in World War II but in Korea as well. That these great players put their lives at risk and their careers on hold speaks volumes about the sacrifices of that generation or, perhaps more accurately, the challenges that the World War II generation faced.

At least since Paul Fussell, himself a veteran of the war, decried the "Disneyfication" of World War II in his 1989 book *Wartime*, scholars have tried to add some nuance to the myths of the war. The iconography of "the Greatest Generation" has made such efforts more difficult, as have the ambiguity and frustrations of America's wars since 1945. It's not that the World War II generation is undeserving of the lavish praise and admiration; indeed, their accomplishments are still awe-inspiring decades later. It's more that we have painted the history of World War II in such black and white terms that it is sometimes hard to see the complexity and the humanity of the people of those critical years.

So it also is with baseball. We idolize our athletes, even those we never saw play the game. I was raised on the tales not just of my uncle who fought in Guadalcanal but, growing up in Pittsburgh, of Roberto Clemente. Although I was born in 1969, my relatives constantly talked to me about Clemente as if I had watched him play his entire career. Even today Roberto's widow, Vera Clemente, can receive standing ovations in Pittsburgh so long that the game gets delayed. Roberto was that big in Pittsburgh. Our heroes, of course, sometimes fall from grace, as players from Joe Jackson to Roger Clemens and Barry Bonds have proved.

What Jeff Obermeyer does in this excellent book is not so much destroy the sacred cows of World War II and baseball as contextualize them. He brings to life the events of these years and shows how much more complicated reality was than the myths would suggest. In doing so he humanizes the men and women of the World War II years. They may not all have been the idols we have in our imaginations, but their complexity only makes them that much more interesting. So turn down the sound on the game and start reading.

Michael S. Neiberg is a professor of history in the Department of National Security and Strategy at the U.S. Army War College. He is the author or editor of more than a dozen books and dozens of articles. His work focuses on the era of the two world wars.

Preface

The origins of this book are, to me, in many ways as murky as the origins of baseball itself. I could simply point to the capstone paper I wrote as the final stage in obtaining my master's degree from Norwich University in 2009 as the inspiration for this project. "War Games: The Business of Baseball during World War II" was not the traditional paper one would expect to see as part of a degree program in military history, and I was fortunate that John Grenier, the "Capstone Czar" of Norwich, saw some promise in my thesis proposal and let me run with it; in fact, he already had the perfect person in mind to act as my advisor — long-suffering Pirates fan and military historian Michael Neiberg.

But my interest in baseball history goes back much further. I could just as easily point to other moments that were essential in putting me on the path to this book. I could make a case for the rush I got the first time I picked up a copy of the *Baseball Research Journal* and realized that scholarly research and writing about baseball really existed, and was not just some fantasy. That find at a local bookstore in 1995 led me immediately to join the Society for American Baseball Research and begin trying to do meaningful research of my own in my spare time. The romantic in me prefers to go back to the summer of 1977, when I was six years old and walked to the local convenience store with my dad to get baseball cards. Living in Philadelphia at the time, I was a die-hard Phillies fan and my favorite player was Greg Luzinski, the huge left fielder who was known for his monstrous home runs. I still remember sitting on the front steps, opening those packs, and coming across that elusive 1977 Topps card of my favorite player, an action photo showing him at the completion of another of his huge swings. I was so excited as I ran up to my dad to show him the card. Just as today I will be excited to show him this finished book for the first time.

* * *

In refining the thesis for "War Games" I reviewed the literature on baseball during World War II, which is extensive. Baseball during the war is covered as parts of broader biographical and historical works, and also in books and articles exclusively devoted to the topic. Many secondary sources focus on the game on the field during the war, and the impact of the draft on baseball. Bill Gilbert's *They Also Served: Baseball and the Home Front, 1941–1945* (1992), William B. Mead's *Baseball Goes to War: Stars Don Khaki, 4-Fs Vie for Pennant* (1998), and David Finoli's *For the Good of the Country: World War II Baseball in the Major and Minor Leagues* (2002) admirably cover this topic, focusing on the game and its players. Some researchers broadened their view to consider baseball as part of the American social environment and how it contributed to the wartime experience, most notably Richard Goldstein, whose *Spartan Seasons: How Baseball Survived the Second World War* (1980) provides an excellent overview (even though its omission of source notes frustrates). More recently some authors looked deeper into the relationship between baseball, its players, and the military. Steven R. Bullock's *Playing for Their Nation: Baseball and the American Military during World War II* (2004) stands out among these for the depth of the author's research and his heavy use (and careful citation of) primary source material. Wanda Ellen Wakefield's *Playing to Win: Sports and the American Military, 1898–1945* (1997), while not devoted exclusively to baseball, is another well-researched work that takes a broad view of the interrelationships between sports, the military, and gender roles.

Some works delve into the business aspects of baseball during World War II. One of the early scholarly works to explore this topic within a broader examination of the game is David Q. Voigt's *American Baseball, Volume II: From the Commissioners to the Continental Expansion* (1970). G. Edward White's *Creating the National Pastime: Baseball Transforms Itself, 1903–1953* (1996) is another excellent piece of scholarship. These two books in particular provided me with examples of what was possible by stepping outside of a simple recounting of events.

In approaching "War Games" I did not look to simply describe *what* occurred during the war but instead *why* certain things happened the way they did. My early research showed that those involved in baseball waved the flag of patriotism in an effort to ensure its continuation, but as I looked deeper into the primary sources a different picture began to emerge, one of a sometimes ruthless business willing to secure its own survival by any means necessary. This was the direction I took in "War Games," and even after its completion and my graduation I continued to examine some of the stories that received only superficial treatment and that appeared to warrant additional research. The story of minor leaguer Al Niemiec provides a useful example. Niemiec, a returning veteran was unceremoniously released by the Pacific Coast League's Seattle Rainiers, engaged in a legal battle with Organized Baseball. The court ruled in Niemiec's favor, citing the Selective Training and Service Act of 1940, which gave veterans still qualified for their previously held jobs the right to return for at least a year following the completion of military service. Here I was aided by a treasure trove of documents in the Seattle Rainiers Baseball Club Records Collection held by the Washington State Historical Society. This led me to write an article called "Disposable Heroes" that appeared in the 2010 *Baseball Research Journal*, and eventually became a key part of one of the chapters of this book. At the same time I had the pleasure of working with Trey Strecker, editor of *NINE: A Journal of Baseball History & Culture*, on the editing and publication of a much more concise version of "War Games" that appeared in that journal in 2010.

Searching for additional primary source material, I struck gold with the 1946 *Report of the Major League Steering Committee* and the complete published record of the 1951 *Hearings Before the Subcommittee on Study of Monopoly Power of the Committee of the Judiciary, House of Representatives*. At this point I knew there was ample material for a book dedicated to the business of baseball during World War II, viewed through the motivations of the major league owners. Research continued throughout the writing process, which caused me more than once to go back to revise what I wrote previously. Ultimately what emerged is a picture of a game and an industry ruled with an iron hand by a small number of men who strove to maintain the status quo, often to their own financial detriment. The result is a book that I believe takes a unique view of the game during the war, and hopefully adds a little to the discussion of wartime baseball.

* * *

A clarification on some of the terms and language used in this book is warranted. The primary focus is on Major League Baseball and its team owners, though the minors, Negro Leagues, and women's professional baseball also play roles. However, in practice I use the word "owners" to refer to the owners of major league teams unless otherwise specified — using the phrase "major league owners" over and over again would be cumbersome. The term "Organized Baseball" refers to the majors and those professional minor leagues that were part of the National Association of Professional Baseball Clubs. It specifically excludes leagues outside these organizations, including outlaw, independent, and black professional baseball leagues, as well as professional women's baseball. Many works use the term "Negro Leagues" to refer to all of professional black baseball, but this is inaccurate since some actual leagues used this terminology (ex. the Negro National League), while others did not (ex. the United States Baseball League). With that in mind I opted to refer to baseball played within the African American community as "black" baseball to differentiate it from the mainstream, racially segregated, and exclusionary "white" game. This decision was made to exclude the potentially offensive term "Negro" except when in conjunction with direct quotes or actual league names, while remaining true to the type of language that was used during the era, before "African American" entered the lexicon. I hope the reader accepts this reasoning and explanation.

* * *

Books are not written in a vacuum, and this one is no exception. I relied on the teaching, help, and support of a wide range of people and organizations to make this project a reality. The faculty and staff of the Norwich University Master of Arts in Military History program taught me a tremendous amount about historical research and writing, and specific thanks go out to John Grenier and Michael Neiberg, both for their support and unwillingness to allow me to take any shortcuts. Editors Nick Frankovich, formerly with SABR, and Trey Strecker from *NINE*, pushed me to do more and helped get early versions of this research published. The staffs at the National Baseball Hall of Fame and the Washington State Historical Society dug deep into their files and provided copies for use in my research. The Society for American Baseball Research is a great organization that provides many resources to researchers, myself included, and my attendance at its 2011 National Convention was a pivotal moment in propelling this project forward, as not only did my receipt of the 2010 McFarland-SABR Baseball Research Award for my work on "Disposable Heroes" give me confidence in my research, I also met my McFarland editor Gary Mitchem for the first time while there. My friends Aaron Wood and Russ Oates gave up some of their time to read a draft of this work, and their comments and feedback were very helpful. Mark Rucker of Transcendental Graphics Publishing was of great help in obtaining rights to some of the photos used in this book, and I owe considerable thanks to my long-time friend Dave Eskenazi for yet again allowing me access to his impressive collection of sports photos and memorabilia.

On a more personal note, I owe thanks to my parents for their ongoing support and love over the years. Also thinks to my fellow Norwich graduate Alan Anderson and our friend, the esteemed historian Timothy Winegard. We make an unlikely trio in many ways, and as probably a thousand or more emails can attest you do not have to live close to people to develop deep and meaningful friendships with them. Lastly, I owe more than I can ever repay to Holly, my wife of 18 years. She willingly sacrificed a portion of our time together to allow me to go to graduate school, and did so again when I spent every Saturday (and parts of some Sundays) for months at a time working on this book. I am fortunate to have her in my life, and she is an important part of anything and everything I have accomplished over the last 20 years.

Introduction

Baseball and World War II. One is "America's Game," a part of the country's social fabric for well over a hundred years; the other is perhaps the pivotal event of the 20th century, one that solidified the United States' role as a world power and was the starting point of the baby boom generation. Both have been extensively studied and written about over the years, individually and in relation to one another, as the war impacted all aspects of American society, including the game of baseball. Most of the era's greatest baseball stars served in the armed forces during the war, some in relatively safe stateside assignments and others in combat. Their experiences, along with those of the boys and men who remained behind and played on ever-changing rosters, have been widely recounted in the baseball literature. From future Hall of Famer Bob Feller insisting on combat duty when he enlisted in the Navy immediately after Pearl Harbor, to one-armed Pete Gray playing with the American League's St. Louis Browns in 1945, individual stories are told as part of the game's history. So too the improbable World Series appearance of the usually dismal St. Louis Browns in 1944, and the creation of the All-American Girls Professional Baseball League, stories that transcend the individual and speak to the game itself.

The origins of baseball are lost to the mists of time. Despite the best efforts of many men to portray it as a purely American game, one created essentially *ex nihilo* by Abner Doubleday in 1839, it is in fact a game cobbled together over time from various other pastimes. In the nearly 100 years between the first formal baseball organizations and the start of World War II, the game developed by fits and starts alongside the society in which it operated. Baseball took on much of the character and flavor of the American people, particularly in the northeastern portion of the country, and was eventually seen as embodying those characteristics that Americans hold dear — a meritocracy on the field, one that used various methods to measure success, and one that celebrated pluck, daring, and toughness. It centered around the one-on-one conflict between pitcher and batter that involved both power and craftiness, without giving prominence to one over the other. Once the ball was put into play it became a team game, with the defense attempting to prevent the offense from scoring, while the runners were one against many on the base paths as they tried to beat the odds and reach home. Baseball was a microcosm of America.

World War II was not the first time that professional baseball faced a wartime government and economy — the owners went through a different global conflict 24 years earlier with America's entry into World War I. While the two wars differed significantly in scope and duration (at least for Americans), professional baseball faced many of the same challenges in both, particularly the perceptions society held of the game and the behavior of the men involved in it. The owners and players suffered a public relations black eye due to their complaining about the hardships the war caused the game during World War I, and their attempts to have it declared an "essential" industry exempt from many wartime requirements resulted in considerable criticism. One would think that they would have learned from this experience, but by the start of American involvement in World War II only two of the World War I era owners remained, and the game was forced to re-learn many hard lessons.

Over the years an image has been built of baseball during World War II as a patriotic game contributing to a patriotic war, and certainly much of this is true. But while individual men and women contributed to the war efforts in various ways, some at home and some overseas, what of Major League Baseball as an organization, a group of 16 team owners, two league presidents, and a commissioner? Certainly the game made many public contributions to the war effort, from bond drives to buying baseball equipment and sending it to the men overseas. However, a critical evaluation of the relationship between Major League Baseball, society, and America's leaders during World War II reveals a sport presenting an image of patriotism but acting strongly in its own best interests to maintain the status quo and protect profits. Even in the face of ever-increasing challenges in finding sufficiently skilled players to fill roster spots vacated by men called to service, the owners steadfastly held to their unofficial policy of racial segregation and refused to sign talented black players. And despite their claims of financial hardship, during the four war years (1942 to 1945) a dozen major league franchises were profitable, while in the four-year period immediately prior to America's entrance into World War II (1938 to 1941) only ten teams finished in the black. In fact the profit margins posted in the last two years of the war were the highest seen by the majors since before the Great Depression.

This is not to say that Major League Baseball, its owners, and executives, did not play a part in the war effort. They most certainly did, and their contributions should and will be recognized. The question is one of intent — were the public statements and actions of the owners really reflective of their true feelings, or merely an effort to avoid the public relations disasters of World War I while keeping their teams afloat financially as the nation transitioned into a wartime economy? When we peel back the shiny veneer the owners put on the game during the war years, we see that what lay underneath was not always solid, and was sometimes full of holes. We must also consider the military officers who collected baseball players like modern-day fantasy league team owners, building professional caliber clubs to represent their bases or service branches. Players who were perfectly healthy and capable of serving in combat roles were kept safely at home to play baseball by men who wanted to satisfy their own egos, while others went off to fight and sometimes die in their places.

The purpose of this examination is not to re-write history and indict Major League Baseball, the players, or the military. It is an attempt to better understand what motivated the actions of the men involved in order to gain perspective on what took place, why certain decisions were made, and how those decisions impacted baseball's place in society during and immediately following the war. The 1950s have often been described as a golden age of baseball, due in no small part to the impact of World War II on the game and the nation. We cannot fully understand that time without considering how both society and the professional game changed during the war years, sometimes proactively, but at other times dragged kicking and screaming into the future against their wills.

CHAPTER 1

Baseball's Relationship with the Military and Society Before World War II

The true origins of baseball are lost to us. It has long been recognized as the "American Game," despite its obvious evolution from countless pastimes that came before it, most notably the English game of rounders and the early American game "old cat." Even Henry Chadwick, the most famous baseball writer in the late 1800s and long-time editor of *Spalding's Official Baseball Guide*, believed the game's origin was linked to rounders. This did not sit well with many Americans, who were tired of their cultural heritage always being tied in some way back to Europe, and usually back to England.[1]

An American Game?

One of the loudest voices in support of baseball's purely American origins was Albert Goodwill Spalding. Born on September 2, 1850, in Byron, Illinois, Spalding first came to baseball prominence in 1866 as the starting pitcher of the semi-pro Rockford Forest Citys [*sic*] when he led his club to an upset 29–23 victory over the touring Washington Nationals. His performance on the mound resulted in offers from stronger clubs, and by 1871 he was playing professionally with the Boston Red Stockings of the National Association of Base Ball Players, helping the club to four consecutive league championships from 1872 to 1875. In addition to being a dominant pitcher, Spalding also had a sharp mind for business, and in 1876 he used an $800 loan from his mother to establish a sporting goods business based in Chicago, A. G. Spalding & Bro. In addition to supplying equipment to professional and amateur players, he launched the annual *Spalding's Official Baseball Guide* in 1878. By 1882 he expanded his baseball business empire one step further, taking over the ownership of the Chicago White Stockings.

As the owner of a sporting goods manufacturing and supply business, publisher of league guides, and owner of a team, Spalding had significant influence in the baseball world. And as a man who saw baseball as the source of his own personal American success story, it was important to him that the game was a uniquely American invention, one that reflected the values that Americans admired and held dear. He could accept that baseball developed out of loosely organized games like "old cat," but sought to distance if not completely separate it from unquestionably English games like rounders and cricket. He faced opposition at home from Chadwick and others, and also overseas during the "World Tour" he sponsored in 1888–1889 to spread baseball to other countries (and thereby open up new markets for his baseball equipment). When the American contingent arrived in England in March 1889, the British press took the opportunity to compare baseball to rounders, concluding it was both English in origin and more suited for children than adult athletes. Spalding was not impressed with this snub and resolved to someday settle the matter once and for all.[2]

The debate continued on and off for another decade until Chadwick brought it back to the forefront again with articles in the 1903 and 1904 *Spalding's Official Baseball Guides*, which was ironic considering that these were Spalding's own publications. In an effort to finally resolve the matter, Spalding created the Special Base Ball Commission (also known as the Mills Commission) in 1905 to investigate and report on the origins of baseball. Though a member of the commission himself, Spalding was savvy enough to realize that he could not be seen as its leader since his pro–American origin stance was well known and he would be seen as biased. Instead he asked his old friend and former National League president Abraham Gilbert Mills to serve as the chairman. He added a number of other cronies to the commission, and as a final touch assigned his personal secretary, James E. Sullivan, to compile materials for the group.[3]

The commission went public with its results in the 1908 edition of the *Guide*, and to almost no one's surprise they announced that baseball was indeed a game of American origin and completely unrelated to rounders. What was perhaps surprising was that the commission also presented a full-fledged creation story of the game's invention, one that included some very specific details. In short, they determined that the first baseball diamond was diagrammed and rudimentary playing rules were established by Abner Doubleday in Cooperstown, New York, in the spring of 1839. The entire basis for this conclusion was the recollections of Abner Graves, a former cattle rancher, real estate speculator, and miner, who was only five years old when the game was allegedly invented. Much of the information Graves provided was contradictory, and his story changed so much over time that in later interviews he claimed to have been in college when Doubleday invented baseball, and that he had in fact played in the very first game, contradicting his earlier recollections that he had been only a child playing marbles at the time he witnessed Doubleday sketch the first baseball diamond in the dirt.[4] Yet despite the total lack of any real evidence, the members of the commission all signed off on the findings and Spalding proudly declared the matter resolved. Though some attempts were made to rebut the Doubleday story, most people simply tired of the argument and went on about their business. Over time Spalding's version gained gradual acceptance, and before long it was firmly entrenched as part of the game's mythology.

Baseball and American Society

Society's view of baseball, and conversely the game's impact on society itself, has changed over time. Ignoring the dubious Doubleday creation myth, we know that baseball developed gradually in the early 1800s, reaching a milestone with the founding of the Knickerbocker Base Ball Club of New York in 1845 and the subsequent formalization of written rules for the game. Alexander Joy Cartwright is often credited with proposing the organization of the Knickerbockers and with playing a prominent role in developing the version of baseball that became the game we know today. Cartwright certainly has more claim to the crown of inventing baseball than does Doubleday. After all, there is ample documentary evidence and oral history from multiple sources that solidly ties him to the Knickerbocker Club, while the only "evidence" linking Doubleday to baseball in any way is the dubious testimony of Abner Graves. That being said, no one person can truly lay claim to being the sole creator of baseball, which clearly evolved from other games over time.

An image has been created of baseball during this period as a genteel game played by young, white-collar professionals who emphasized sportsmanship and invited their opponents to banquets after their matches, and this certainly was one side of the game. There was also another side, one comprised of teams drawn from the working classes who took a more rowdy approach, both on and off the field. Regardless of which group was under discussion, baseball was generally looked upon at the time by society as a waste of time, men playing a children's game, and certainly not a potential vocation.

Slowly, however, interest in baseball games began to build. Some newspapers ran stories and reported game results, and this attracted the attention of a group of people who, while they did not play the game, eventually had an important role in shaping it: gamblers. When gambling becomes involved in an amateur sport, such as baseball during this period, the outcomes of games quickly become much more serious matters than when the game is simply a competition between groups of men seeking recreation. A cycle starts to form in which the gambling increases interest in the games and therefore attendance, which in turn generates more media coverage, which then in turn generates even more interest, including people who are not going to the games to gamble, but simply to watch. Before long pride is no longer the dominant driving force behind the sport, replaced instead by money, with gamblers, promoters, and players all looking to cash in.

Early baseball teams were strictly amateur affairs. After all, the teams were simply clubs organized and run by groups of men with similar interests. A club had no owner and no sources of income other than the dues paid by its members, so paying players made no sense. As more money began to surround baseball, however, so too did the specter of professionalism. With gambling and the press generating enough interest in games that teams could charge admissions, suddenly there arose a financial benefit associated with winning. There was also money to be made by players placing bets on their own teams to win. Or, at times, to lose. The earliest professionals were often paid in non-direct ways, receiving a local job paying considerably more than the going wage that required them to do minimal amounts of work, freeing them up to practice and play. As professionalism became more overt, so too did the payments, and some organizations no longer tried to create a false front to hide what they were doing.

In 1869 the Cincinnati Red Stockings came out publicly as a completely professional baseball club, one created in order to make money through touring and gate receipts. With the floodgates now opened, overt professionalism quickly became a common practice. Though some leagues attempted to maintain an amateur basis, the era was rife with stories of paid ringers who were brought in to play for local clubs to improve their chances of winning. As the money involved and popularity increased, so too did the potential for gamblers to look for ways to improve their odds. Players were offered money to throw games intentionally, and gambling scandals rocked professional baseball throughout the 1870s. Gambling continued to be a concern well into the 20th century, culminating with the infamous 1919 Black Sox scandal in which eight members of the Chicago White Sox were alleged to have been part of a plot to lose the World Series to the Cincinnati Reds.

Along with gambling problems, "rowdyism" was another common criticism of baseball by its detractors. Drinking and violence in the stands hindered the ability of the professional game to grow, and umpires sometimes faced down angry crowds that threatened to turn into violent mobs. In many cities and towns, blue laws prohibited baseball games from being played on Sundays, in part because they were not seen as wholesome activities, and some locales attempted to curb the poor behavior by prohibiting the sale of alcohol at games.

Slowly but surely professional baseball took steps to get its house in order. Attendance was the key to success for team owners, and that meant they had to get the gambling under control to ensure the integrity of the game and maintain fan interest. They also had to improve the overall environment within the ballparks themselves in order to attract customers who would otherwise avoid the ballpark out of fear or distaste for the experience. With a growing financial incentive, owners worked hard at improving society's image of the game.

By the end of the 1800s professional baseball had grown by fits and starts. At the pinnacle stood the eight-team National League, founded in 1876, which represented the highest level of professional baseball and garnered the most attendance and press attention. Its power base was the heavily populated and industrial Northeast and Midwest, with St. Louis representing its furthest outpost both to the west and south, and by 1899 league attendance reached an impressive 2.5 million. There were also at least ten professional minor leagues servicing various parts of the country, owned and operated independent of the National League in this era before the farm system had been invented.

One major threat faced by the owners was competition from rival major leagues. Interleague wars were not uncommon, nor was contract jumping as some players sought to earn the most money possible and were willing to go wherever necessary to get it. Rivals were treated ruthlessly using any tactic available, from roster raids to blackballing players who left to join other leagues. Attempts by players to improve their lot, such as the formation of the Players' League in 1890, were crushed by the owners. Baseball owners had investments in their teams as businesses, and they were not going to give up their money without a fight, a singular focus on the bottom line that only intensified over time.

A distinguishing feature of baseball at the end of the century was its color — the professional game had become the exclusive domain of white players. While technically no rules existed that barred black players from joining white teams, the offensively named "Gentleman's Agreement" kept owners from signing black players, relegating them to either outlaw organizations or, more profitably, their own all-black leagues, something they did frequently and often with a degree of financial success. In an odd twist, most other ethnic minorities were allowed to play professional baseball, including Native Americans and so-called "light skinned" Cubans, though they often faced the taunts of both fans and opposing players, as did Jews and other ethnic minorities, for many decades to come. Like American society, baseball was a melting pot, though one with a pecking order, and one that completely separated blacks from everyone else.

The first two decades of the 20th century were pivotal in solidifying the structure of the professional game into something very similar to what we know today. The new century opened with a baseball war between the National League and the upstart American League, which contributed to the founding of the National Association of Professional Baseball Clubs in 1901, the organization created by the minor leagues to protect the rights of member clubs and formalize the relationship between the majors and the minors. The 1903 peace agreement between the warring major leagues brought much more stability to the world of professional baseball, establishing a 16-team major league comprised of two distinct eight-team circuits and offering protection to the contracts of the various member leagues of the National Association, eliminating the threat of player contract jumping across leagues and forcing non-member leagues into an outlaw status. This framework created an environment that strengthened ownership control over their teams and players, and in turn increased fan loyalty to their hometown clubs as rosters became more stable from season to season.

The Black Sox gambling scandal was a publicity disaster for baseball that had the potential to cause the game to take a big step backwards. In response the major league owners hired Judge Kenesaw Mountain Landis in 1920 to be the first commissioner of baseball. His first order of business was to deal with the Black Sox situation, which he did ruthlessly, banning from baseball for life eight members of the White Sox. While many questioned the severity of the punishment and whether or not all of the banned players were indeed involved in the plot, Landis' decisive action sent a message to the fans and the players alike that he would not allow gambling to ruin the integrity of the game.

As America entered the "Roaring Twenties" so too did baseball, carried in part on the shoulders of a larger-than-life hero in Babe Ruth. The game and society moved in parallel as the swift economic boom propelled them forward. Prohibition may have had a somewhat positive effect on attendance, as it eliminated legal drinking at the ballparks and reduced rowdy behavior, though the resultant gains in attendance may very well have been offset by the loss in concession sales in those cities that had allowed alcohol to be sold at the ballparks. In 1930 the majors peaked in popularity and set an attendance record of just over 10.1 million fans through the turnstiles, a level they would not reach again until 1945.

Professional baseball slowly improved its status in the eyes of American society, and by the 1930s it was entrenched as the "National Pastime." It was now a game not only followed by men of a certain class, but by a broader spectrum of fans that also included women and especially children, who could collect images of their heroes on baseball cards which were now being packaged with candy and gum instead of tobacco. Baseball was a way for new waves of immigrants to integrate into the American social fabric, with fandom creating at least one common element between different ethnic groups, though blacks were still excluded and relegated to their own leagues. Star athletes were treated much in the same way as other celebrities, with some earning substantial salaries. Outside of the elite level, players could still earn good salaries, certainly better than those of a laborer, and for many uneducated youths with limited prospects the meritocracy of baseball offered a way out of poverty. Owners were not concerned about a player's education or manners, but only wanted to know how well he could hit, run, and throw. Baseball was a microcosm of society, valuing success above all else. At least so long as your skin was the right color.

Baseball and the Military Prior to World War I

Even during its infancy, baseball had a relationship with the military. The Civil War broke out in 1861, between the time of the Knickerbockers' initial codification of rules and the establishment of the fully professional Red Stockings. The game was already popular in the North, with the New York and Massachusetts versions of the game vying for acceptance. Other versions were played south of the Mason-Dixon Line, though these more resembled older versions of town ball than the game played in the North. Regardless of the rules in use, ballplayers packed up their equipment and took it to the camps and battlefields of the Civil War, where their play was often encouraged by officers who saw it as a positive form of recreation that built relationships and provided exercise. Contests took place within units, between rival units, in prison camps, and even supposedly between guards and prisoners.[5] Even if guards and prisoners never actually played together, one can surmise that watching prisoners playing a version of baseball may well have helped humanize them in the eyes of their captors, who could see them as men with common interests.

Civil War military baseball, in both units and prison camps, exposed considerable numbers of men to the game for the first time and contributed significantly to its rise in popularity in the post-war years. This was especially true in the South, where prisoners brought the game back with them upon their return home. It also solidified the standing of the rules of the "New York game," which outlasted its rivals and became the most popular version of baseball, eventually becoming the sport we know today.[6]

The Civil War has one interesting direct tie-in to the history of the game, at least the history as reported by the Mills Commission. Abner Doubleday, the alleged "creator" of baseball, was a noted Union general during the war. He was at Fort Sumter, South Carolina, in 1861 when the Confederates launched the attack that opened the war, and his men fired the first Union shots of the conflict. His troops later saw heavy combat at the Battle of Gettysburg, during which Doubleday was wounded. As a relatively well-known Civil War hero, he was in many ways a perfect choice as the inventor of baseball and one who emphasized the alleged American roots of the game, regardless of the fact that he was a student at West Point at the time he supposedly laid out the first baseball diamond in Cooperstown, half a state away, and had nothing other than Abner Graves' story tying him in any way to baseball.

In 1898 the country entered another war, though instead of occurring on American soil the Spanish-American War was fought away from the mainland, primarily in Cuba, Puerto Rico, and the Philippines. Though the fighting was often bitter, the war itself was brief and the hostilities lasted less than four months, after which American forces found themselves in often monotonous occupation duty. Organized and recreational sports, including baseball, were quickly recognized by military leaders as an important form of entertainment and a way to stave off the inevitable boredom of their troops. At overseas outposts black and white players sometimes competed together, something not tolerated at home, and this too contributed to cohesion among the soldiers. Team sports also offered opportunities for the occupiers to interact with the local civilian population through friendly competitions, and the Cubans in particular embraced the American game as a way to cast off the influences of Spanish culture on their society.[7] Even with the subsequent outbreak of the Philippine-American War in 1899, baseball retained its foothold in the Philippines at American bases and eventually became popular with the Filipinos.

For much of American history the military, and in particular the Army, operated in a repetitive cycle. Immediately following the end of a war, the Army rapidly demobilized and was left with a small, ill-equipped, and underfunded, peace-time force. When hostilities began again in a new war, there was an immediate surge in manpower through enlistments and/or conscription, with an infusion of capital and material that often lagged behind the rapid increase in size. After the new conflict concluded, the cycle began anew with another rapid demobilization. During the period between the Spanish-American War and the outbreak of World War I, sports were seen as an important part of maintaining the fitness of soldiers in the small peace-time Army, not only for the physical and health benefits they provided, but also for the emphasis on teamwork and the building of camaraderie. According to historian Wanda Ellen Wakefield, "Acting on their belief that participation in sports would help prepare any man for competition not only on the ball field or in the boardroom, but on the battlefield as well, military commanders began looking to athletics as a crucial part of preparation for war."[8] Baseball was part of that plan.

World War I

The United States was a latecomer to the battlefields of World War I. The war broke out in Europe in July 1914, and the Americans did their best to maintain neutrality while still providing financial support for their traditional allies, most notably Great Britain and France. When Germany announced it was resuming unrestricted submarine warfare in the Atlantic in

The American military has a long history with the game of baseball, as seen in this picture postcard from the early 20th century. Military leaders viewed sports as a valuable training tool to promote physical health, teamwork, and competition (author's collection).

January 1917, it was only a matter of time before the first American merchant ships would be sunk. Following a number of such attacks and sinkings in the first months of the year, the United States declared war on Germany in April and immediately began the process of mobilization. As usual, however, the Army found itself woefully unprepared for war, which is surprising considering the massive scale of the conflict that had raged in Europe for nearly three years. At the start of 1917 the Army had barely 100,000 full-time soldiers in its ranks, with another 132,000 on the rolls of the National Guard. To put this into the perspective of World War I as a whole, the British suffered roughly 60,000 casualties (dead or wounded) on *the very first* day of the Battle of the Somme in 1916. With the losses being incurred daily on the Western Front, the Army need to increase its manpower, and do it fast. And they did, rapidly building a force that numbered over four million men in uniform by the end of the war in November 1918.[9]

But what of baseball? Major league owners had very little experience in how to deal with managing their business during a time of war, and certainly not during a war with such a huge impact on society as a whole. There had been no organized business of professional baseball during the Civil War, and the wars with Spain and in the Philippines did not involve the broad conscriptions of vast numbers of men and the shift of the economy to a wartime footing. The majors were coming off of a very successful 1916 season which saw attendance spike to over 6.5 million fans, a nearly 34 percent increase over 1915. Thirteen of the major leagues' 16 clubs improved at the gate, led by the Chicago White Sox, who drew just under 680,000 paying customers.[10] Overall 1916 gave the league its fourth highest attendance ever, and expectations for another profitable year were running high, but the declaration of war made the future uncertain.

At least one baseball executive had been thinking about the possibility of war and the impact it could have on the game. American League President Byron Bancroft "Ban" Johnson recognized that if war came, and if Major League Baseball wanted to continue to operate during wartime, the game would need popular approval. In an effort to show that the game supported the military, Johnson instructed American League clubs to incorporate military-style drill practice as part of their spring training regimens, even going so far as to arrange to have actual army drill instructors put the players through their paces. With the declaration of war in April, the teams quickly arranged for public close-order drills to be carried out by players in front of the press and fans, and ensured that photos of the players, their drill instructors, and the flags of America and her allies appeared in print.[11] The actual impact of this ploy is difficult to determine, but it did make a favorable impression on the press and at least enabled the 1917 baseball season to get off to a positive start despite the news of war. For the most part the minor leagues echoed the sentiments of the majors that 1917 would be business as usual, though only 21 minor leagues opened that season compared to 26 in 1916. The impact was greatest in the low minors, as all the leagues that folded were Class C or lower, classifications usually reserved for the youngest players.[12]

One of the earliest attempts to influence public opinion, and one that would be revived during World War II, was the establishment of the Ball and Bat Fund to provide baseball equipment to soldiers serving overseas. Clark Griffith, the manager and part-owner of the American League Washington Senators, was the leading force behind this program, which he announced in an open letter to the fans that appeared in *The Sporting News* on April 26. Griffith asked each fan to send him 25 cents for the purchase of equipment, and to forward a copy of his appeal to four other fans in order to raise money for the Fund.[13]

Military drill continued into the regular season and was also taken up by the clubs in the National League. The owners were concerned about the prospect of conscription decimating the ranks of their teams, which were comprised primarily of physical fit, relatively young men. They hoped that if the professional players could show that they were already proficient in much of the basic military training it might earn baseball a little breathing room, and possibly push back player military inductions until at least sometime after the conclusion of the 1917 season.

It did not take long, however, for professional baseball to stub its toe publicly. Johnson, accompanied by executives from some of the minor leagues, went to Washington in early May to ask Congress to give special consideration to professional baseball when it came to the application of the 10 percent war tax. They told Congress that major league clubs operated at very slim profit margins and that most minor league clubs actually lost money, so an additional tax on admissions would be an undue burden on the game and could force it to shut down for the duration of the war.[14] There was also talk of increasing ticket prices to account for the tax, a move that surely would not be popular with the fans, who would see this as a way of forcing the citizen to pay it instead of the business. Asking for the concession was bad enough, but implying that the cost of the tax would be passed on to the consumer was even worse for the game's image.

On May 18, conscription became a reality with Congress' passing of the Selective Service Act of 1917, which initially required all men between 21 to 30 years of age to register for the draft (the age ranges were expanded later in the war). Of the roughly 480 men who appeared in at least one major league game that season, 411 were potentially eligible for the draft — almost 86 percent of the league's players. Needless to say the potential impact on the majors, and in fact on all of professional baseball, was enormous. In July *The Sporting News* published its first list of major league players known to have been drafted, 35 in all, though this included a number of players who had already entered the service as volunteers. Ironically, most players were not even aware of their draft numbers, and it was often the club owners who tracked down the relevant information and notified the players that they had been called to serve.

While the 1917 season continued its normal course, there was concern as to whether or not the World Series would be played. A reporter contacted the White House and received the response, "The President sees no necessity at all for stopping or curtailing the baseball schedule."[15] This was a bit of good news for the owners, at least at the major league level, even though the overall financial outlook was bad as attendance dropped noticeably from the peak of 1916.

Though players were entering the service both through the draft and enlistment, voices were raised asking why more of these professional athletes were not volunteering, a question that would again haunt baseball during World War II. The always pro-baseball *The Sporting News* attempted to offer an explanation to rebut those who publicly referred to ballplayers as "slackers":

> 'Tis [*sic*] true that he did not make haste to volunteer, but it is also true that the influences governing him were against such a course. He was made to feel that the public did not see the necessity of baseball being interrupted until there came an emergency that warranted, and the highest government authority endorsed that stand.[16]

This was not exactly a ringing endorsement. In effect *The Sporting News* implied that society itself was to blame for the small number of voluntary enlistments among professional baseball players. *The Sporting News*, as a weekly publication devoted exclusively to baseball, certainly had a vested interest in supporting the actions of the players and owners, and its bias often became apparent as it attempted to defend the actions of men involved in the game. It continued to publish articles emphasizing the patriotic nature of the game and its contributions to the war effort throughout the conflict.

In the post-season the Chicago White Sox defeated the New York Giants in the World Series, wrapping up the title on October 15. The league raised an additional $8,000 for the Ball and Bat Fund during the Series from a portion of the ticket sales, fan donations, and a contribution from the Player's Fraternity. Attendance for the Series was off, with all the games in New York played before less than sellout crowds, including a Game 4 that was played in front of 10,000 empty seats. That kind of a turnout did not bode well for the state of the game.

A season that looked promising when it opened, 1917 proved to be a very difficult year for the majors and all of professional baseball. Historian David

Quentin Voigt summarized the poor decisions that damaged the majors' reputation in the eyes of the public:

> It mattered little that baseball men gave bats and balls, or drilled players, or sported flags on uniform sleeves; what hurt the game's image was the scarcity of voluntary enlistments, the reluctance of owners to accept a 10 per cent admissions tax, and the players' demand for higher salaries. For these reasons, baseball was accused of not sacrificing enough, and its status as an essential activity was much clouded.[17]

Some post World Series exhibitions played at military bases by major league clubs earned them a little more credibility, as did a purchase of $100,000 in Liberty Bonds by the league (it had purchased $60,000 worth of bonds earlier in the year), but it was important for baseball's leaders to come up with a plan to improve public perceptions going into 1918.

A number of important topics were on the table for discussion during the off-season. It was clear that the 1918 major league schedule would have to be shortened from the normal 154 games due to travel restrictions, but two separate camps emerged, one which supported a 140-game season and the other which wanted to shorten it even further to 110 games. Regardless of the option chosen, player salaries and roster sizes were additional concerns, one or both of which would likely need to be reduced in the event of a shortened season. There was also still the 10 percent war tax that had to be applied to ticket sales, and teams needed to decide if this warranted ticket price increases for all types of seats, or just some. The minors were struggling badly, and there was talk of realignment to strengthen some leagues so they could continue in 1918.

As if that wasn't enough, in November Johnson made some comments that were interpreted by the press as indicating that he planned to ask the government for draft exemptions for 285 major leaguers to ensure that teams had enough suitable players for the upcoming season. Johnson attempted to clarify what he meant to say:

> Could the draft fall upon all clubs with equal force, then some semblance of a favorable "lineup" might be obtained. It would be the height of folly to send a club over blindfolded into the campaign next summer. Common sense and prudence must prompt us to get our bearings. This can only be brought about by an open and frank discussion of the subject. If the public demands baseball of the highest grade, that fact will be developed during some period in the winter months.[18]

Though Johnson insisted his original comments had been misinterpreted, this situation further damaged the reputation of an already struggling game. This was made clear in a separate article in the same issue of *The Sporting News* that carried Johnson's attempted clarification.

Justly or otherwise, it is a fact that professional baseball players of the United States have been placed into the "slacker" class by the general public. Attention has been called time and again to the large number of representatives from all other branches of sport who have enlisted or are now serving their country, and to the very small number of ball players who have entered the ranks.

Far be it from this writer to criticize the ball players for the course they have pursued. Doubtless, each man, in his own mind, has a complete justification for the course he has pursued. Nevertheless, the fact remains that the public do not believe there is any justification for the failure to enlist in large numbers.[19]

The players and owners faced a huge credibility issue with their fan base and society as a whole, attracting a lot of unwanted attention upon themselves.

A further embarrassment arose in February 1918 when Congressman James A. Gallivan of Massachusetts submitted a request to Secretary of the Navy Josephus Daniels to give special consideration to Boston Red Sox manager and Navy captain Jack Barry. Gallivan asked that Barry be placed on inactive status for six months during the summer of 1918 based on the fact that President Wilson previously wrote that professional sports should continue during the war, further noting that Barry was essential to the club and that it would suffer a significant financial loss should he be called away for the 1918 season. By all appearances Barry knew nothing of the request until it became public and the resultant drama played out in the press, but it still caused the Red Sox and baseball to suffer from yet more negative publicity.[20] Now the owners were not only suffering as a result of their own missteps, but from those made by others outside of baseball as well.

Some owners began to take proactive steps to protect their franchises for the upcoming season through the judicious signing of players ineligible for the draft. The Brooklyn Dodgers signed Cuban-born ballplayers who were exempt from the draft[21], while the Dallas Giants of the Class B Texas League made a point of signing veteran players who were too old to qualify for the draft as the age range stood at that time. The Giants bragged they could field an entire starting lineup that was above draft age,[22] a gamble that paid dividends and gave Dallas a 3.5-game lead in the Texas League pennant race at the end of the season, which unfortunately for the Giants came on July 7 when the league suspended operations for the remainder of 1918.

Representatives of the American and National Leagues met with tax officials in January to discuss possible options for dealing with the war tax on tickets for the upcoming 1918 season. In February the two leagues took the unusual step of holding a joint off-season meeting to discuss a number of issues, most notably schedule length and the application of the tax. The cost of the war tax was to be passed on to the consumer at the rate of 10 percent, but with bleacher seats normally costing 25 cents, this created a problem — not only would ticket sellers have to make change on most tickets sold, there was also the issue of the resultant pesky half-cent. Government officials proved willing to work with the leagues, and a price structure was established that increased the prices of all types of seats while also adding a tax onto season pass holders for every game they actually attended. Unfortunately the buyers of the lowest priced tickets felt the greatest impact, as bleacher seats went from 25 cents to 30 cents per ticket, an increase of 20 percent, a larger percentage increase than that applied to the more expensive reserved seats.[23]

While the resolution of the tax issue was positive news, the majors quickly suffered another blow as a number of players returned their 1918 contracts to their clubs unsigned, demanding more money. Every professional baseball contract offered by National Association and major league clubs included the infamous "reserve clause," which essentially made the ballplayer the property of the team so far as his baseball career was concerned. The club retained its rights to the player even in the event he refused to sign a contract, which prevented any other team from signing him. This gave the owners tremendous power when it came to negotiating contracts, leaving holding out and not playing the only option open to a player in hopes of pressuring the owner to meet his demands. So while some players held out for pay increases for the 1918 season, others had been offered contracts by their clubs that resulted in pay cuts from the prior year, and they were simply refusing to sign in an effort to earn the same salary they had in 1917. This distinction did not matter in the eyes of most fans, who simply saw professional athletes who were not in the military during a time of war refusing to play unless they were paid more money, a fact made even harder to swallow considering that many players earned salaries well in excess of the average working-class American. The press was merciless.

> The demands of the strikers once more prove that the average player has no sentiment or civic pride. He is hungry for coin and if he doesn't get it he sulks. Surely this is a fine state of affairs with the war threatening businesses of all kinds and the magnates apprehensive of what may happen between April and October.[24]

Certainly the pro-owner bias of *The Sporting News* can be seen in the above quote, but this was still a very strong sentiment and one that certainly had the potential to damage the game as a whole, including the bottom line. These holdouts drew exactly the kind of attention the game did not want or need.

The 1918 season stumbled out of the gate in April, and only ten minor leagues opted to field teams. The expanding military draft began taking able-bodied players at an ever-increasing rate, and travel restrictions made it harder for teams to get from city to city. In the majors the owners looked for any way possible to control costs in a season that might not play out the full schedule. Many players received contracts for lower salaries than they earned in 1917, daily meal money was reduced, and incidental player expenses previously incurred by the teams were eliminated entirely. The game, like society, faced considerable uncertainty now that the country was fully engaged in World War I.

It did not take long for the season to begin to unravel. In late May two clubs in the Pacific Coast International League disbanded, and by the end of the June the Virginia League, the Blue Ridge League, and the Southern Association called it quits. In the majors the owners continued to complain about the impact of the war on their businesses, and there was talk of trying to work with the government and railway officials to allow ball clubs to travel at reduced rates. Even the normally supportive *The Sporting News* was getting weary of the owner's missteps.

> And going before the government with such a presumptuous request as it is said will be made won't be likely to make the government any more favorably disposed when it comes to asking for exemptions under the "war work or fight" order either. The magnates had better be careful how they pile it on these ticklish times.[25]

Many players had already heeded the "war work or fight" order and took jobs in various war industries. However, even this did not help the game's reputation with Americans, as much of society believed that these professional athletes were perfectly capable of serving in the military and only chose war industry labor out of cowardice. Even when baseball men operated within the laws of the land, they still came out as losers in the eyes of the public.

In July Secretary of War Newton D. Baker announced that baseball was no longer considered "essential," and the leniency previously shown to ballplayers with regards to the "war work or fight" edict was over. While Baker indicated he was willing to listen to an appeal of his decision, the minors quickly folded up shop and every circuit other than the International League ceased operations before the end of the month. As for the majors, Baker was open to allowing them to continue and even discussed the particulars with President Wilson. Baker announced his final ruling later in the month, and he made certain to explain fully the thought process behind the decision so that there would be no confusion on the part of the American people or of baseball.

> As to the first: The situation of professional baseball differs in no wise [*sic*] from other civilian peace-time business, which, by reason of the stress of war and its demands upon the industries and energy of the country, must be content to bear whatever burden is imposed by temporary inactivity. While the number of men affected by the order may be sufficient to disor-

ganize the business, many of the players are beyond the present draft age, and it is by no means certain that complete disorganization of the business would follow adherence to the order as made.

As to the second: Baseball players are men of unusual physical ability, dexterity and alertness. It has been necessary for us in this country to institute processes of rapid industrial training and it is quite inconceivable that occupations cannot be found by these men which not only would relieve them from the onus of non-productive employment but would make them productive in some capacity highly useful to the nation. This change will be welcomed by the individuals involved and its usefulness to the country, both direct and indirect, is obvious.

The third consideration is, of course, the serious one, and is the one which has brought about the present appeal to the president. The stress of intensive occupation in industry and commerce in America in normal times, such as to give the highest importance and social value to outdoor recreation. It may well be that all of the persons who attend such outdoor sports are not in need of them, but certainly a very large preponderance of the spectators in these great national exhibitions are helped, physically and mentally, and made more efficient industrially and socially, by the relaxation that they there enjoy.

But the times are not normal; the demands of the Army and of the country are such that we must all make sacrifices and the non-productive employment of able-bodied persons, useful in the national defense either as military men or in the industry and commerce of our country, cannot be justified. The country will be best satisfied if the great selective process by which our Army is recruited makes no discriminations.

I am therefore of the opinion that the regulation in question should not be changed, but rather that the scope of its provisions should be so enlarged as to include other classes of persons whose professional occupation is solely that of entertaining. Our people will be resourceful enough to find other means of recreation and relaxation if there be not enough persons beyond the useful military or industrial age to perform such functions, and they will be wise and patriotic enough not to neglect the recreation necessary to maintain their efficiency merely because they are called upon, in the obvious public interest, to sacrifice a favorite form of amusement.[26]

Baker's decision clearly reflected the feelings of a large portion of Americans, that professional athletics were not essential and that the athletes themselves should contribute to the war effort just like other citizens.

On the surface Baker appeared to end the baseball season immediately, but the majors were given a little leeway to wrap up their business, and the ruling indicated that ballplayers should be working or serving by September 1. Ban Johnson recommended that the majors shut down on August 20, but the National League had other ideas and pushed for the season to run until September 2, to be followed immediately by a best-of-seven World Series. Ultimately the majority of owners supported the National League plan, and yet again despite the flexibility shown by the government, baseball's owners believed that they knew best how things should be handled. They got their way, however, as government officials agreed to give leniency to those players participating in the Series.

While the World Series between the Chicago Cubs and Boston Red Sox should have been an opportunity for a baseball celebration, the owners and the players used it as an opportunity to shoot themselves in the foot publicly one more time before the end of the year. Players on World Series teams were allocated "shares" of the profits from the series as a bonus for their successful seasons. In 1918 the players on the winning club were allocated $2,000 apiece, while those on the losing team would receive $1,400 each. Attendance was low in the early games, however, and as a result the decision was made to cut the player shares to $1,200 and $800 respectively, thereby putting more money into the pockets of the owners. The players did not take kindly to this unilateral change in arrangements, and they threatened not to play the upcoming fifth game unless the old share plan was put back into place. Baseball's executives convinced the players that a strike over money, and specifically one coming after the September 1 "war work or fight" deadline, would not be well received by the public. The players begrudgingly agreed and the Red Sox went on to win the series in six games, but not before word of the dispute got out to the press and gave baseball one last black eye in 1918.

The Lessons of World War I

The World War I experience was a humbling one for professional baseball, particularly at the major league level. A game that had been moving in the right direction in terms of popularity took some major blows in a relatively short period of time following the country's entrance into the war. Average attendance dropped from 5,279 per major league game in 1916 to 4,237 in 1917, and to a paltry 3,062 per game in 1918, a decrease of 42 percent in just two years. The number of professional minor leagues dropped from 26 in 1916 to just ten in 1918, with only one completing the 1918 schedule. There is no doubt that war took an economic toll on the game, though the question remains as to how much of the impact was due to the war, and how much was due to the decisions made by baseball men themselves?

The owners came across as complainers who were more interested in their own businesses than in the war effort. They went to the government on multiple occasions and sought concessions for baseball, attempting to paint the game as the patriotic national pastime and an essential part of America's social fabric. They sought draft exemptions for their players, different rules for the application of the war tax, and preferential treatment with regards to travel. These were men used to getting their way, men who operated their teams as fiefdoms and, because of the reserve clause, treated their players like serfs or indentured servants — relatively well-paid serfs to be sure, but still men whose careers were completely at the mercy of the owners who held their contracts. They had weathered challenges from player unions and rival leagues, having just crushed the upstart Federal League in 1915, but they behaved more or less as they had before the war, making unilateral decisions even in the face of government edicts, and for the most part they got away with it.

The players too behaved much as they normally had before the war. There was the often warranted griping about salaries and bonus money, and the continued expectation of the various perks of the job such as first class travel and accommodations. Many players, though certainly not all, sought to avoid military and war industry service, which resulted in public cries that they were cowards and slackers. It was not until the government stepped in and enforced the "war work or fight" order that the majority of the players got the message, though within a few months of the September 1, 1918, deadline the war in Europe was over, meaning the impact on most players was minimal or non-existent.

Many of the criticisms laid against baseball in the press may have been unfair, with the game and its players taking the brunt of the attention simply because the sport was a public spectacle and therefore very visible throughout society. Doubtless many business owners attempted to maintain the status quo in their industries to minimize the impact of the war on their bottom lines, though they were able to do so less publicly. Many other large businesses also had the ears of those in government and quietly sought concessions, though small business owners were relegated to trying to work within the system. The players too were not unique. Many men in all walks of life sought to avoid military service or war industry work in an attempt to continue with their normal lives. They, however, had the benefit of not working in the public eye, and their day-to-day activities were only visible to those within their local communities, meaning they often remained unnoticed, unlike the player who worked in the public spotlight.

Hundreds of professional baseball players did serve in the military during World War I, including some of the game's greatest stars like Ty Cobb, Christy Mathewson, and Grover Cleveland Alexander. Even some executives served, such as Branch Rickey of the Cardinals. Of the estimated 227 major leaguers who donned military uniforms during the conflict, many served overseas in combat roles, including the aforementioned Alexander, who came home shell-shocked and hearing-impaired after his experiences in the artillery. Mathewson too was permanently injured due to the war, suffering exposure to poison gas during a training exercise that badly damaged his lungs and considerably shortened his life. Eddie Grant, the one-time captain of the New York Giants, was the only major leaguer killed in combat, falling in France on October 5, 1918, just five weeks before the end of hostilities on the Western Front.[27] A significant number of players, executives, and owners supported the war effort in various capacities, though baseball as a whole did not do enough to publicize these contributions as a way of counteracting the criticisms laid against those who remained with their teams.

Eddie Grant was the only major leaguer killed in combat during World War I, falling in France on October 5, 1918, shortly before the end of the war (author's collection).

* * *

Did baseball men, and in particular the owners and executives who exerted so much control over the game for such long periods of time, learn any lessons from their experiences during World War I, and would they be able to use what they learned in the event a future conflict jeopardized the future of the game? Perhaps a better question is did the owners think they would even need to do anything differently in the future? After all, despite the bad publicity the game rebounded immediately in 1919 and major league attendance jumped back up to over 6.5 million fans, the same level it was at in 1916, the last full season before America became involved in the war. It surged again in 1920, this time increasing by nearly 40 percent as the majors set a new attendance record, drawing over 9.1 million fans and crushing the previous mark of 7.2 million set in 1909. Despite the gambling scandal that resulted from the 1919 World Series, major league attendance remained over 8.6 million per season throughout the 1920s. The game was riding a wave of popularity, so was there really any need to learn anything from the gaffes of World War I? While the answer was most certainly yes, it did not appear so from the vantage point of the owners, and this would come back to haunt them 23 years later when America once again went to war.

CHAPTER 2

Baseball at the Outbreak of World War II

You could not have made the two decades between the world wars much more different from one another if you tried. The "Roaring Twenties" was a decade of excitement and exuberance, of economic growth, rising incomes, and relatively low unemployment. The future looked bright, and anything seemed possible. At least it did until October 29, 1929, "Black Tuesday," when the American stock market crashed, signaling the start of the Great Depression that came to define the 1930s. The new decade was one of inflation, skyrocketing unemployment, farm failures, and a worldwide economic collapse. People saw their life savings wiped out almost immediately in the stock market crash and the insolvency of thousands of banks. American society went from overconfidence to deep despair in a matter of weeks.

Baseball in the Twenties and Thirties

The story of the on-the-field game of baseball during the 1920s and 1930s has been widely told and celebrated. It was an era of many of the game's greatest stars, including arguably the greatest of them all, George Herman "Babe" Ruth. Ruth helped bring the home run into fashion with his monumental clouts, and his regular assaults against his own single season home run records were followed throughout the country. His fame was truly national, more akin to a Hollywood star than a baseball player, and even extended overseas where he was idolized in baseball-hungry Japan. While it may be excessive to point to one man as the cornerstone to baseball's popularity, a strong case can be made for Ruth's contributions to the game during his career.

At the end of World War I, baseball's reputation was tarnished in the eyes of many, though the sporting public, reinforced by the servicemen returning

31

from overseas who wanted to get back to their normal lives, were quick to forgive the national pastime, and in 1919 returned to the game at pre-war attendance levels. The majors drew over 9.1 million fans in 1920, shattering the previous record of 7.2 million set in 1909, and the minor leagues were back on track with 22 leagues operating at the start of the decade.

Despite the sharp rise in attendance, there were dark clouds on the horizon and the owners were nervous. The reason was baseball's oldest nemesis — gambling. The game had weathered various gambling scandals throughout its history, regularly facing questions surrounding unusual losses by heavily favored clubs. There were murmurs following the 1918 World Series that everything might not have been above board, and the same was true of the 1919 Series when the heavily favored Chicago White Sox fell to the Cincinnati Reds in a Series that saw many of Chicago's stars play poorly. Unlike many previously rumored incidents, the doubts surrounding the 1919 World Series exploded into a full-fledged scandal in late 1920, with some very strong and public allegations that accused specific White Sox players of accepting money to throw the Series.

Previous baseball gambling incidents were internal affairs handled within the framework of the leagues. What became known as the "Black Sox Scandal" was different, however, in that government prosecutors got involved and called a grand jury to investigate the allegations. Suddenly the baseball owners found themselves outside of the situation looking in and unable to contain it within the veil of secrecy of their boardrooms, with this investigation being played out in full view of the public. This was the type of publicity they could ill afford. The public could forgive and forget the missteps of World War I because at the end of the day they really wanted to continue watching baseball; but if they lacked confidence in the integrity of the outcome of games, the entire purpose of attending a sporting event was undermined and it would surely wreak havoc on attendance, and therefore the bottom line.

The major league owners had to act quickly, and they did so by hiring federal judge Kenesaw Mountain Landis to be the league's first commissioner. Landis first came to the attention of the owners as the presiding judge in the antitrust suit brought against the majors by the upstart Federal League in 1915. The Federals thought they had an ally in Landis, who had a reputation for taking a hard line on monopolies from the bench, but they failed to consider that the unconventional and unpredictable judge was

Opposite: Judge Kenesaw Mountain Landis became the first commissioner of Major League Baseball in 1920. While the owners gained credibility from his handling of the Black Sox Scandal, the stubborn Landis proved impossible for the owners to control (Transcendental Graphics).

also a baseball fan, and he saw that a verdict in favor of the Federals could throw professional baseball into chaos by eliminating the reserve clause and causing massive financial instability within the professional game. At one point during the trial the exasperated Landis asked, "Do you realize that a decision in this case may tear down the very foundations of the game, so loved by thousands, and do you realize the decision must also seriously affect both parties?"[1] In lieu of making a ruling Landis did nothing, and instead sat on the case throughout the entire 1915 season. The Federal League owners had had enough after that season and reached an agreement of sorts to sell out to the majors for $600,000,[2] while many of the individual clubs made separate deals to sell their franchises (and players) to major league clubs. The litigation cost the owners over $5 million, but once again they outlasted their rivals.[3] In their eyes Landis established himself as a man who respected the game of baseball and who could be trusted to deal with their problems. The desperation the owners felt was evident in the sweeping powers they granted Landis, essentially binding themselves and the players to his decisions. This was a major step for men who were used to operating their businesses with complete control, as they now had to answer to a higher power instead of trying to build a coalition of fellow owners to support their positions.

Landis dealt swiftly with the Black Sox and on March 13, 1921, the day before the trial of the players was to begin in a Chicago courthouse, he announced that the eight accused players were all being placed on baseball's ineligible list, effectively banning them from playing for any team under the National Association umbrella. Other players involved in gambling scandals or criminal activity quickly felt Landis' wrath as well, finding themselves on the ineligible list and out of professional baseball.[4] When the jury acquitted the Black Sox players later that year, Landis held firm to his stance:

> Regardless of the verdict of juries, no player that throws a ball game; no player that undertakes or promises to throw a ball game; no player that sits in a conference with a bunch of crooked players and gamblers where the ways and means of throwing games are planned and discussed and does not promptly tell his club about it, will ever play professional baseball.
>
> Of course I don't know that any of these men will apply for reinstatement, but if they do, the above are at least a few of the rules that will be enforced. Just keep in mind that, regardless of the verdict of juries, baseball is entirely competent to protect itself against crooks, both inside and outside the game.[5]

Landis' quick and decisive action, while certainly upsetting to White Sox fans and owner Charles Comiskey, who lost many of his best players as a result, sent a clear message to players and fans alike that threats to the integrity of the game would be dealt with severely.

With public confidence restored, professional baseball took advantage of the economic boom of the 1920s. Major league attendance during the 1920–1929 era averaged just under 9.3 million fans per season. The New York Yankees, who opened their brand new stadium in 1923 known as "The House That Ruth Built" were the most economically successful club of the period and reported earnings in excess of $3.5 million for the decade. Not all organizations were so fortunate, however, and many failed to turn a profit in the 1920s despite the positive economic climate.[6]

The minors expanded to 26 leagues by the end of the decade, and the relationship between the majors and minors was solidified with the Major-Minor League Agreement that outlined the relationship between the leagues, including rules for player drafts and acquisitions. Limiting the number of players a minor league team could lose each year to teams in higher classifications provided a level of stability for clubs by eliminating the need to replace a large number of players each off-season. For their part the minors agreed to defer disputes to Landis, who was now the *de facto* czar of all of professional baseball.

Baseball faced one significant challenge during the 1920s in the form of a residual lawsuit left over from the Federal League days. The owners of the Baltimore Federal League club refused to give in to the majors and instead pursued their own antitrust suit against the majors and the National Association (some former Federal League officers were also named as defendants), taking their case all the way to the United States Supreme Court in 1922. The stakes were high, just as they had been in the original Federal League suit, and the owners knew their position was shaky at best. The question at hand was whether or not professional baseball fell within the scope of the Sherman Antitrust Act. Justice Oliver Wendell Holmes wrote the opinion in this famous, if not misguided, ruling as the Court determined that professional baseball was not interstate commerce, and therefore not subject to the Sherman Act.[7] The ruling was a huge victory for professional baseball and a continuing source of consternation for those attempting to challenge Major League Baseball.

The Major-Minor League Agreement wasn't the only thing that brought the majors and minors closer together in the 1920s, as Branch Rickey of the St. Louis Cardinals began the process of building the first formal "farm system." By signing contractual agreements with minor league clubs, or in some instances by purchasing them outright, Rickey ensured the Cardinals not only had access to the talent developed by those teams, but could also actively prevent competitors from obtaining the players under his umbrella of control. Rickey was notorious for signing talented young players, locking them into his farm system, and using them as a lucrative source of both playing talent and revenue for the Cardinals, which was important since the club did not draw nearly as well as its eastern counterparts. The capital generated by selling minor league players to other major league clubs was an integral part of the team's financial success, and the depth of talent certainly contributed to the Cardinals five World Series appearances between 1926 and 1934. Other teams quickly took note, and despite Landis' objection to the concept of the farm system it became an integral part of the business of baseball.[8]

The stock market crash came after the conclusion of the 1929 season, and it was certainly a cause of concern for professional baseball. Ironically the majors experienced its best attendance ever in 1930, breaking the ten million fan barrier for the first time as 10.1 million people came out to the ballparks. The effects of the Great Depression made themselves felt in 1931, and the next four years were lean ones for baseball, just as they were for most other segments of the economy. Consumer expenditures on professional baseball fell more than 36 percent from 1930 to 1933, dropping from $17 million to $10.8 million in just four years.[9] For an industry that relied upon admissions as the principle source of revenues,[10] this was a significant blow. In 1931 only five clubs managed to turn a profit. The following year the number dropped to four, and by 1933 only two teams finished the season in the black. Not until 1935 did more than half the teams turn a profit in the same season once again, and the second half of the decade was more stable, a trend that continued through the 1940 season.[11]

The minors struggled as well, and by 1933 there were only 14 remaining in operation, down from 23 in 1930. Of the 101 minor league teams that played in 1933, 31 were farm clubs tied to the majors, and some insiders later stated that had it not been for the farm system and the infusion of capital from the majors, many if not most of the minor leagues would have gone defunct during the Depression.[12] The system expanded further as the economy improved, and by the end of the decade there were 42 leagues and 173 farm teams populating the minor leagues.

The passing of St. Louis Browns owner Phil Ball in the winter of 1933 was a cause for reflection by the editors of *The Sporting News*. A few owners had died in the recent years, and *The Sporting News* noted a trend in baseball of teams moving away from the traditional single owner model toward a more corporate structure, a change that was deemed both favorable and inevitable.

> When it was a question of fighting for one's rights, the one-man type of club was not only the best, but really the only system that could hope to be successful. The personality of the owner, his ability to make quick decisions and courage to hang on were prime requisites. It was these qualities that conceived and made the American League successful.
>
> But the requirements are different today. The administration of a base-

ball club is the same as that of a business. Its board of directors must be men of diverse interests, whose talents are varied and who can bring to the club the support of the leading elements of the city which it represents. In other words, baseball has ceased to be a personal venture and has become a co-operative or syndicate affair.

Instead of searching for some angel with a lot of money and enthusiasm for baseball to succeed the men who are passing as the years take their toll, the game should be looking forward to a system of ownership vested in a corporation of sportsmen who are interested both in the sport and in the benefits which a club brings to a city. Under such an arrangement, the death of no one man would result in uncertainty for the future; instead, the association of a group would assure uninterrupted operation.

The days of so-called angels seem to be about ended. Baseball now must be sold to communities, both large and small, as civic enterprises, which the different cities owe to themselves to continue and which may or may not be profitable, but which can be made so when the proper amount of co-operation is displayed. Thus the game will be established on a permanent basis and thus it will attract the necessary amount of support from the varied interests of each city to make it self-sustaining, besides re-building the community spirit that once revolved around the ball club and made it the focal point of local pride.[13]

Professional baseball had always been a business to a great extent. For some owners, like chewing gum magnate and Chicago Cubs owner William Wrigley, it was not their primary source of income and they could handle the financial ups and downs that came with operating a franchise. For others, like Philadelphia Athletics owner Connie Mack, baseball was their livelihood. As men such as Ball, Wrigley, and Charles Ebbets passed away, their teams often ended up in the hands of ownership groups, and as *The Sporting News* noted more and more teams were being operated as corporations.

The 1930s closed on a positive note for the game. Attendance was back at pre–Depression levels and personal consumption expenditures on baseball by the public reached a record $21.5 million by 1939, an increase of over 26 percent from 1930.[14] The minors were flourishing due in large part to the ever-widening impact of the farm system that provided many clubs with financial subsidies. The game had a number of popular stars, including an impressive crop of young talent just making its way to the majors. The last thing baseball needed was another war.

Baseball, Business and Society in 1940

At the start of the new decade the majors were riding a wave of economic success and popularity. Baseball was truly America's game, though in truth it was more like America's professional game. In 1940 baseball's revenues were approximately equal to those of professional football, professional hockey, and animal racing (horses and dogs) combined; however, it was still a distant second behind college football, which generated almost twice as much money from the sports consumer.[15] Regardless, baseball was more popular than ever and still commanded a considerable following in American society.

The majors were comprised of the same 16 teams that opened the 1903 season, a run of 37 years with no team relocations or failures. Teams were spread out among ten different cities (including Brooklyn as part of New York City) — Boston, Chicago, Cincinnati, Cleveland, Detroit, New York, Philadelphia, Pittsburgh, St. Louis, and Washington D.C. Five cities had teams in both the American and National Leagues (Boston, Chicago, New York, Philadelphia, and St. Louis), while New York boasted three major league teams. Half the teams were located on the eastern seaboard, while the other half were in cities known for their industrial output and status as railway hubs, with St. Louis both the western-most and southern-most outpost. This was not a broad cross-section of America, but teams were limited to a great extent by the primary form of transportation available during the era, which was rail. It was not until the rise of affordable air travel that locating major league teams west or south of St. Louis became feasible.

That is not to say that the west and south were without professional baseball. Just about anywhere that was not big enough for the majors had some classification of minor league ball in the general vicinity. In fact the quality of play in the Pacific Coast League was said to be of high enough caliber to almost qualify as a third major league. With the broad minor league classification system, it was potentially economical to place teams even in some relatively small towns. The reach of the minor leagues helped solidify baseball as the national game, something that would have been very difficult, if not impossible, had only the 16 major league teams existed in this era before television.

While the locations of major league teams remained constant, the ownership of those teams had changed significantly since World War I. Only two teams can be said to have remained with the same primary owner: Col. Jacob Ruppert's Yankees and Connie Mack's Athletics. Clark Griffith was an important part of the Senators franchise during World War I, including as a minority owner, and had taken over ownership of the club in the intervening years. The other teams had traded hands either through sales or inheritances. As *The Sporting News* noted, major league teams were beginning to resemble multi-owner businesses more than the sole-proprietorships they had been earlier in the century. In this regard they were becoming more in line with the large companies of the day, often with many shareholders to answer to and far-flung business locations to manage in the form of their minor league farm teams. Instead of only employing one coaching staff and perhaps a handful of scouts, major league franchises now needed coaching and business staffs in many different cities, and an even wider network of scouts to get a leg up on their competition.

In many ways the baseball workforce was similar to that of the nation. Players had varying levels of education, though most did not advance past high school. For many, baseball was seen as their best chance of financial success given the limited educational and vocational opportunities available to them locally, and this helped fill the minors with hard-working players. The national publicity achieved by the game and its stars made sporting success seem both attainable and desirable, though in reality the overwhelming majority of players never made it to the majors, and even those who did often needed to work at other jobs in the off-season to make ends meet for their families. Baseball could certainly be lucrative, but only for the chosen few who were the most talented.

Though on occasion a promoter might field a team of female players (for instance, the so-called "Bloomer Girls") and take them on a barnstorming tour, professional baseball was an exclusively male vocation. There were some examples of women involved on the field at the minor league, semi-pro, or industrial league levels, but these were very rare exceptions, and society generally did not support women playing sports, especially alongside men. This is not an attempt to diminish the accomplishments of those women who tried to break into the game, but simply a matter of how baseball and sports were viewed at the time. Like many jobs during the era, baseball was an exclusively male domain.

Women were not the only group excluded from Organized Baseball. So too were black men. The discrimination against blacks playing alongside whites went back to the 19th century, and the "Gentlemen's Agreement" kept them out of major and minor league baseball even in the absence of any formal rule banning their participation. This exclusion did not prevent blacks from playing baseball, though it did limit their options. The first all-black professional team, the Cuban Giants, appeared in 1885, and they and other all-black teams played in the white minor leagues until 1890. Once they were shut out of the minors, the opportunities rested primarily in the various segregated all-black leagues that came and went over the subsequent decades, along with assorted barnstorming teams that toured the country and took on all comers. In the 1920s and 1930s the Negro Leagues and black baseball fielded a number of exceptionally talented teams and performed in front of some very large, and quite often mixed race, crowds. The Negro Leagues in many ways mirrored the majors, hosting their own All-Star Game and championship series to rival the World Series. Though popular, the various leagues often struggled to remain afloat, finding themselves in competition with white teams for dates at ballparks and forced to play inconsistent schedules. There were many black players of major league caliber during that period who were kept out of the majors only due to the color of their skin, the only racial/ethnic group discriminated against to that extent.[16]

The business of baseball in many ways resembled the American business structure as a whole. The teams were primarily run as corporations, though a few single-owner operations still existed. The workforce had an average level of education for the period, was exclusively male, and excluded blacks. There were also some differences, most notably the reserve clause and the antitrust exemption given by the Supreme Court. In no other part of society was a man likely to be prevented from leaving his current employer to ply the same trade elsewhere, whereas a man who wanted to play professional baseball had to sign a contract with a reserve clause that tied him to his team and made it impossible for him to offer his services to any other club within the National Association, which controlled the industry. Combined with the antitrust exemption that made it so difficult for potential competitors to establish themselves, baseball was a type of indentured servitude. Certainly a player could opt to retire from the game at any time and move into another line of work, but if he wanted to play baseball he had to do so under the reserve clause or risk playing in an outlaw league. Players were also at a disadvantage due to their lack of a union, something available to workers in many other industries. Various attempts at unionization had failed, and players feared blacklisting if they tried to organize and bargain collectively.

Selective Service

When did World War II actually start? The most common date given is September 1, 1939, the day that Nazi Germany invaded Poland. This is, of course, a very Euro-centric view of what was a global conflict, and one could just as easily point to Japan's 1931 invasion of Manchuria or its 1937 attack on China, not to mention the host of smaller conflicts that occurred during this general period. Some historians even take the stance that we should look at World War II as nothing more than the continuation of World War I, lumping the entire 1914–1945 period into one global conflict.

Regardless of the date selected, by 1940 it was obvious to Americans that there were significant wars going on in both Asia and Europe, and that given the escalation of hostilities it was becoming more and more difficult for the country to stay on the sidelines and out of direct military involvement. The country's small standing Army was woefully insufficient for any type of meaningful involvement in either of the primary theaters, and the buffer zone provided by the two oceans meant that there was no obvious, imminent threat to American territory, so there was no rush to enlist voluntarily as the public warily watched events unfold overseas. But with the stunningly rapid fall of France to the German blitzkrieg that summer, it was apparent that the conflict in Europe would not be over any time soon, and President Franklin Delano Roosevelt turned to conscription to begin the process of building up the armed forces. On September 19, 1940, Roosevelt signed the Selective Training and Service Act of 1940 into law, and America established its first-ever peacetime draft. The act required all men between 21 and 36 years of age to register for the draft, which selected candidates using a lottery system. Those chosen had to appear before their local draft boards for evaluation, and if selected and inducted into the military they served for 12 months, after which they were guaranteed the right to return to their former jobs. The local boards had considerable discretion, and with the rush to start the first round of the lottery many of the rules, guidelines, and exceptions remained to be worked out. As a result, a considerable number of men gained exemptions for a wide range of reasons, and many observers felt the draft boards favored certain classes and groups.

In the baseball world the owners were a bit nervous. The first rounds of the draft were scheduled to take place during the off-season, a time when clubs would be attempting to sign their players and solidify their rosters for the upcoming 1941 campaign, leaving them facing the very real possibility that players they signed and expected to play would in fact be working for Uncle Sam instead. Publicly the major league owners indicated that baseball would contribute to the nation's manpower needs. Senators owner Clark Griffith had many contacts in the government owing to his team's location in the nation's capital, and as such he exerted a certain amount of political influence. In the days leading up to the signing of the act, Griffith made it clear that baseball was ready to heed the call to arms. "Baseball will do what the country wants. We're all ready. Why, by sin, at my age I'm ready, too, if they want me."[17] Players reported as ordered to their local voting precincts on October 16 to register for the first draft selection that was just over a month away. Many, such as the DiMaggio brothers and Bob Feller, posed for publicity photos during their visits to show that baseball players were indeed doing their part.

The owners were cautiously optimistic about the first rounds of the draft. Because their players came from all over the country, their corresponding risk of selection was well distributed. Also, major leaguers were generally seasoned ballplayers who were typically older than those in the minors and therefore more likely to be married and have dependents, making them better able to obtain deferments or exemptions. The lowest levels of the minors were likely safe as well, but for the opposite reason — Class D teams tended to have the youngest players, many of who were not yet of draft age. It was the mid-level minors that stood to suffer the most, as they did when the country entered the war in 1941 and significantly ramped up the draft.

Another group of men were keeping close tabs on the possibility of high-level baseball talent being drafted, as many military officers were already contemplating the possibilities of fielding teams to represent their units or branches of the service. According to *The Sporting News*, "There will be draft army ball teams all over the country next summer, and army officials would be delighted to have these teams feature as many big leaguers as possible."[18] The controversy surrounding healthy, capable men playing baseball on service teams gained considerable attention once the war started, with the public asking why these men remained safe at home while others were sent overseas to fight. But in this period prior to America's entry into the war, service teams attracted little if any attention.

The pending draft also impacted the business of off-season player transactions. A number of teams had been interested in acquiring Philadelphia Phillies pitcher Hugh Mulcahy, but when word got out that the bachelor Mulcahy held a low draft number, interest evaporated. Teams were not willing to take risks on players of draft age who had no dependents because their futures were very unclear.[19] Teams like the Athletics and Reds, which had large portions of their roster spots held by draft-age bachelors, faced very uncertain futures going into the 1941 season. Overall, however, few of the leagues' top players held low draft numbers, which was a cause for relief.[20]

Commissioner Landis was adamant that no requests would be made for any type of special treatment for ballplayers. A group of owners wanted Clark Griffith to lead a committee to work directly with the War Department and draft officials, but Landis immediately put a halt to any such efforts. Landis himself was taking charge of all draft-related issues, and no contacts with the government were to be made by anyone else associated with the game.[21] Landis for one had learned the lessons of World War I, when attempts by major league owners to exempt players from service caused a swift backlash and a public relations nightmare, and he was not going to allow the owners to repeat their mistakes. Much to Landis' dismay, Griffith continued to talk to his political contacts and make statements to the press that proved embarrassing for the league:

> The authorities here are sympathetic towards baseball. They don't want to see it hurt. There is the question of national morale and baseball. In times of trouble, people want to be entertained. If we aren't crippled, we should have the biggest season in baseball history. Then, there is *the status of base-*

ball as a vast business with big investments, and appreciable revenues for the government through the various forms of taxes. Yes, we deserve some consideration, but we are not going to the War Department to seek it[22] [emphasis added].

Griffith was playing his own brand of politics in the press, attempting to show that baseball was important to society for its morale value and to the government due to its tax revenues. As such it certainly deserved special considerations, according to Griffith, but the game was above actually asking for any concessions, implying that they should originate from the government itself. It is unclear whether anyone was really fooled by this rhetoric, that surprisingly originated with someone who had been involved in the game during World War I and saw first-hand the damage done by talk of concessions. Painting the game as "a vast business" was also a questionable tactic, and certainly not one likely to generate any sympathy from the public.

The majors survived the initial draft selections without the loss of any established players. Bill Embrick of the International League's Harrisburg Senators became the first professional ballplayer selected, and he joined the Army at the end of November. It wasn't until 1941 that the first man on a major league roster entered the service when Bill Stack reported for duty on January 10, though Stack had never actually appeared in a major league contest (and in fact never would). The first established major leaguer to heed the call to duty was none other than Hugh Mulcahy, who entered the service on March 8, much to the dismay of the Phillies and with sighs of relief from those teams that had held off on trading for him during the off-season. As Opening Day approached it looked like baseball would come through the early rounds of the draft relatively unscathed.[23]

The first serious blow to rock the majors was the announcement that Detroit Tigers star slugger Hank Greenberg had been selected, and by mid–April found fit for duty. Greenberg was signed to a $55,000 contract for the 1941 season, a far cry from the $21 per month he would initially earn in the Army. It was rumored, however, that Tigers owner Walter Briggs would continue to pay Greenberg his contracted salary during his service in an effort to keep his biggest star happy.[24] Greenberg went out with a bang, hitting two homers in his last game before reporting to the Army. He also made certain to maintain a positive attitude about his situation when speaking in public, knowing full well that the spotlight was on him as the first star player to be drafted. "If there is any last message to be given the public, let it be that I'm going to be a good soldier,"[25] he said. Greenberg was eligible for early release from his commitment and was discharged from the Army on December 5, 1941. Two days later the Japanese bombed Pearl Harbor and he immediately re-enlisted, not to return to the baseball diamond until 1945.

Hugh Mulcahy was the first established major leaguer inducted into the military via the Selective Training and Service Act of 1940. A number of teams were interested in obtaining Mulcahy prior to the 1941 season, but his low draft number scared them all away (Transcendental Graphics).

In 1941 the nation found itself being dragged ever closer to active participation in the war. The signing of the Lend-Lease Act paved the way for the country to supply even more war materials to the struggling Allies, and the sinking of the merchant ship SS *Robin Moor* by a German submarine on May 21 outraged the nation. That outrage, however, did not equate to a call to join the war, as many Americans still sought to avoid becoming involved in combat. A May survey of college students by sociologist Delbert Miller showed that only 21 percent of respondents "Agreed" or "Strongly Agreed" with the statement "Every able bodied single man who calls himself an American should volunteer now for military service," and only 22 percent chose those responses for the statement "The U.S. should declare itself an ally of Britain and send air force, navy, and army if necessary to defeat Hitler."[26] Even with the war in Europe nearly two years old, many Americans still believed the country could stay outside of the conflict.

The 1941 season was a success for both the owners and the players. The majors drew almost 9.7 million fans, slightly less than they had in 1940, but still respectable. On the field the nation was captivated by the progress of two dramatic achievements, as serious and casual fans alike checked the papers daily to follow the progress of Yankee Joe DiMaggio's eventual record-breaking consecutive game hitting streak, and later followed Red Sox slugger Ted Williams as he attempted to break the .400 barrier, which he succeeded in doing on the season's last day to finish the year with a .406 mark. The owners also made some moves to improve the game's standing in the arena of public opinion, with many teams admitting servicemen in uniform to the ballparks free of charge. The league did its part, too, donating the receipts from the 1941 All-Star Game to the United Service Organization to be used for providing recreation for those in the military. Other than Griffith's gaffe in the spring, which went largely unnoticed, 1941 was a resounding success.

Not all teams were doing well financially, however. The woeful St. Louis Browns finished seventh in the eight-team American League and had by far the worst attendance in the majors, attracting a mere 176,240 fans in 1941, an average of less than 2,300 per game. The Browns shared their ballpark with the National League's St. Louis Cardinals, and the Cardinals drew 633,645 fans to the same stadium that year. Over the course of the prior 12 seasons the Browns finished in the bottom half of the American League standings every year, each time doing so with a losing record, and recorded the league's lowest attendance 11 times. The team simply could not compete against the consistently successful Cardinals for the attention of St. Louis baseball fans, and owner Donald Barnes was looking for a way to save his struggling franchise.

For an answer to his problem, Barnes looked west. St. Louis was the westernmost outpost of the majors at the time, but there was plenty of baseball being played in the western part of the country, and the Pacific Coast League drew very well in cities such as Los Angeles, Oakland, San Francisco, Portland, and Seattle. With its rapidly growing population centers, California in particular looked promising as the home for a major league franchise. It was not as easy as just picking the team up and moving it across the country, however, as there were a number of hoops to jump through. Not only did Barnes need the approval of the other major league owners and Landis, there was also the issue of the territorial rights to Los Angeles, the Browns' potential new home, which were held by the Pacific Coast League franchise there under the National Agreement. Other considerations included the extra time and expense involved with traveling to and from the coast, and the associated scheduling issues.

Throughout the 1941 season Barnes laid the groundwork with his fellow owners to approve the Browns' move to Los Angeles for the 1942 season. He accounted for everything, securing agreements and arranging to pay a fee to the Pacific Coast League for expansion into its territory. It appeared that everyone wanted the relocation to happen, and the city of Los Angeles offered the Browns a financial guarantee of 500,000 spectators per year, with the city paying the difference if attendance was below that level, a figure nearly three times the team's 1941 attendance. Even the Cardinals contributed, agreeing to pay the Browns $200,000 to cover moving expenses and taking over their lease at Sportsman's Park, the stadium the two teams shared, glad to be rid of even the minimal competition the Browns provided. Everything was in place for a mere formality of a vote scheduled for Monday, December 8, at the league meetings.[27] That vote, needless to say, never took place.

America Enters World War II

In the early morning of Sunday, December 7, 1941, the Japanese navy launched a surprise attack on the American naval base at Pearl Harbor, Hawaii. Using carrier-based aircraft, the Japanese badly damaged the U.S. Pacific Fleet and forced America's entry into World War II. By December 11 the United States had declared war against Japan, Germany, and Italy, and began the process of rapidly expanding the draft to increase the size of the military quickly.

The annual baseball meetings continued in the days following the attack, as professional baseball still had business to attend to. Players were traded, schedules discussed, and the merits of night baseball debated, but all under a cloud of uncertainty. Would there even be a 1942 season? Would the draft be expanded? How many players would voluntarily join the military? There were more questions than answers facing the men who made baseball their business. They took the opportunity to make one initial positive public gesture in relation to the war effort, reviving the Professional Baseball Equipment Fund, also known as the "Ball-and-Bat Fund," that served them well during World War I. The Fund provided kits of baseball equipment that were shipped to servicemen both at home and overseas so that they could play at least rudimentary baseball wherever they happened to find themselves. The majors launched the Fund in December with a $24,000 contribution form league coffers, plus an additional $1,000 coming from the Baseball Writers' Association of America, and declared that all of the receipts from the 1942 All-Star Game would be donated to the Fund.[28] Griffith headed the Fund and placed the first order for 1,500 kits, comprised of 4,500 bats and 18,000 baseballs, on December 31.[29]

Many ballplayers joined in the wave of voluntary enlistments immediately following the attack on Pearl Harbor. Among them were Hank Greenberg, who had just been discharged from the Army on December 5 after fulfilling his draft obligations, and 23-year-old pitching sensation Bob Feller, who led the American League in wins over the previous three seasons with the Cleveland Indians. Feller even insisted on combat duty, a request the Navy gladly obliged, and he served with distinction as a gunner on board the USS *Alabama* through most of the war. Others followed suit as both major and minor leaguers signed new kinds of contracts, very much like their baseball contracts in that they had no say in where they would be from year to year, with Uncle Sam playing the role of team owner.

Facing complete uncertainty as to the future of professional baseball during the duration of the war, Landis found himself in an unenviable position. The owners appeared to believe that the game had done its part during World War I, though this line of thinking resulted from a certain amount of revisionist history. They conveniently forgot about all the public missteps they made and the poor press the game and players received for continuing their petty squabbles while Americans were being sent to Europe to fight and die. Bob Quinn, president of the Boston Braves, proved this point when he discussed the future of the game in days immediately following Pearl Harbor:

> In the World War baseball was slow to alter its routine. As a matter of fact, when Ban Johnson and John Heydler went to Washington with the suggestion that the schedules be suspended, the high authorities there vetoed the idea. But in 1918, when the "work or fight" slogan became so popular, the players themselves became so impatient to get into the "big fuss" that the season was shortened and ended on Labor Day.[30]

The league representatives certainly met with government officials, but there is no evidence that baseball ever suggested the canceling of the 1918 season and that the politicians "vetoed" the idea. Furthermore, it was not the players who pushed to end the season early, it was an order from the government, and the owners actually pushed for the World Series to be played *after* the government's September 1 deadline. This inaccurate view of the game's involvement in the war was reinforced by the tremendous growth in the popularity of baseball immediately following its conclusion. In reality the owners' actions told a much different story as they tried to wrangle concessions and have the game, and therefore their businesses, declared essential. Landis saw baseball at a similar crossroads at the beginning of 1942, but recognized that any efforts to have the status of the game addressed by the government required much more tact than the owners exhibited on their own in 1917–1918.

Landis was also a patriot, something that certainly influenced his approach and ideas about how the game should try to navigate the war, which he could plainly see would not be a short one. His father, Dr. Abraham Hoch Landis, was a Union surgeon in the Civil War, and was badly wounded when a cannon ball struck his leg at the Battle of Kennesaw Mountain. The battle had such a significant impact on his life that he later named his son after it, though omitting one "n" in Kennesaw. Landis' son Reed joined the Illinois National Guard in 1916, and by 1917 was a fighter pilot serving with the American Expeditionary Forces in France. Reed served with distinction, rising to the rank of Captain and earning the Distinguished Flying Cross. Landis was tremendously proud of his son's service and achievements, and was a vocal supporter of the war effort, making appearances to promote the sale of war bonds. He presided over a number of cases during World War I that involved both draft dodgers and foreign agents, dispensing some harsh punishments and harsh words from the bench for those who failed to support the war effort.[31] Landis was not going to allow himself and the game he loved to come across as whining and not doing their parts during this new war, not only because it was bad for business but also because it was against his personal ethics.

The situation was complicated by Landis' relationship with President Roosevelt, whom the judge had criticized publicly over the years. The staunchly Republican Landis was no fan of the liberal Democrat Roosevelt due in part to his social and economic policies, but perhaps even more importantly because of his handling of the growing world conflict. According to *The Sporting News* editor and baseball supporter J. G. Taylor Spink, during a conversation he had with Landis the day after the Pearl Harbor attack, the commissioner blamed Roosevelt for not having done more to prepare the nation for war. "Do you realize, Spink, that we now are a secondary power in the Pacific?," Landis is said to have asked rhetorically.[32] Regardless of whatever personal animosity he felt towards the president, Landis needed his support if baseball was to continue during the war, and he knew it. Fortunately,

Roosevelt had already opened the door a crack, sending a letter to the New York chapter of the Baseball Writers' Association of American to be read at their annual off-season dinner following the close of the 1940 season, in which he extolled the virtues of the game and its value for national morale.[33] The president was a well-known baseball fan and regularly took his presidential prerogative of throwing out the first pitch to open the season in Washington. He also had a good relationship with Senators owner Clark Griffith, who regularly traveled to the White House each spring to present the president with his season's pass to the club's ballpark. The fact that Roosevelt willingly posed for publicity photos during Griffith's visits further emphasized the president's fondness of the game.

Behind the scenes it appeared that Griffith was already tapping his political contacts despite Landis' announcement that he was personally taking charge of the war situation as the game's spokesman, and that the owners were to stay out of it. A number of politicians made public statements in early January 1941 in support of baseball, and one wonders if such men would have even given any thought to the future of baseball while dealing with the nation's very recent entrance into the war unless someone suggested the idea to them. Griffith is a natural suspect, though certainly many owners had strong political connections, and any evidence is circumstantial. Congressmen from both sides of the aisle were quick to speak out in support of continuing the 1942 season. "It would be foolish to do otherwise. Morale must be maintained," said House Minority Leader Joseph Martin of Massachusetts, a Republican. Democrat Edward A. Kelly from Illinois also supported the continuation of the game at all levels. "I'm for keeping it going. It's a matter of morale and recreation. And by keeping pro ball going we encourage amateur baseball, which in turn builds up bodies of our youngsters. And that's what we need today." Representative Walter G. Andrews of New York pointed to the patriotic examples set by Bob Feller and Hank Greenberg in volunteering for service in the aftermath of Pearl Harbor.[34] Baseball was not only good for national morale during a time of war, but it would also build the physical skills of young men who might be called upon to fight.

The support from members of Congress was positive, but what the game really needed was the blessing of the baseball-fan-in-chief, Roosevelt. With this in mind, Landis wrote a letter to Roosevelt asking for his input as to how the game should proceed for the upcoming 1942 season, while at the same time pledging his and the game's support for the war effort. Dated January 14, 1942, the letter read:

Dear. Mr. President

The time is approaching when, in ordinary conditions, our teams would be heading for Spring training camps. However, inasmuch as these are not ordinary times, I venture to ask what you have in mind as to whether professional baseball should continue to operate. Of course my inquiry does not relate at all to individual members of this organization, whose status, in the emergency, is fixed by law operating upon all citizens.

Normally we have, in addition to the sixteen major teams, approximately three hundred and twenty minor teams — members of leagues playing in the United States and Canada.

C
O
P
Y

BASEBALL

TPF 227

Kenesaw M. Landis
   Commissioner
Leslie M. O'Connor
Secretary-Treasurer

333 North Michigan Avenue
Chicago

Jany. 14, 1942

Dear Mr. President

    The time is approaching when, in ordinary conditions, our teams would be heading for Spring training camps. However, inasmuch as these are not ordinary times, I venture to ask what you have in mind as to whether professional baseball should continue to operate. Of course my inquiry does not relate at all to individual members of this organization, whose status, in the emergency, is fixed by law operating upon all citizens.

    Normally we have, in addition to the sixteen major teams, approximately three hundred and twenty minor teams - members of leagues playing in the United States and Canada.

    Health and strength to you - and whatever else it takes to do this job.

    With great respect

        Very truly yours,

      (Signed) KENESAW M. LANDIS

The President
Washington,
D. C.

Commissioner Landis wrote to President Roosevelt on January 14, 1942, roughly six weeks after Pearl Harbor, to ask for direction with regard to the upcoming baseball season. While Roosevelt's famous response has been widely quoted over the years, the contents of Landis' original letter are often overlooked (courtesy Franklin D. Roosevelt Presidential Library and Museum, Hyde Park, New York).

Health and strength to you — and whatever else it takes to do this job. With great respect

Very truly yours,
KENESAW M. LANDIS[35]

This was almost certainly a difficult letter for Landis to write, forcing him to swallow his enormous pride and put the fate of the game he represented and loved into the hands of another, even more so because he had in the past been highly critical of Roosevelt, of which the president was well aware. In fact Griffith once quipped, "Landis wasn't much more welcome at the White House than the Japanese ambassador."[36] Despite his personal feelings, however, Landis used considerable finesse in his letter to Roosevelt, wisely not asking for any concessions or special considerations, but only a statement as to whether or not the game should continue. There was nothing in the letter that, if it appeared in the press, could hurt the game's reputation with its fans and society as a whole. In addition, the onus was placed entirely on Roosevelt, so that if the outcome proved to be unpopular it would be easy to distance baseball from the decision and point the finger directly at the president.

Landis' letter was delivered to the president on the 14th, and Roosevelt wasted no time in responding, sending a return note a day later that became known as the "Green Light Letter."

My dear Judge—

Thank you for yours of January fourteenth. As you will, of course, realize the final decision about the baseball season must rest with you and the Baseball club owners — so what I am going to say is solely a personal and not an official point of view.

I honestly feel that it would be best for the country to keep baseball going. There will be fewer people unemployed and everybody will work longer hours and harder than ever before.

And that means that they ought to have a chance for recreation and for taking their minds off their work even more than before.

Baseball provides a recreation which does not last over two hours or two hours and a half, and which can be got for very little cost. And, incidentally, I hope that night games can be extended because it gives an opportunity to the day shift to see a game occasionally.

As to the players themselves, I know you agree with me that individual players who are of active military age should go, without question, into the services. Even if the actual quality to the teams is lowered by the greater use of older players, this will not dampen the popularity of the sport. Of course, if an individual has some particular aptitude in a trade or profession, he ought to serve the Government. That, however, is a matter which I know you can handle with complete justice.

Here is another way of looking at it — if 300 teams use 5,000 or 6,000 players, these players are a definite recreational asset to at least 20,000,000

January 15, 1942.

My dear Judge:-

Thank you for yours of January fourteenth. As
you will, of course, realise the final decision about the
baseball season must rest with you and the Baseball Club
owners -- so what I am going to say is solely a personal
and not an official point of view.

I honestly feel that it would be best for the
country to keep baseball going. There will be fewer people
unemployed and everybody will work longer hours and harder
than ever before.

And that means that they ought to have a
chance for recreation and for taking their minds off
their work even more than before.

Baseball provides a recreation which does
not last over two hours or two hours and a half, and
which can be got for very little cost. And, incidentally,
I hope that night games can be extended because it gives
an opportunity to the day shift to see a game occasionally.

As to the players themselves, I know you agree
with me that individual players who are of active military
or naval age should go, without question, into the services.
Even if the actual quality of the teams is lowered by the
greater use of older players, this will not dampen the
popularity of the sport. Of course, if any individual
has some particular aptitude in a trade or profession,
he ought to serve the Government. That, however, is a
matter which I know you can handle with complete justice.

Here is another way of looking at it -- if
300 teams use 5,000 or 6,000 players, these players are
a definite recreational asset to at least 20,000,000
of their fellow citizens -- and that in my judgment is
thoroughly worthwhile.

With every best wish,

Very sincerely yours,

Hon. Kenesaw M. Landis,
233 North Michigan Avenue,
Chicago,
Illinois.

Roosevelt responded to Landis' letter quickly with what became known as the
"Green Light Letter," paving the way for the continuation of baseball during the
war (courtesy Franklin D. Roosevelt Presidential Library and Museum, Hyde
Park, New York).

of their fellow citizens — and that in my judgment is thoroughly worth-while.

With every best wish,

Very Sincerely Yours,
Franklin D. Roosevelt[37]

The last thing the president wanted to do is to alarm the public any more than necessary by taking action to shut down parts of their normal, pre-war lives, which could have a disastrous effect on morale. However, he was also wise enough not to make any commitments of his own that he might be forced to go back on as the war progressed, and the result was a somewhat vague response that put the decision back on Landis and the owners. Roosevelt thought it was best to keep the game going for now, but he wasn't going to force that decision on them.

In later years Griffith would claim considerable credit for brokering this correspondence between the commissioner and the president, and while it certainly shows signs of his participation, the actual level of his involvement is impossible to determine. One part of Roosevelt's letter does lend credence to Griffith's claim, however, and that is the president's "hope" that the majors would increase the number of night baseball games, his only specific request. Night baseball was a contentious issue among the owners, with the teams that struggled financially viewing it as an avenue to increase ticket sales, while profitable teams looked at it simply as an additional expense due to the additional equipment and electricity required. Griffith was initially in the anti-night baseball camp, but in the years immediately preceding the war had changed his views and become perhaps the strongest proponent of night baseball among the owners. In fact at the league meetings in December 1941 Griffith wanted to increase the number of night games allowed per team from seven to 28, a significant expansion even among the other owners who wanted more night ball.[38] It is quite possible that Griffith made this suggestion to Roosevelt, and that the president included it in his letter as a favor to his friend, or possibly even as a jab at Landis.

* * *

The Green Light Letter solved baseball's immediate problem — the 1942 season would go on, and the owners and players could begin making the necessary plans and arrangements. However, many questions remained unanswered. Some players were enlisting in the military, while others would surely be lost to the expanding draft. Schedules needed to be drawn up but it was unclear what impact the war would have on transportation, both in the availability of rail berths for train travel and gasoline for buses. The potential for government ordered blackouts in coastal cities to help protect shipping from German submarines, along with general curfews, threatened to impact the start times for games. Perhaps the most important question for the owners was: would the fans come to the ballparks, especially if news from the front became bad? The minor leagues had the most to lose, with their tight budgets and so much of their support coming from the majors. Roosevelt's letter ensured that the 1942 season would indeed start. But no one could tell how or when it would end.

CHAPTER 3

Baseball and the War Effort

The press immediately reported on the Green Light Letter, using head-lines such as "Roosevelt Urges Continuation of Baseball During War and More Night Games" in the *New York Times* and "Stay in There and Pitch F.D.R." in *The Sporting News*. There was no denying its impact on the baseball world, where it was received with a sense of tremendous relief. *Baseball Magazine* described the letter's importance as, "If the shot that was fired at Lexington in 1775 was 'heard around the world,' it is equally true that the 'Play Ball' of President Roosevelt in his letter to Commissioner Landis recently, was heard and applauded around the baseball universe."[1] Esteemed baseball writer Dan Daniel called it "the most important approval the game has got in all its history."[2]

Even with the go-ahead from Roosevelt and some very public comments of support from members of Congress, the owners were still aware of the need to proceed cautiously. Though they certainly had some very selective and often completely inaccurate memories of the game's experiences during World War I, at least some executives realized the importance of projecting the correct image to the public and not requesting any special treatment for the game. Larry MacPhail of the Dodgers felt the need to emphasize this just a week after the Green Light Letter was sent:

> One thing must be made very clear to the players and the public. Landis did not write to the President looking for favors. He did not write in order to get players deferred. On the contrary. He asked if the White House wanted us to fold up until after the war. The President sent the Judge an emphatic "No."[3]

MacPhail was not just a savvy businessman but also a World War I veteran, having served overseas as an artillery captain. He was often at the fore-front of the league's early efforts in support of the war effort and became the unofficial voice of baseball in the first months of 1942. "We cannot run on any 'business as usual' slogan now," he said. "The fan, who digs down in his jeans and clicks the turnstiles in the 300 communities where professional ball hopes to carry on in 1942, expects us to work out a definite program of unselfish co-operation with agencies of the government needing help."[4] MacPhail's inclusion of the minor leagues in his comments was also telling, as 148 of those teams were farm clubs for the majors, which had a vested economic interest in the future of their talent development organizations.

Professional baseball's strategy for continuation was built on the premise that the game would provide three primary contributions to society during the war: morale at home and overseas, economic benefits, and manpower. This strategy was not laid out in any formal sense, but instead developed over the opening months of the war as the owners looked for ways to show that the game was an important part of American society and one that would "do its part" in the new conflict. Baseball publications were full of hyperbole, patriotic proclamations, and catchy headlines, all intended to assure the baseball fan that being a fan was in and of itself patriotic. James Gould wrote in *Baseball Magazine*, "With the treacherous attack on Pearl Harbor, an unsought but not totally unexpected war has come to menace the most truly NATIONAL sport in the world—BASEBALL."[5] The implication was that an attack on America was an attack on baseball since they were essentially one in the same, harkening back to the findings of the Mills Commission decades earlier. For the most part this type of talk was confined to the sporting press, but the view of baseball as an American institution was widely accepted in society.

Morale

The argument that baseball was good for morale was an old one that was previously used during World War I, and the owners brought it out again when faced with the potential loss of players to the draft in 1941. The idea gained a stronger foothold during the new war and was a talking point for the politicians who spoke in support of the game in early January 1942, but it was the Green Light Letter that gave it real validity. While Roosevelt never actually used the word "morale" in his letter, he wrote of the recreation value of spectator sports in taking people's minds off of their work, and that was enough. Baseball men took the morale baton and ran with it, making it a frequent rallying cry during the war whenever times got tough and the game faced opposition.

The concept of morale was at the forefront of American thought during the war years, both before and after America's direct involvement, and many experts viewed recreation as an essential component to maintaining positive attitudes and good morale in the face of the conflict. Sociologist Eduard Lindeman, writing in November 1941, concluded that the morale of both the military and the workers on the home front was essential to America's success, regardless of whether or not it entered the war as a belligerent, and one of the ways to maintain and improve morale was through sports and recreation. Unlike some who insisted that it was the physical participation in sports that provided value, Lindeman believed that attending sporting events was beneficial, creating an environment of shared experience. "Some experts in physical education disparage mere attendance at sport events; they regard this as a form of vicarious experience and hence not fruitful," he wrote. "My opinion is contrary; I have witnessed some of the finest types of shared experiences on the part of spectators at baseball games."[6] While Lindeman wrote about the impact of sports in general, references to baseball appeared throughout his article, further emphasizing the importance of the game in society as a whole. Though supportive of the place of sports in society, Lindeman also astutely pointed out that sports did not promote equality in that "racial discrimination, for example, is almost universal in certain of our sports,"[7] and given that the democratic nature of any wartime mobilization would surely include ethnic minorities, there could be a social backlash after the war when minorities would be expected to return to their previous place in society. His recommendation of racial inclusion and integration was one that would play out in society and in baseball as the war progressed.

If baseball wanted to live up to its claims as being important for national morale, then it was essential to make the game itself available to as many Americans as possible, and this was the impetus for Roosevelt's request for more games to be played at night. Prior to the start of the 1941 season the majors announced that the number of night games was indeed being increased, with teams now permitted to play up to 14 home evening contests in contrast to the seven originally allowed, and the Senators were granted 21 night games due to their proximity to so many government employees and servicemen in Washington D.C. Publicly it appeared that the owners and president were in agreement, but in reality night baseball had been a contentious issue in the majors ever since the first game was played in Cincinnati in 1935. Ironically Roosevelt played a part in that historical event, pushing a button in the White House that supposedly turned on the lights at Crosley Field, a masterful piece of publicity arranged by none other than Larry MacPhail. However, owners of many of the game's most successful franchises did not want to incur the expenses involved in equipping their stadiums for nighttime play when they were regularly profitable with exclusively day games, and Landis too supported keeping strict limits on night games. New York Yankees president Ed Barrow once quipped, "Night baseball is a passing attraction which will not make it wise for the New York Club to spend $250,000 on a lighting system for the stadium."[8] There was considerable resentment among some owners that the president was basically forcing them to schedule more night games by his request in the Green Light Letter. Even some of night baseball's strongest proponents like MacPhail did not want to see the night schedule expanded considerably, and hoped that it would be reined back to seven games per team after the conclusion of the war. Even though attendance at night games was almost always significantly higher than day games in the majors, most owners saw it primarily as a novelty and feared that a broader night schedule could negatively impact the abilities of their players, who would not be able to establish a routine in their training and playing. This concern did not deter the minor leagues and even some barnstorming black teams from embracing the technology, as they recognized the economic benefits of playing at night. There was the additional problem that only 11 major league clubs were

Washington Senators owner Clark Griffith presents President Roosevelt with his annual major league pass. Griffith's relationships with Roosevelt and other Washington politicians proved beneficial to the owners over the course of the war (Transcendental Graphics).

equipped to play night baseball in 1942, with the two clubs in Boston, the Chicago Cubs, the Detroit Tigers, and the New York Yankees now potentially facing the expense of adding lights to their stadiums.

Regardless, the president got his way and the night schedule was expanded. At least some teams got a reprieve, however, when the military authorities banned evening games in New York City due to fears that excessive light from the city could make ship silhouettes more visible, and therefore present better targets for the German submarines that were beginning to operate off the American coast. As a result New York fans had to be content with day games until the ban was lifted in 1944.[9] Though night games continued throughout the war, the debate continued behind the scenes and many owners looked to reduce the frequency of night games as the war progressed. They were further confounded by other government "suggestions" such as the one made by War Manpower Commission Chairman Paul V. McNutt, who in 1943 asked the owners to consider scheduling some games in the morning to make them more available for swing-shift war industry workers, an idea that was too radical for the owners, who quietly ignored the suggestion.[10]

In addition to improving accessibility by playing games at night, teams also made efforts to make the game more available to servicemen. In February 1942, MacPhail announced that the Dodgers would work with the military to admit 150,000 servicemen in uniform to games at Ebbets Field that season, and other teams, including those in the minors, quickly followed suit with their own plans for opening their parks to servicemen. By the end of the 1944 season an estimated 4.5 million servicemen had been admitted free of charge at major and minor league ballparks.[11] The Dodgers also indicated they would make members of their scouting and coaching staffs at both the major and minor league levels available to work with the military on recreational opportunities for their men.[12] In addition there were games between major leaguers and military service teams, often heavily stocked with major league talent of their own, played at various military bases or in front of exclusively military crowds. USO tours took major leaguers to the corners of the globe to visit the troops, play games, and conduct clinics. Even regular games played before the public took on a patriotic and military feel as the national anthem became a regular part of the pre-game ritual, and many games featured military parades and induction ceremonies.

Making the game more accessible was fine for servicemen who were stationed within the United States, but what of those who were overseas? Baseball remained a popular pastime throughout the war, and those in the business of baseball looked for ways to keep the troops connected to the game back home. Readers could purchase subscriptions to *The Sporting News* to be sent to servicemen overseas, and the majors provided highlight films of important

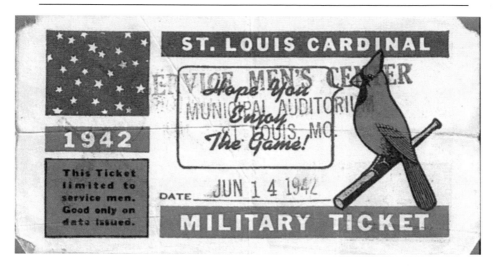

ST. LOUIS CARDINAL

1942

This Ticket limited to service men. Good only on date issued.

SERVICE MEN'S CENTER
MUNICIPAL AUDITORIUM
ST. LOUIS, MO.

Hope You Enjoy The Game!

DATE___JUN 1 4 1942

MILITARY TICKET

One of the many ways baseball's owners publicly supported the military was by allowing servicemen in uniform free tickets to attend games, both at major and minor league ballparks (author's collection).

events, All-Star Games, and the World Series, that were shipped to bases around the world. General Dwight D. Eisenhower even demanded that a full broadcast of the 1943 World Series be made available to troops overseas as a morale booster.[13] In 1944 short-wave radio broadcasts of some regular season games were carried by the military, both actual play-by-play and recreations, further expanding the reach of the game to its fans who were stationed far from home.[14] For those men who had returned from duty but were convalescing and unable to make it to a ballpark, the league even experimented with television as a means to broadcast games to New York hospitals.

Early in the war the public responded favorably to the continuation of baseball. A Gallup Poll in April 1942 asked Americans, "Do you think that professional sports should be continued during the war, or should they be stopped until after the war?" The continuation of professional sports during the war was favored by 66 percent of respondents, with only 24 percent in favor of shutting them down for the duration. While the survey question covered professional sports in general, the American Institute of Public Opinion, which ran the Gallup Polls, identified baseball as the number one sport in the eyes of American fans, noting that Americans prefer baseball "above all others to watch." While the outlook was rosy for baseball, America was still new to this war, having only been involved as an active belligerent for less than four months. A similar poll in Canada found that only 50 percent of Canadians supported the continuation of professional sports, and another showed that only 45 percent of Australians wanted their sports to continue.[15] Canada and

Australia had both been actively involved in the war for much longer than the United States, a fact that surely contributed to the results and did not bode well for the continuation of support at the current levels.

As the war dragged on and casualties mounted, the game in general and the players in particular encountered a growing amount of criticism for continuing to play a sport during a time of war. There was a growing feeling within society that if a man was fit enough to play a sport professionally, then he was certainly fit enough to be in the military, or at the very least work in a war industry. To some extent this missed the point, as professional athletes were in no way exempted from military service, nor were they eligible for any special deferments not available to others. The primary difference between the players and the average citizen was that the players were in the public eye and therefore more visible to all of society. Even with the increased grumbling, professional sports still enjoyed support from some in government such as Representative Samuel Weiss, who stated to the House of Representatives in 1943, "It is my firm conviction that soldier and civilian morale demands that the government permit spectator sports to continue for the duration. The Administration ought to have the courage to clarify its position on wartime sports."[16]

Arguably the group whose opinion should have mattered most was servicemen. After all, they were the ones serving in the military while the ballplayers remained safe at home playing baseball. Throughout the war, servicemen showed a much greater level of support for the continuation of professional sports in general, and baseball in particular, than did the public. One poll of 130,000 servicemen in early 1943 indicated that almost 95 percent of the respondents wanted to see professional baseball continue throughout the war.[17] Just how important was baseball to these men? Perhaps the best evidence can be found in their own words. Veteran John C. Woods of Amherst, New York, wrote to the National Baseball Hall of Fame and Museum in 2001 about the importance of the baseball equipment he carried with him during World War II:

> I carried these two mitts and balls thru [*sic*] 22 months in European Theatre and came home with them in early 1946. I've had them all these years, occasionally as a younger man teaching my four sons some basics about baseball.[18]

Louis Repetto also wrote to the Hall of Fame, describing his experiences editing his unit's newspaper:

> It was 2:00 A.M. in the morning across the International Date Line when two sleepy G.I.s turned on the radio to listen to the Mosquito network's broadcast of the sixth game of the 1944 World Series. They were Corporal

Young Man Kwon & Private First Class Louis A. Repetto, the P/R staff of the 298th Infantry Regiment on Guadalcanal. They were joined by T/5 Harold K.Y. Kam who was the Charge of Quarters that early morning.

For the next three hours they listened, recorded, and then issued "The Warrior"'s [sic] World Series Extra of the St. Louis Cardinals winning the Series from the St. Louis Browns. By 5:30 A.M. Headquarters jeeps were delivering copies throughout the regiment.[19]

Army Major Gordon Jones wrote to American League President William Harridge in 1945 to tell him the impact a traveling group of former major leaguers (including Fred Fitzsimmons, Carl Hubbell, and Harry Heilmann) had on his soldiers who were stationed in Iran, probably one of the most distant outposts of the war.

> I am not exaggerating the facts when I tell you that the baseball unit won acclaim wherever it went. No remote outpost was too small. Wherever there were 15 GI's, the baseball men stopped, cut up old touches, spun a few fancy diamond tales and signed their names to anything.
> [...]
> The Special Service Branch of the Persian Gulf Command takes this opportunity to express sincere thanks to organized baseball, to the major leagues and to these fine men for their wonderful work. Without question their series of appearances will go down in P.G.C. history as epochal. Their contribution to the morale of Persian Gulf Command personnel was great, to say the least. You can be proud of them.[20]

Baseball, whether playing, watching, or talking about it, was an important slice of home for many soldiers serving overseas, something they could relate to that reminded them of their lives before the war and what awaited when they returned home. As a symbol of America for men of military age, it is easy to see why support for the continuation of the professional game was much higher among those in the military than those at home.

Economic Contributions

The most immediate and objectively measurable contribution of baseball to the war effort was the money it raised in support of various charities and in war bond sales. At the winter meetings immediately following Pearl Harbor the league re-established the Ball and Bat Fund and endowed it with $25,000 start-up money for the purchase of baseball equipment for the military. Soon after, it was announced that every team in the majors would contribute all of the receipts, both from the home and away team shares, from one of its 1942 home games to the Army-Navy Relief Fund. In addition, the majors decided to follow the regularly scheduled July 6 All-Star Game in New York with a second exhibition the following night in Cleveland, with the winning team from the first game facing a squad of professionals who were currently in the service in the second. The ticket prices for the New York game were doubled with all the proceeds earmarked for the Ball and Bat Fund, while tickets for the Cleveland game were regular price but included a request that the bearer purchase a one-dollar war stamp. To top it off, every league in Organized Baseball agreed to contribute the receipts from one game of its league year-end championship series, including the World Series.[21] A number of teams used other methods for raising funds as well, such as the Brooklyn Dodgers playing spring exhibitions against service teams with all the proceeds going to military charities.

MacPhail's Dodgers led the charge by hosting the first of the war relief contribution games on May 8, selecting a twilight 4:50 P.M. game against the cross-town rival Giants to ensure maximum attendance. MacPhail required everyone who attended to pay admission to get in the door — including the players, umpires, and reporters. The Dodgers sold 42,822 tickets for the game and raised $59,859 for the military charities, getting the program off to a quick start. The Giants reciprocated with a home game against the Dodgers as their charity game later in the season.[22]

By the end of the 1942 season, Organized Baseball had raised a reported $1,314,825.03 for various charities and relief organizations, with $1,054,953.16 coming from the majors and another $259,871.87 contributed by the various minor leagues. According to *Baseball Magazine*, the sources of money were:

American League Relief Games	$238,205.24
National League Relief Games	$267,895.55
New York All-Star Game	$ 89,314.58
Cleveland All-Star Game	$ 71,611.14
World Series	$362,926.65
League and BB Writers — Ball and Bat Fund	$ 25,000.00
Minor Leagues	$259,871.87

Below is a breakdown as to how this money was distributed:

Army-Navy Relief Fund	$567,026.51
Ball and Bat Fund	$125,000.00
United Service Organization (USO)	$362,926.65
Assorted contributions to various organizations by the Minor Leagues	$259,871.87[23]

The Cubs and White Sox also played a year-end "city series" that raised another $40,926.84,[24] though it is unclear if that amount was included in the accounting above. Most of the players and executives agreed to spend 10 percent of their salaries on war bonds, and the same held true for the season-ending bonuses paid to the players from the top four major league teams.

Teams regularly advertised for and sold war stamps and bonds, and though it is impossible to know exactly how much was raised using these methods, they certainly added to the game's overall contributions.

Not to be outdone, the Negro Leagues also held exhibitions to raise money for war charities, despite the fact that blacks were still not treated as equals in baseball, in the military, or in society as a whole. A pair of games in 1942 pitted the Kansas City Monarchs against a team comprised of former big leaguers and a handful of professional ballplayers who were currently serving in the military, led by Dizzy Dean. The games were played in front of large crowds, but there were questions about whether or not these were official charity games and how much, if any, of the proceeds were actually donated to relief causes. Reacting to the confusion, Commissioner Landis issued an edict prohibiting teams or players from participating in such non-sanctioned games, including a ban on renting out ballparks and facilities to such barnstorming events. "The activities of promoters of games allegedly played for relief but actually as commercial enterprises misled the public into the erroneous belief that such games are for the Army and Navy relief funds and thereby interfere with games actually played for those funds," noted Landis in his memorandum to the various teams and leagues.[25] The commissioner was not going to tolerate baseball looking bad in the press and to the public due to the greed of others.

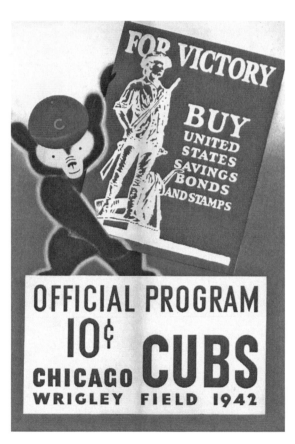

Teams frequently hosted war bond sale drives at their ballparks, and players made public appearances at businesses and factories to further support the bond efforts (author's collection).

Baseball was not unique among sports in contributing economically to the war effort.

Football, golf, and tennis did their parts to various degrees, and horse racing contributed over $3,000,000 to relief funds.[26] Boxing's heavyweight champion, Joe Louis, fought two exhibition bouts in 1942 with all the proceeds going to military charities. Immediately following the first of these fights against Buddy Baer on January 9, Louis enlisted in the Army where he was assigned to the Morale Branch and was heavily involved in athletic training and speaking engagements on the home front. In addition he appeared on a famous recruiting poster that featured his quote, "We're going to do our part ... and we'll win because we're on God's side," and in a training film for new enlistees called *The Negro Soldier.*[27]

Baseball opened the 1943 season using the same plan it had in 1942, with each team contributing the receipts from one home game to war relief, plus funds from the All-Star Game and a portion of the World Series receipts. Some new ideas cropped up as well. In June the three New York teams formed the Baseball War Bond League at the suggestion of John Callen, an assistant administrator with the Treasury Department who was looking for new ways to encourage war bond sales. What Callen and the New York clubs created was essentially the first baseball fantasy league, with local business owners bidding for the rights to specific players to represent them in the league. It was a rousing success, with the player auction selling $123,850,000 in war bonds, led by the $11,250,000 paid for Brooklyn Dodger Dixie Walker, a popular player nicknamed "The People's Cherce," a play on the way Brooklynites pronounced the word "choice."[28] The event cost baseball nothing except some time, and it was a huge public relations coup. Teams also participated in material drives, offering free admission to fans bringing certain items useful to the war effort to the ballpark. While these drives usually collected metals, there were some unusual ideas, including a "Kitchen Fat Day" hosted by the Dodgers in July 1943 to collect used grease, which could be used to make glycerin for artillery shells.[29] The model continued in 1944 with each team again donating the receipts from one home game, plus all the All-Star Game receipts and some of the World Series revenues. New novelty events such as the "Tri-Cornered Baseball Game" on June 26 that featured the Dodgers, Giants, and Yankees all playing against one another in the same game, with the teams rotating between fielding, hitting, and sitting out every third inning, were also popular.

After three years of benefit games and donations, Major League Baseball raised an estimated $2,630,460 for war relief charities, including the Ball and Bat Fund, according to Earl Hilligan of the American League Service Bureau. Of that amount, $1,161,168 came from the receipts of the regular season games donated by each team during that period, with another $1,062,918 from the World Series.[30] The rest of the funds were from the All-Star games, radio broadcast rights, and donations directly from the leagues and the commissioner's office. The primary beneficiaries of these funds were the Ball and Bat Fund, the USO, the Red Cross, and perhaps most importantly the Army-Navy Relief Fund, an organization that provided money to military families who were left temporarily without pay and benefits when a soldier went missing. The majors were also responsible for the sale of $1,027,923,225 in war bonds, according to National League President Ford Frick.[31] Though in subsequent years baseball failed to eclipse the amount it raised in 1942, the financial contributions made by the majors and all of professional baseball were an important part of the war effort and a great way for the game to ensure a positive connection with society during a period when its future was tenuous.

Manpower

The draft that began in 1940 called to service a number of professional ballplayers, including a handful of major leaguers. During that first year, deferments were not difficult to obtain, and draft boards were even willing to work with draftees to push back their reporting dates if they had seasonal work to complete. This type of postponement was particularly common in agriculture, but sometimes it was also applied to baseball players. Local draft boards exercised considerable control and discretion over the process, though when the country entered the war in 1941 things became much more formal and consistent.

Landis made it abundantly clear in 1940 that baseball would not request any special considerations or treatment related to the draft on behalf of its players, re-emphasizing the point again in his letter to Roosevelt in early 1942. The commissioner had very firm convictions about the importance of military service and support during times of war, and he was not going to allow the owners to try to keep players out of the armed forces. At times various parties complained about the impact of the draft on baseball, but Landis was never one of them, and he consistently held firm to the stance that the game and its players should not be treated differently from anyone else. When baseball writer and war correspondent Quentin Reynolds suggested in 1943 that the game should have some sort of lobbyist in Washington to represent its interests, the commissioner was quick to put an end to any such thinking.

> Unless some sort of rule is passed that makes it impossible to put some sort of men out on a field for each side, baseball is not dead. We haven't gone to Washington to plead our case, because we didn't want any inference placed before the 130,000,000 people in the country that we are seeking any favorable treatment in time of war.

But no matter how feeble are the nine men we'll put on the field, I think they'll be strong enough, without the help of any lobby in Washington, to survive.

We do not want baseball in America exempt from the liabilities of common life in America. We want the same rules applied and enforced on us as on everyone else.

When I give thought to the statutes ruling our lives in war, I think of those fellows in New Guinea crawling in trenches and those fellows in Africa. They have complied with those statutes.[32]

As long as Landis was in charge, this would be baseball's official stance. However, he did not live to see the end of the war, and following his passing on November 25, 1944, the owners were left to their own devices and quickly reverted to asking the government for help.

Throughout the war the baseball press reported on the number of minor and major league players who entered the military, along with updates on where they were serving. The May 1942, issue of *Baseball Magazine* listed 60 major leaguers who were in the military. Assuming a roster size of 25 players per team, in the opening months of the war 15 percent of major league caliber players had already traded their baseball uniforms for military garb.[33] By the end of the year the same publication reported that nearly 2,000 former professional players were in the armed services or in war production work.[34] Over the course of the war an estimated 473 major leaguers and 4,076 minor leaguers served in the military,[35] and countless others left their baseball careers for work in war industries. There can be no question that professional baseball players heeded the nation's call to duty.

Criticisms of Baseball's Perceived Contributions to the War Effort

On the surface baseball successfully impacted the war effort in the areas of morale, economic contributions, and manpower. However, questions remain as to how real these impacts were, and how much control, if any at all, the men who ran baseball actually had over what occurred.

Everyone who supported the continuation of the game consistently touted the morale benefit of baseball as its primary contribution to the war effort. Executives, players, politicians, and soldiers routinely used the word "morale" when discussing the game, and the baseball press in particular went out of its way to portray it as a truly American and patriotic pastime. *The Sporting News*, the self-proclaimed "Baseball Paper of the World" and "The National Baseball Weekly Devoted Exclusively to Organized Baseball," was at the forefront of these efforts, and editor J. G. Taylor Spink was one of the game's most vocal and at times controversial supporters. In an ironic twist of fate, the foreign country with the greatest interest in America's national game in 1941 was Japan, where the game was extremely popular prior to the war. If baseball embodied those values that made America great, such as fair play, hustle, and teamwork, did Japan's love of the game mean that the Japanese exhibited these qualities as well? Spink was quick to provide an answer in an editorial on December 18, 1941, less than two weeks after Pearl Harbor.

> Baseball was not a new development in Japan. It dates back some 70 years, not so long after our American Civil War. It was introduced by American missionaries, who wanted to wean their boy pupils away from such native sports as the stupid Japanese wrestling, fencing with crude broadswords, and jiu-jitsu. Having a natural catlike agility, the Japanese took naturally to the diamond pastime. They became first-class fielders and made some progress in pitching, but because of their smallness of stature, they remained feeble hitters. In their games with visiting American teams, it was always a sore spot with this cocky race that their batsmen were so out-classed by the stronger, more powerful American sluggers. For, despite the brusqueness and braggadocio of the militarists, Japanese cockiness hid a natural inferiority complex.
> [...]
> So, we repeat, Japan never was converted to baseball. They may have acquired a little skill at the game, but the soul of our National Game never touched them. No nation which has had as intimate contact with baseball as the Japanese, could have committed the vicious, infamous deed of the early morning of December 7, 1941, if the spirit of the game ever had penetrated their yellow hides.[36]

Spink used his editorial as an opportunity to claim that the Japanese never *really* understood baseball, while also making racially disparaging remarks about the Japanese stature and character. Americans were bigger, stronger sportsmen, while the Japanese were small, weak, and burdened by an inferiority complex. Of course America would win the war against a foe like that.

There were three primary ways for people to experience professional baseball during the war years — attending games in person, listening on the radio, and following the game in the press. Television was still a novelty, and though movie newsreels often included pieces on baseball, both casual and serious fans had limited avenues through which to experience the game. In-person attendance was of paramount importance to team owners because it generated the majority of each team's revenue. Fans with access to a radio, newspaper, or copy of *The Sporting News* could follow the game and gain enjoyment from it independent of how many people were actually in the ballpark, so one would assume the owners would be open to ways to get more paying customers in the door. Going to games was good for morale, as they were quick to point out, and it was also good for the bottom line.

Roosevelt's request for more night games appeared on the surface to be a reasonable request. According to baseball writer Arthur Anderson, writing in 1942, the average attendance at night games during the period was roughly two-and-a-half times that of day games. Anderson recognized that while there was a certain novelty value to night games, ultimately fans would continue to come out at night in greater numbers than during the day because more of them were available to attend after their workdays concluded, with the added benefit that evening temperatures were generally more comfortable than during the daytime in the dog days of summer. The owners and Landis, however, were not sold on night baseball, which had been a regular topic of debate between the wealthy teams that generally opposed it and the teams that struggled economically, who saw it as a way to increase attendance and therefore revenues. Regardless of the side they took, teams were almost unanimous in their belief that the president's request went too far. According to Anderson, who had contacts among the major league owners:

> Until President Roosevelt's request, extension of night baseball beyond seven games per season per club was bitterly opposed by most club owners, who were upheld by Landis. Even Larry MacPhail, the pioneer of arc-light baseball in the major leagues against nearly universal opposition, opposes additional night games in normal times.[37]

In their first league meeting after Landis' passing, the owners again revisited the issue of night baseball and indicated that a reduction of night games for the upcoming 1945 season was likely.

> On night ball, it is believed the league will continue their wartime program of permitting "home rule" to determine the number of nocturnal games to be scheduled. This agreement was reached when it was learned that neither President Barnes of the Browns nor Clark Griffith, owner of the Senators, avid supporters of night ball, intended to *abuse the privilege* and likely of their own accord would reduce the number of night games they play, as against last year[38] [emphasis added].

Black barnstorming teams had been using portable lighting systems to stage night games on their tours across the country since 1929,[39] and in the 1930s many established minor league clubs proved that night baseball was more than just a novelty and could contribute significantly to their profits.[40] Despite the evidence to the contrary, the majors still resisted expanding the night schedule, even though doing so would enable more fans to come out to the games and therefore gain the oft-touted morale benefit of being a spectator. While those teams that did not already have lighting in place in 1942 would not have been able to acquire the necessary materials during the war to build new lighting systems, the resistance to making the game more accessible in those stadiums equipped with lights stood in stark contrast to what the owners identified as the game's primary contribution to the war effort, morale.

Soldiers, sailors, and airmen regularly offered their support for the continuation of baseball on the home front during the war, and were more adamant in their support than was the civilian population. Even if they themselves were not able to see a game at home, or a game involving one of the many service teams, the infrequent news of the diamond that arrived from home gave them a sense of continuity in their lives and something to look forward to when the war ended. The majors provided this level of support simply by continuing to exist, since it did not matter to servicemen overseas at what time or on what day games were played, only that they were indeed played and the news shared with them.

The economic contributions of the game can be measured objectively to some extent, and without question the majors and minors combined to donate considerable funds to various charities and promoted bond sales. A handful of creative ideas came out of the war years, many of them involving the Brooklyn Dodgers. Contributions also came from the All-Star Game and World Series receipts. The majors raised $1,053,951 in 1942, $725,104 in 1943, and $851,405 in 1944, through assorted sources, and made every effort to utilize these donations to improve the game's public image.

On occasion the methods used to determine contributions resulted in some head scratching. One of the most important and visible sources of funding came from a portion of the World Series receipts. In 1943 the Yankees and Cardinals faced off in a Series that went five games and drew 277,312 fans, generating total gate receipts of $1,105,784 (the additional broadcasting receipts of $100,000 were donated in full, as they were in 1944). The following year the intra-city 1944 World Series between the Browns and Cardinals went six games, but drew a paltry 206,708 fans as the clubs were forced to play all their games in the relatively small confines of Sportsman's Park. In part as a result of the lower attendance, the receipts for the 1944 Series were only $906,122. While the 1943 World Series receipts were greater than those recorded for 1944, the amount contributed to war relief was actually higher in 1944, with $308,373 in Series money donated in 1943 and $391,620 donated in 1944. Why? This seemingly odd disparity was caused by how the World Series receipts were divided, particularly with regards to how the players' shares were calculated. The players' pool was based on a percentage of the receipts for the first five games of the Series only. As a result, the players received a percentage of all the gate receipts from the highly attended, five-game 1943 Series, while in the meagerly attended 1944 Series they did not receive any shares from the sixth game. Because of this, even though the attendance was considerably lower in 1944, the total donations were greater than they were in 1943 because the bulk of the 1944 game six receipts went to war relief. To an outside observer it would seem odd that despite significantly higher attendance in a shorter Series in 1943, the war contributions were actually less, a situation that perhaps should have been rectified.[41]

The one thing that every team contributed, at least from 1942 to 1944, was the total receipts from one home game for each team (including the visitor's share). This represented 1.3 percent of a team's games, one home and one road game out of a 154-game schedule. With 55.9 percent of annual team revenues coming from home admissions and another 19.2 percent coming from road admissions,[42] a team could expect these games to contribute a little more than one percent of its revenue to war relief. In 1942 these games generated $506,100, nearly 12 percent of which came from the first-ever charity game staged by the Dodgers on May 9, 1942. Unfortunately the second such game of the season, played in Philadelphia between the Phillies and the Pirates on May 19, was a huge disappointment, drawing a meager 3,366 fans and raising only $3,732.[43] While the Philadelphia fans were criticized in the press for their failure to support the war effort, unwanted attention quickly turned to the Phillies themselves. Whereas the Dodgers picked a lucrative Friday afternoon game against the cross-town rival Giants, the Phillies picked a Tuesday date that came on the heels of a Monday doubleheader (which drew 10,079 fans). The choice of opponent was not as egregious, as each team was paired up with another team in the same league to play their relief games, so the Phillies were slated to play both their charity games against their cross-state rivals from Pittsburgh. Accusations were made that some teams intentionally chose less attractive dates for these games in an effort to minimize the impact on the club's bottom line.

A more detailed accounting is available for the war relief games played in 1944, and below is a summary by team:

American League		*National League*	
Boston Red Sox	$55,530	Boston Braves	$ 4,208
Chicago White Sox	$32,564	Brooklyn Dodgers	$11,820
Cleveland Indians	$30,685	Chicago Cubs	$15,888
Detroit Tigers	$33,288	Cincinnati Reds	$12,911
New York Yankees	$34,587	New York Giants	$12,924
Philadelphia A's	$10,319	Philadelphia Phillies	$15,678
St. Louis Browns	$24,394	Pittsburgh Pirates	$23.008
Wash. Senators	$17,374	St. Louis Cardinals	$25,833[44]

The two St. Louis clubs raised similar amounts, and given that they played in the same ballpark and both teams finished the season atop their respective leagues, this makes sense. The two Boston franchises also played in the same park, and while both finished in the middle of the pack (the Red Sox fourth in the AL, the Braves sixth in the NL), the Red Sox raised by far the most money of any team in the majors, while the Braves had by far the worst result. It's true that the Red Sox drew 2.5 times as many fans as the Braves in 1944, but that does not come close to accounting for the large dollar variance between the two clubs. The two Chicago clubs finished the 1944 season with almost identical overall attendance, the White Sox outdrawing the Cubs by only about 700 fans, yet the seventh-place Sox still significantly outraised the fourth-place Cubs.

The trend in regular season game contributions did not match the overall trend in league attendance. The majors drew 8,553,569 fans in 1942, and in 1943 league attendance dropped 12.7 percent to 7,465,911. However, the contributions from relief games fell by 35.5 percent over the same period. In 1944 attendance not only went up, but it actually exceeded the level of 1942 with 8,772,746 fans turning out to major league parks. But despite this large increase in attendance, the contribution amount increased by less than one percent compared to that of 1943. The fans were coming out to the ballparks, but the teams were not raising significantly more money. Was this due to apathy on the part of the fans, who perhaps were no longer making a special effort to go to the charity contests as the war progressed? Or was it due to decisions made by the owners in selecting dates and marketing the games? Most likely it was the combination of a number of factors, but the intentional selection of some less desirable dates appears to have played a part, at least enough to draw the attention of the press at the time.

The owners were not unified regarding the distribution of the game's revenues to the war effort. The majors failed to turn a profit in 1943, with the leagues as a whole finishing the season 2.2 percent below the break-even mark,[45] and attendance dropped to the lowest level since the Great Depression. Had the teams kept the profits from their charity games, the All-Star Game receipts, and the World Series money, the majors would likely have at least broken even. The World Series money was especially controversial according to baseball writer Dan Daniel, who had many high level sources within the majors. "There is a feeling in some quarters that in giving away most of the profits of the World Series, Judge Landis has been too lavish, that it would have been wiser to set up a sinking fund against possible trouble with finances,"[46] wrote Daniel. In fact some owners had sought to cancel the entire 1943 season, but only if they could convince the government to order the shutdown, which would provide them certain legal protections from contractual obligations to players and suppliers. Such a directive would likely have come from War Manpower Commission Chairman Paul V. McNutt, and while McNutt did not issue such an order, he acknowledged discussing various baseball issues with Clark Griffith though he did not elaborate on the specifics.[47] This was hardly the posture of a sport that considered itself essential to the morale of the population and viewed itself as a source of financial aid for the war effort.

In 1951 National League President Ford Frick testified before the House of Representatives Hearings on Monopoly Power. While the primary purpose of those hearings was to review Organized Baseball's monopoly status and determine whether or not it should be allowed to continue, a number of other topics were discussed with those who testified. Frick opened his testimony with a statement regarding the role of baseball in society that touched upon the game's contributions to the war effort during World War II. The economic figures he presented did not precisely match those reported in other sources, but his comments are still meaningful in other ways. According to Frick,

> During the war period, major league baseball contributed $416,052.92 to the United Service Organizations. Contributions totaling $567,026.51 were made to Army-Navy Relief; $163,279.42 was contributed to the American Red Cross during the season of 1943 alone and a similar contribution was made to the National War Fund during that same season. In addition, from the 1943 world series [sic], $154,186.74 was contributed to the American Red Cross and a similar amount to the National War Fund.
>
> Baseball contributed $250,814.96 to the baseball equipment fund for the armed services — all of this by your major leagues. To that you can add $259,871.87 contributed by the national association [sic].
>
> These represent a total in cash contributions from baseball's coffers of $2,128,698.58 made in years in which baseball on the whole *finished in the red.* All of this was over and above the contributions of the individual clubs[48] [emphasis added].

Reconciling Frick's figures with those provided in other sources is problematic, in part because he did not provide a detailed breakdown. For instance, he provided specific figures on the 1943 World Series, but not for 1942 or 1944, nor did he provide any kind of year-by-year breakdown. Regardless, the financial contributions were certainly in the millions.

What was troubling, however, was his statement that all this money was contributed "in years in which baseball on the whole finished in the red." What did Frick include in "baseball on the whole?" Was this meant to include the minors as well? It is impossible to determine with any certainty as he did not elaborate. What is certain, however, is that his statement was not true for the major leagues as a whole. The major leagues were required to submit financial information as part of the monopoly hearings, and an examination of the profitability of the 16 franchises revealed that they as a group were profitable in three of the four wartime seasons (1942 to 1945), only finishing "in the red" in 1943. In fact, over the entire war period the major league clubs operated at an estimated overall profit of 4.5 percent.[49] Frick appears to have fallen into the habit that was so common among major league owners and executives, telling the same revisionist version of events so often that he came to believe it was in fact the truth.

With regards to manpower, the number of professional baseball players who entered the service during the war was considerable. That being said, the owners did nothing to contribute to more players either entering the service or working in essential industries, yet they regularly touted the manpower contributions of the game. Simply continuing professional baseball during the war years meant that men who could otherwise have contributed to the war effort in the military or industry did not do so, or at least not during the baseball season, so for the game to take credit for manpower contributions is not legitimate.

As early as the start of the draft in 1940, Landis made it clear that baseball would not ask for concessions or favors with regard to the draft status of players, something he continuously reiterated until his passing in 1944. There is no evidence that he ever wavered from this position or asked the government for anything more than clarification on specific issues. He understood that baseball had to remain consistent on this point, both because it was the game's duty as an American institution and to protect the business of baseball from public backlash. His order to the owners not to discuss this issue publicly implied that he was concerned that some of them would make comments in the press lamenting the impact of the draft on their businesses, or worse yet actually approach government or draft officials to seek special considerations for their players. Clark Griffith's statement in April 1940, that referenced "the status of baseball as a vast business with big investments" and noted that "we deserve some consideration, but we are not going to the War Department to seek it" was one example of the type of comment the game could ill afford.[50] Fortunately it was made prior to the country's entrance into the war.

Some owners were dissatisfied with Landis' handling of baseball's wartime policy and completely disregarded his edict, going to government officials to seek support on some issues. In 1943 the baseball owners learned of a bill before Congress and supported by the Secretary of Agriculture that would have banned the sale of food at locations that did not serve regular meals, including concession stands at sporting events. With most teams working on thin margins during the war years, the loss food sales would have proved disastrous as an estimated seven percent of team revenues came from concessions.[51] The owners received the tip from someone in the horse racing community, a group that took a more active role in government lobbying. Without advising Landis, an unnamed "club official" went to Washington to fight the bill, and it eventually died in Congress without being passed. Dan Daniel described that club official as a "magnate," a word generally reserved for club owners or presidents, and that person told Daniel, "I intend to go right on snooping in Washington and protecting the game regardless of the Landis order."[52] While not specifically a manpower issue, it is evidence that some in the ownership ranks were willing to oppose Landis by going directly to the government to seek support for their businesses.

The minors faced an even bigger manpower issue than did the majors. By 1943 there were only ten minor leagues left struggling for survival, down from 41 leagues just two years prior. Because minor leaguers generally made considerably less money than their major league counterparts, they were much more likely to leave professional ball and move on to industrial work, which often paid the same or better than what they earned playing ball. Some large war industries created their own "defense leagues," baseball leagues with teams tied to specific companies that played against one another. This generated competition for talented baseball players who could earn very comfortable salaries "working" for these defense contractors, when in fact much of their work involved practicing and playing ball on the company team. National Association President William G. Bramham considered this contract jumping, though since the players did not sign baseball contracts with their defense employers he was left without a legal avenue to prevent the practice. When four members of the Richmond Colts left the club to go to work for a shipyard in Jacksonville, Florida, Bramham placed them on the ineligible list, baseball's version of blacklisting. Not only were the players banned from playing for any team that fell within the National Association, but any person who played in a game against one of the players also became automatically ineligible. One of the players, pitcher Owen Wright, wrote to Bramham and asked to be placed on the retired list, but Bramham was clear about his opinion in a response letter to Wright. "You are just a plain contract-jumper and I'm placing you on the ineligible list and like action will be taken against the others who have followed the same course,"[53] wrote Bramham, who found himself in the unenviable position of banning players who were, at least on the surface, leaving their baseball jobs to work in defense industries. It was a questionable move to take such drastic action while still claiming that baseball supported the manpower needs of the war effort.

When Landis passed away in November 1944, the owners did not immediately replace him with a new commissioner. After 24 years of nearly dictatorial rule during which he often stymied their goals, the owners were relieved to have some breathing room, and they did not waste any time in having public discussions with the government regarding the players. Within weeks James F. Byrnes, director of the Office of War Mobilization, made it clear that there would be a crackdown on professional athletes who were not currently in the service or working in war industry, and the owners faced their first post–Landis crisis. One of baseball's proponents during this period was Senator Albert B. Chandler of Kentucky,[54] a man whose support would be remembered by the owners when they later got around to looking for a new commissioner. Larry MacPhail was confident a compromise could be reached, while also noting that he too had been in regular contact with government officials about the state of baseball throughout the war. Regarding any decision about baseball's future, he stated:

> We all admit that baseball is unessential just like many other industries such as cosmetics and whiskey. Baseball, unfortunately, depends on manpower. The fundamental problem is whether the indirect contribution that the game makes is worth the expenditure of manpower and transportation that baseball calls for.
>
> That decision, however, can only be reached by the Government [*sic*] and armed forces. For the past two and a half years I have been working with Under-Secretary of War Robert P. Patterson and I know he is of the opinion that such an expenditure is worth while. I will even go further and say that I believe that Jimmy Byrnes will ultimately come around to that way of thinking, too.[55]

Byrnes agreed to meet with the presidents of the two major leagues in the absence of a commissioner to see if the parties could reach an understanding regarding the potential 1945 season.

The meeting with Byrnes was scheduled for mid–March, and Griffith took advantage of the fortuitous timing to pay a visit to the White House on March 12 to give Roosevelt his annual pass and talk baseball. Griffith insisted that the two did not discuss the future of the game,[56] yet the very next day Roosevelt made a statement during a press conference that he was in favor of the game continuing in 1945 so long as it was within government manpower guidelines.[57] The timing could not have been better. On March 21 McNutt and Byrnes announced that baseball would be allowed to continue in 1945, and that ballplayers who were ineligible for military service but who were working in war plants were free to leave their industry jobs to return to the diamond. This was a huge victory for baseball, one achieved by making public statements and working directly with government officials to ask for special consideration for the game. The government's decision was criticized by those who did not believe baseball merited special treatment, but the owners used the carefully cultivated image of baseball as America's national game and a contributor to the war effort to their advantage. The politicians certainly took into account the progress of the war, with all signs pointing to an Allied victory by the end of 1945 or sometime in 1946, and such a decision might not have been made had the country faced a more dire situation. Not only would the game continue in 1945, but players were allowed to leave the factories to play, ironically *removing* manpower from the war effort.

* * *

Despite the regular public proclamations about baseball's morale value and its economic and manpower contributions to the war effort, a deeper look at the words and actions of the men who ran professional baseball reveals that they never lost sight of the fact that the game was first and foremost a business. Landis did an admirable job of balancing the needs of the game with the needs of the country, but the owners continued to work behind the scenes with or without his knowledge to move their individual and group agendas forward. Though baseball certainly made positive contributions to the overall war effort, putting these contributions into the proper context sheds light upon the motivations of the men involved and paints a picture that does not look as rosy up close as it does from a distance.

CHAPTER 4

The Professional Game on the Field

World War II impacted baseball at many levels, most visibly on the field of play. At the major league level, the draft and voluntary enlistments claimed large numbers of players, including most of the day's greatest stars, resulting in a constant cycling in and out of new players who were often hastily called up, then lost almost as quickly when they too entered the service. Teams were comprised of men at opposite ends of the age spectrum who were not eligible for the draft, and those with medical conditions or other life situations that kept them out of the military. For the minors the struggle was even greater, with the uncertainty regarding the war's duration keeping many young men who would have entered the lowest levels of professional baseball out of the game, while working-age men transitioned to war industries. Minor league teams scrambled to find enough men to fill out their rosters, not just at the start of the season but often from week to week, and the number of active minor leagues dropped significantly during the war years. The lack of available talent, which for baseball in the 1940s was limited to non-black men, led some enterprising entrepreneurs to look "outside" the traditional pool to either fill their rosters or create whole new leagues, much to the chagrin of the baseball establishment.

The Majors

While the draft claimed a handful of players in 1941, the attack on Pearl Harbor and the country's entrance into hostilities upped the ante. Whereas before Pearl Harbor voluntary enlistments of established professional ballplayers were rare, in the days and weeks immediately following the attack many players joined the service out of a sense of patriotism and duty. This changed the dynamic for the owners. During the 1941 season the number of players selected in the draft was relatively small, and for the most part local draft boards showed a certain leniency in allowing many players to finish up the current season before actually reporting for duty. Not only did Pearl Harbor add volunteerism to the mix, it also assured that the parameters of the draft would be quickly expanded to call more men to arms much more quickly than it had in 1941.

The Green Light Letter provided professional baseball the mandate it needed to continue operating, at least during the beginning of the war, so now the owners had to scramble to figure out who was available, who might be called up soon, and who intended to enlist. All the major league clubs struggled to find players, though those with well-developed farm systems like the St. Louis Cardinals saw less of an immediate impact as they had a deep pool of minor league talent to use in filling roster spots. In fact the Cardinals shrewdly sold off a number of high-priced, veteran players in 1940 and 1941 and replaced them with their much younger and less expensive minor league talent. Many of the players whose contracts the Cardinals sold entered the service by 1942, depleting their new teams' rosters while the Cardinals kept the proceeds of the sales.[1] With an average age of 26.4 years,[2] the 1942 Cardinals were the youngest team in the majors, yet still went on to win the World Series over the Yankees in October.

Over 100 rookies appeared on major league rosters in 1942, a record number[3] necessitated by the swift military call-ups. The June 1942 issue of *Baseball Magazine* reported that 76 major leaguers and over 725 minor leaguers were already in the service,[4] and by the end of the year roughly 2,000 professional ballplayers were either in the armed forces or had left the game for war industry work.[5] The owners could not even rely on their young rookies to provide stability. For example, Johnny Pesky, who led the American League in hits with the Red Sox during his first major league season in 1942, entered the military and did not return to baseball until 1946. Players came and went quickly, and only some eventually returned to the game.

The suddenness of Pearl Harbor caught the mobilization effort flat-footed, though not entirely unprepared. A framework was in place due to the Selective Services Act of 1940, but the system was not prepared for the rapid call-up now needed. As a result, many professional ballplayers who were in perfectly good health were granted draft deferments in 1942 for various reasons, often due to being the sole financial supporter for their families. While this was a perfectly legitimate deferment reason, and one granted by the draft boards, many deferred players encountered a backlash from segments of the public. They wanted to know why a man who was in good enough physical condition to play professional sports at the highest level had not only failed to volunteer, but was also deemed ineligible for service by the draft boards. It was a war of words that played out in the newspapers, both in editorials and in letters to the editor such as this one that appeared in the *New York Times* in May 1942:

> Are Larry MacPhail and the Brooklyn Baseball Club so politically powerful as to persuade a draft board to reclassify a draftee from Class 1-A to Class 3-A? Don't they realize that our country is at war for the preservation of our rights and freedom and that we need all the man power [*sic*] available, both for active and non-combat service?
>
> It would seem not, since their only desire appears to be the serving of selfish ends and ambitions; another pennant for Brooklyn, no matter what the cost to our country and its people.
>
> Pete Reiser, 22 years of age and in perfect physical condition, prefers playing baseball to giving his aid to the defense of the country. And there are many more professional athletes of the same ilk.
>
> If these young men are more indispensable to their baseball clubs than to their country, then it is high time for baseball parks to be boycotted until they are brought to the realization that we are at total war with ruthless enemies who would destroy every vestige of liberty and democracy.[6]

In countering these charges, baseball supporters focused on the fact that all deferment decisions were made by the draft boards, and that baseball players followed the same set of rules as everyone else. Also, since players worked with the draft boards in the communities where they lived, which were often not the same places where they played, there was less chance of a biased fan of the player's team granting a deferment for which the player did not qualify. For the most part those arguments fell upon deaf ears and baseball continued to confront this issue throughout the war years.

Players encountered such critics not only in the press but also at the ballpark, with the stars often singled out for the greatest share of the heckling. Joe DiMaggio was classified 3-A in 1942, but in every stadium the Yankees went to he heard the jeers asking why he was still playing ball and not in the service. This was difficult for DiMaggio, a long-time superstar, to take coming off the 1941 season during which he had captivated the nation with his record 56-game hitting streak. Eventually the pressure became too much for him to bear and he volunteered for the Army in February 1943.[7] Ted Williams, who like DiMaggio chased a milestone in the limelight in 1941 as he attempted to finish the season with a batting average of .400, also felt the barbs at the ballpark. Like DiMaggio, Williams was classified 3-A at the start of the 1942 season. But unlike DiMaggio, Williams quickly silenced most of his detractors by meeting with his draft board in May, where it was agreed he would enter the Navy at the end of the season.[8]

The majors made it through 1942 successfully with some stars still in the game and a crop of rookies who played well, but the owners and fans knew that baseball faced even tougher challenges ahead. "Last year major league baseball suffered comparatively slight losses because of the nation's military demands," wrote John Drebinger during the off-season. He noted that only a few of the game's top stars were impacted in 1942. "But these defections will prove as nothing compared with the heavy inroads the military demands will make before even the next campaign gets underway."[9] Drebinger was right.

As the parameters of the draft expanded, more and more men became eligible for selection, not only because the age ranges were broadened but also because deferments were much more difficult to obtain. War Manpower Commission Chairman McNutt also made it clear that baseball was not an essential industry, and that baseball players would receive no special consideration. "When a ball player's number comes up he is not given any special privilege by the local board simply because he plays baseball," said a commission spokesman, clarifying comments previously made by McNutt. "The only persons who get such consideration are those with jobs essential to the war effort."[10] The commission did confirm, however, that ballplayers who went to work in a war industry during the winter were free to leave those jobs and return to their teams in the spring, which was certainly a consolation to the owners. However, a player who made such a move would be unable to maintain any existing deferment status he held as a war industry worker, nor would he be able to claim such a deferment if his draft number was pulled during the baseball season,[11] which certainly diminished the appeal of returning to the diamond for most.

At the start of the 1943 season there were 219 former major leaguers in uniform, with hundreds more working in war industries.[12] The owners now faced a new challenge when the draft criteria were expanded to include many men who previously held 3-A deferments as the sole supporters for their families. Men who worked in specific industries were still eligible to receive the deferment, but the potential impact on baseball was enormous — the Cardinals had 22 players on their 29-man spring training roster holding 3-A deferments, while the Browns had 24, all of whom now faced possible inclusion in the draft.[13] As the season progressed, players continued to be lost to the service, including 14 American Leaguers called away from the game during the pennant race.[14] The quality of play continued to suffer, as did the attendance, which dropped by roughly 12 percent to just under 7.5 million, the lowest level since 1935.

The owners turned where they could to find talent. Clark Griffith looked to Latin America, as Latinos were allowed to play in Organized Baseball even though blacks were still excluded. Some looked to players too old or too young to be called up in the draft, such as Joe Nuxhall, who appeared in one game for the Cincinnati Reds less than two months shy of his 16th birthday.[15] Others turned to 4-Fs, men who had been excluded from military service due to physical, mental, or moral reasons. On the surface it may seem strange to think that a man could have a physical condition that made him unsuitable to serve in the armed forces yet still left him capable of playing a professional sport, even in the admittedly watered-down talent pool of the war years. However, there was a wide range of conditions that, while not physically debilitating, could cause problems in military life and prove liabilities in the service. Ailments from epilepsy to chronic ulcers, or prior injuries such as a punctured eardrum or torn-up knee cartilage, could be effectively managed at home but not in a combat zone. Others were either too tall or too short to serve, and even bad teeth could keep a man out of the military.[16] To the owners, men already labeled 4-F who had the necessary skills to play were valuable resources since they were unlikely to have their draft status changed. The Browns in particular looked to these men to fill their rosters, with 18 4-Fs playing for the club in 1944, plus two more who had received medical discharges from the military. By comparison, the rest of the majors averaged ten 4-Fs per team.[17] The Browns were not only competitive, but even good enough to win the American League pennant for the first and only time in franchise history. League-wide attendance rebounded to a little under 8.8 million, not only reclaiming the fans lost during the prior season but also showing an increase of roughly 200,000 over the 1942 draw. The successful D-Day invasion and consistent advances in the Pacific gave Americans a more positive outlook on the eventual outcome of the war, and they were able to relax just a little more than they could during 1943, when they faced a more tenuous war situation.

The war also impacted the game on the field in some less obvious ways. Many raw materials that were abundant in peacetime were now needed in massive quantities in support of the war effort, resulting in changes to the tools of the game. While not visible to the public, this hurt the quality of play. As early as 1942 ball manufacturers were forced to use a different type of horsehide covering, lesser quality yarn to wind the core, and recycled rubber in the core itself instead of the normal high quality crude rubber.[18] By 1943 baseball was forced to make do with reclaimed yarn and recycled cork in the ball's core.[19] These lower quality baseballs surely had an impact on the game, though the magnitude is difficult to estimate given the different caliber of players on the field during the war years. Contemporary estimates were that the new baseballs were 10 percent less lively than pre-war balls, and combined with a lower level of playing talent, the impact on the game was even more severe.[20] As the war progressed, wool shortages made uniforms and workout clothing more expensive and of inferior quality, and the leather shortage impacted the quality of gloves. Even wood for bats increased in price, though fortunately bat manufacturers kept large stocks of ash on hand to be seasoned and aged, so while there was no actual shortage at the major league level, the bats being produced were of less seasoned wood and therefore of lower quality.[21]

The end of 1944 brought more bad news when Office of War Mobilization Director James F. Byrnes announced that all athletes currently classified as 4-F would have their draft status re-evaluated, and that he would ask Congress to pass a bill requiring all 4-Fs to transition into some type of war industry work or a limited role in the military. With over half the major league roster spots occupied by 4-Fs, this was potentially the death knell for baseball for the duration of the war. Response to Byrnes was divided. Democratic National Chairman Robert E. Hannegan came out in support of the game, noting, "In the last three years draft boards have made no exceptions for baseball players. If a board finds a ball player fit for military service, it inducts him."[22] Others, such as House Military Affairs Committee Chairman Andrew May, agreed with Byrnes, declaring, "Any man who is able to play baseball is able to fight or work in a war plant."[23] It was a divisive issue both politically and socially. The people who really suffered in this debate were the 4-Fs themselves, who never asked to be put in this position and had complied with all the required examinations. According to *New York Times* reporter Arthur Daley, "The unfortunate part of all the fuss over 4-F athletes is that it placed them in a position they didn't deserve, almost as though each of them had sought and gained deferment by Machiavelian [*sic*] means."[24] Eventually cooler heads prevailed, and while 4-Fs were re-evaluated by their draft boards and many inducted this time around, Roosevelt's public support for the continuation of baseball in March 1945 paved the way for another season. McNutt even agreed to allow ballplayers once again to leave their war industry work and return to their teams if they chose.[25]

Even with the support of the president and McNutt's permission for players to return to their teams, the majors still faced challenges going into the 1945 season with the draft expanding and the pool of 4-Fs shrinking. The talent pool was so thin that the St. Louis Browns started the season with Pete Gray on their roster, a 30-year-old outfielder who stood out because he was missing his right arm (the result of a childhood accident). While undeniably a talented athlete who was good enough to continue playing professional ball in the minors after the war, Gray almost certainly never would have advanced to even the high minors had it not been for the manpower shortage of the war years.

The schedule makers faced challenges when in February the Office of

Defense Transportation asked the majors to reduce rail travel by 25 percent for the upcoming season, along with the cancellation of all exhibition games not being played for the benefit of the military.[26] This eliminated some lucrative pre-season games, though even more importantly resulted in the cancellation of the All-Star Game. The request also put the World Series in jeopardy, leaving it in limbo and dependant on the war situation in the fall. By the spring it was apparent that an Allied victory was inevitable, and the only questions remaining were how long it would take and how many more people would have to die. Germany surrendered in May, allowing the Allies to focus all their resources on the Pacific, though the prospect of an invasion of Japan conjured up nightmares of hundreds of thousands of new casualties. Japan held out until August until it too surrendered, ending World War II and ensuring that the 1945 World Series would be played.

The end of the war allowed some players to return to their clubs in time to finish out the 1945 season. Hank Greenberg, the first major league star to enter the military via the draft, returned to the diamond with the Tigers on July 1 and quickly made an impact. Greenberg appeared in 78 games in 1945, and his home run in the last game of the season gave the Tigers the pennant. He stayed true to form in the World Series, hitting .304 with two homers and seven RBI as the Tigers knocked off the Cubs in seven games. Another returning veteran who had been away for a considerable amount of time was Bob Feller, who returned to the Indians in time to appear in nine games and post a 5–3 record. The league also had some feel-good stories, most notably that of Bert Shepard, a minor leaguer who entered the service and became a fighter pilot. Shepard's P-38 was shot down over Germany in May 1944, and as a result of injuries sustained in the crash a portion of his right leg was amputated below the knee. Undeterred, Shepard practiced his pitching while a prisoner of war, and upon his return home in early 1945 as part of a prisoner exchange, he came to the attention of Larry MacPhail, who in turn put him in contact with Clark Griffith. Griffith gave the pitcher a tryout, signed him as a coach for the Senators, and even managed to get Shepard onto the mound in a major league game in a relief appearance against the Red Sox in August, when he pitched five innings and surrendered only one earned run.

As the war news improved over the course of the year and the first veterans returned to the field, fans came out to major league stadiums in droves. Not only did major league attendance reclaim all the ground lost during the first two years of the war, it set a new record with over 10.8 million fans coming through the gates, eclipsing the previous record of 10.1 million set in 1930. One of the things many veterans looked forward to upon their return to the states was a visit to a ballpark, a desire that extended all the way up to General Dwight Eisenhower who, when asked what he looked forward to doing upon his return home, answered, "One 'must' on my list of things to do when I get back to New York is to see a ball game."[27] The war was over and major league baseball not only survived, but also stood on the threshold of an era of incredible growth in popularity and profit.

The Minors

The war experience of the minor leagues differed significantly from that of the majors. The war years were an era of enormous struggles in finding players, arranging for transportation, and overcoming reduced attendance. Even with the financial support of the farm system that tied many minor league teams to parent clubs in the majors, giving the majors a vested interest in their success, it was simply too difficult to find enough players to fill the rosters reliably. The majors were forced to look outside of the minors for talent as the war progressed, often focusing their attention on 4-Fs and older players who fell outside of the draft age range. The minors, to some extent, had lost their primary purpose of being a feeder system for the majors, moving ballplayers from level to level and culminating in the majors.

During the 1941 season there were 41 minor leagues in Organized Baseball (not including the independent Mexican League), comprised of 291 ball clubs. The majors controlled 148 of these teams as part of their farm systems, led by the St. Louis Cardinals, who built a deep, 26-team organization that spread from coast to coast.[28] The Cardinals' system served a dual purpose, providing talented young players for the major league club while also allowing the organization to sell off players to other teams. Those whose contracts were sold were often older, experienced major leaguers who commanded large salaries, who could then be replaced by younger and significantly less expensive players. The sale of players was very lucrative for both the franchise owners and for Branch Rickey personally.

The military draft in 1941 called a number of active minor leaguers to service, but many were able to obtain deferments, postponing the start of their enlistments until after the conclusion of the baseball season. At that stage, prior to the country's entrance into the war, obtaining deferments was not terribly difficult. When asked about the deferments, General Lewis B. Hershey, who was in charge of the Selective Service System throughout the war, stated:

> We postponed a lot of people for a lot of reasons. I grew up on a farm, and I had no problem in my mind with a guy in July or August being deferred to get his crop in. A crop's a crop; I have no quarrel with baseball players, no prejudice against them. Another thing, when you're inducting 10 or 15

thousand, well, you had so many more that were just as obligated to go, and if a fellow was going anyway, you didn't have to worry too much about public opinion if the guy goes eventually.[29]

While many received deferments, by August there were 193 minor leaguers in the military undergoing their one-year commitment,[30] less than one player per team on average.

Pearl Harbor changed everything, and the impact was much more dramatic in the minors than it was in the majors. The draft was accelerated, and the men who normally played in the minors were the ideal candidates for military service, both in terms of age and physical fitness. By the start of the 1942 season over 600 minor leaguers had been lost to military service.[31] Roughly a quarter of the leagues that played in 1941 failed to come out of the gate to start the 1942 season, which opened with 31 active minor leagues. The initial losses were all felt at the lowest levels of the minors, with two Class C and eight Class D leagues shutting down. As if those losses were not enough, four leagues folded during the course of the season. The Class D Florida East Coast League shut down on May 14 after it lost two of its member teams in April, and it was quickly followed by the Class D Evangeline League (May 30), Class D Kitty League (June 19), and Class C California League (June 28). Other leagues stayed afloat but lost franchises during the season, like the Class D Appalachian League that saw two of its six teams fold in June. Of the 41 minor leagues that started the season, only 27 made it through to the end, an inauspicious start to the war years.[32]

The leagues that remained in operation tried to do their parts to contribute to the war effort, following the lead of the majors. Exhibitions were played against military service teams, servicemen were often allowed into games for free or at reduced costs, and various bond and material drives were held at the ballparks. The financial sacrifices made by the minors, while nominally less than those of the majors, had a much greater impact on the solvency of those teams, a fact that was noted at the time by baseball writer L. H. Addington. "Down in the small minors, the folks haven't been behind. Perhaps their contributions haven't been so widely publicized outside their immediate territories. But their sacrifices, in many instances, have been proportionately greater."[33] During the war's first year the minors contributed more than $250,000 to relief organizations and sold roughly $380,000 in war bonds based on their reports to the National Association, though in all likelihood the totals were higher.[34]

Only ten minor leagues opened the 1943 season, and all but one finished out the year. Major league farm teams made up an increasing percentage of the remaining franchises, with 46 of the 62 teams that finished the season tied to a major league parent team.[35] In many circumstances teams found their lineups changing daily as players entered the service in rapid succession. The quality of play suffered, though that did not appear to keep as many fans away from the ballparks as did longer working hours and less disposable income. The further expansion of the draft announced at the end of 1943 that eliminated many of the deferments for fathers put the upcoming 1944 season in jeopardy, but ten minor leagues cobbled together enough players to make a go of it, and this time every league went the distance. By the time the season came to a close nearly 4,000 minor leaguers were in the armed forces, while thousands of others put their baseball careers aside and went to work in war industries. The minors, though decimated, continued to make financial contributions to the war effort, raising over $7 million through donations and war bond sales, a considerable effort given the massive contraction of leagues and teams.[36]

For some of the minor leagues, 1944 represented a turning point after bottoming out in attendance in 1943, similar to the trend experienced in the majors. The Pacific Coast League in particular witnessed an attendance explosion, reaching a low point with 1.1 million fans in 1943 before bouncing back to an astounding 2.3 million in 1944. Many PCL cities were active in war industry work, with growing work forces that earned good wages resulting in a larger fan base. PCL attendance jumped drastically again in 1945 to 2.9 million fans, an increase that far outpaced that experienced by the majors and promised to usher in a new era of popularity and economic success when the war ended.[37]

The minors expanded slightly in 1945, increasing to 12 leagues, but the push by the government to re-evaluate 4-F athletes for possible military or civilian service put the entire professional baseball season at risk. National Association President William Bramham was left in an unenviable position, not knowing whether the season would take place. "Our helplessness in being able to give you authentic information is, of course, obvious to you,"[38] he wrote in a statement to the league and club presidents. Roosevelt's support for the continuation of baseball came in March, and while most press attention focused on the impact this had on the majors, it was also a green light for the minors to move forward. The season went ahead as planned and all 12 leagues completed their schedules. With the war concluding during the 1945 season, Bramham expressed confidence that in the upcoming years the minors would expand and eventually get back to pre-war levels.[39] In fact that took less time than Bramham or anyone else expected, with 43 leagues opening the 1946 season, two more than played in 1941. In 1946 the minors had an embarrassment of riches from a manpower perspective as millions of servicemen returned home and looked to start or continue their baseball careers, and a baseball-hungry public was anxious to watch them play.

The Negro Leagues

Organized Baseball garnered most of the national attention during the war years, deemed by the majority of sports fans to represent the highest caliber of professional ball. This, however, was not entirely true. Despite the references to baseball being "America's Game," it was only America's Game if you happened to be male and did not have dark skin. While it is true that only a handful of women may have been skilled enough to play minor league baseball during the 1940s (due in part to women having no opportunities to play ball in any kind of organized fashion while growing up), the exclusion of blacks kept roughly 10 percent of the nation's men out of Organized Baseball. The baseball powers-that-be regularly asserted that technically there were no formal rules prohibiting teams from signing black players, though they conveniently ignored the fact that there were no black players in Organized Baseball, nor had there been for decades. Like many other areas of American society, if you were black you were not welcome and need not apply.

The black community did not allow the discrimination they encountered in American society to keep them from enjoying baseball. With their banishment from the white professional ranks, it was not long before they began forming their own teams. Sometimes groups of teams coalesced to form leagues, while others made their money barnstorming, traversing the country by bus alongside other teams to put on exhibitions or to play against local town teams, ironically often in front of primarily white crowds and against white opponents. In general the term "Negro Leagues" is used to refer to all segregated black baseball, though in reality some very talented and famous clubs did not play in actual organized leagues. Regardless of the level of organization involved, there were opportunities for black men to play baseball at a high level and make a living at it.

The Negro Leagues struggled for the most part in the 1930s, and black baseball faced many challenges not encountered by its white counterparts. The lack of a stratified minor league system made identifying and developing talent difficult, and the lack of an over-arching organizational structure and set of agreements between leagues left rosters open to raids from rivals and contract jumping by players. Lacking the structure of Organized Baseball meant that there were few if any repercussions for those who did not honor contracts, and because teams fought over a limited number of top athletes, those who jumped contracts would sometime later be brought back by the same teams they had left, because the teams needed them to draw fans and stay afloat. Black teams not only faced raids from other American teams, but also Caribbean, Central American, and South American leagues that welcomed black players and often promised much higher salaries than were available back home. White players saw less benefit from playing outside the United States and Canada, both financially and with respect to career advancement, and they also faced the possibility of banishment from Organized Baseball if they jumped their contracts to head south, so they seldom did. For black players, however, playing outside the United States and Canada represented an opportunity to earn more money, in a more accepting culture, with little or no professional risk to the future of their careers.

While the Negro Leagues did not face competition from Organized Baseball for playing talent, the two organizations did compete at the gate — though the competition was for the most part one-sided. Black teams rarely had their own ballparks, instead playing in stadiums owned by major and minor league owners and promoters who gave the most favorable dates to the white teams. They also competed for fans, for while very few whites attended Negro League games, black fans often attended games played by white teams, especially in major league cities. New York Black Yankees owner James Semler lamented that while his club would only draw about 5,000 fans per game, the same number or more black fans could be found in Yankee Stadium at Yankees games, even though tickets cost twice as much as they did to see his team.[40] It was hard enough to make ends meet when drawing from a much smaller fan base than that of Organized Baseball; it was even harder when your core fan base split its money between your leagues and the competition.

Following a financially challenging decade in the 1930s, the Negro Leagues rose to new heights of popularity starting in 1940 and continuing throughout the war years. The Depression hit black society hard, and unemployment rates in that community remained significantly higher than those of whites into the 1940s. The war that was engulfing much of the rest of the world certainly stimulated the economy, but blacks still faced discrimination in the workplace and found it hard to break into many industries. Roosevelt's Executive Order 8802, issued in June 1941, made discrimination in defense industries and the government illegal, opening the door a little for black labor. But ultimately it was a matter of increased demand for industrial labor that reduced black unemployment from over 900,000 in 1940 to roughly 150,000 by 1944. Blacks migrated in large numbers from rural areas to cities to work in war industries, creating larger concentrations of employed and fairly well paid black populations that became the fan bases for Negro Leagues baseball during the war years.[41]

The 12 teams of the Negro National League and the Negro American League dominated black baseball between 1940 and 1944. The two six-team leagues included clubs in the major league cities of Chicago, Cincinnati, Cleveland, Philadelphia, Pittsburgh, New York and Washington (the Homestead Grays played in both Pittsburgh and Washington), along with minor league cities such as Baltimore, Birmingham, Indianapolis, Kansas City, Memphis, and Newark. Attendance climbed steadily during the war years, and the Negro Leagues avoided the decreases suffered by the majors in 1942 and 1943. Even more importantly, the teams were profitable, and the annual East-West All-Star Game drew crowds that sold out major league parks.[42] However, the Negro Leagues still faced many of the same challenges as Organized Baseball. As the war progressed, more and more men entered the armed forces and shifted to war industry work, while others were lost to the raids of rival leagues south of the border. A new challenge arose in 1945 with the establishment of a third Negro League, the United States Baseball League (USL), but the threat proved a minor one as only four of the league's six teams managed to complete the 1945 season and most players remained with their Negro League clubs.

While the war years proved very financially successful for the Negro Leagues as a whole, their future remained in doubt due in large part to the very thing most sought by the black community — integration. Roosevelt's administration pushed for more and more integration in society, labor, and the military during the war years. While this represented a tremendous opportunity for black Americans to improve their positions in society, it threatened to destroy the proud Negro Leagues tradition. If Organized Baseball removed the barriers that excluded black players, the top black players would almost certainly move to the majors and high minors, leaving the Negro Leagues teams without their biggest draws and further incentivizing blacks to attend major and minor league games to see their favorites play. Jackie Robinson's signing of a minor league contract with the Brooklyn Dodgers in late 1945 was a tremendous step in terms of racial integration, but it was also the beginning of the end for the Negro Leagues.

The All-American Girls Professional Baseball League

Blacks were not the only group kept out of Organized Baseball. So too were women.

Like blacks, women had a long history of playing baseball. Some colleges in the second half of the 19th century fielded teams, and barnstorming clubs traveled to play exhibitions, often against teams of men. These so-called "bloomer girl" teams were quite popular attractions,[43] though some included a number of male players dressed as women, all part of the fun in staging exhibitions. Women continued to play baseball in the new century, often using different sets of rules developed especially for them, including versions of indoor baseball. Schools and companies sponsored teams, and by the 1930s the growth in popularity of softball as an alternative to baseball drew an increasing number of women and helped create a new generation of female ballplayers who had years of experience on the diamond.[44]

Another similarity between women and blacks was that America's entrance into World War II opened up new economic opportunities for both groups. Millions of men were drafted into the military, and war industries needed an ever-increasing number of workers, paving the way for black and female workers. The famous "Rosie the Riveter" character symbolized a new type of American woman, one who was confident and capable, who could work in the factory by day while still maintaining her femininity. New opportunities became available to women, one of which was playing organized professional baseball.[45]

The father of women's professional baseball was Philip Wrigley, owner of the Chicago Cubs and the Wrigley Gum empire. Unlike with most major league owners, baseball was nothing more than a side project for Wrigley, who had inherited the team from his father William Wrigley, as he primarily focused on the fortunes of his gum company. Wrigley was an innovator and a smart businessman, and by the fall of 1942 he saw an opportunity for a women's league, though initially the focus was on a professional softball league, not baseball. He saw the potential economic benefits of such a league, one that could exploit the markets opened by the failure of so many minor leagues and do so without worrying about its players being drafted. He also recognized the morale and recreational benefits such a league would provide, especially to the growing army of women in the workplace. Among those charged with developing the new league was Arthur Meyerhoff, Wrigley's chief advertising agent.[46]

Wrigley's new league got underway in 1943 as the All-American Girls Softball League (AAGSBL) in four cities that were all relatively close to one another: Racine and Kenosha, Wisconsin; Rockford, Illinois; and South Bend, Indiana. The intent was to expand later into larger cities including Chicago, where the ambitious Wrigley envisioned league games being played in his own ballpark and home of the Cubs, Wrigley Field. Like its other professional counterparts, the AAGSBL promoted itself as recreation for war industry workers, while also providing a family-friendly environment. The players were not only expected to compete on the diamond, but were to be ambassadors to the communities, so in addition to their baseball coaching they received "training" in etiquette, manners, and makeup application. It was essential to Wrigley that the players portray what he and society expected from women, and in addition to the coaches and etiquette instructors, teams also had chaperones that helped keep the women out of any potentially compromising situations. Documents in Meyerhoff's files indicate that players were to exhibit "the highest ideals of womanhood" and "dress, act, and carry themselves as befits the feminine sex."[47]

The AAGSBL also supported the war effort in more direct ways, and the 1943 all-star game played at Wrigley Field was used as a Women Army Air Corps (WAAC) promotional and recruiting event. Over 7,000 fans turned out to watch an exhibition between two women's military teams followed by the all-star contest, which was likely the very first game ever played at night at Wrigley Field, under temporary electric lights. As in other professional leagues, servicemen (and women) in uniform were admitted to games free of charge, and exhibitions were often held at or near military bases.[48] The teams played an ambitious 108-game schedule in 1943 and the league drew 176,612 fans, averaging just over 800 fans per game. The Racine Belles, winner of the split-season's first half, were crowned the league's first champions.

In 1944 the league switched from softball to baseball and became the All-American Girls Professional Baseball League (AAGPBL), though the ball remained larger than a standard baseball and pitching was still underhand. It expanded to six teams, moving into larger cities by adding franchises in Milwaukee and Minneapolis, both of which had established high-level minor league teams in the American Association. The addition of Minneapolis caused the league some difficulty. The team received limited support from the city and was located well outside the geographical region occupied by the other five clubs, increasing travel times and costs. By July the Millerettes were forced to pack up their equipment and become a nomadic traveling club for the remainder of the season. The six teams played a roughly 116-game season, though some clubs played one or two games more or less, and experienced an impressive jump in popularity by drawing 259,658 fans.[49] One of the league's new teams, the Milwaukee Chicks, claimed the league title. The women's game certainly had its niche, with lower ticket prices and overhead compared to men's professional teams making it financially viable. Support from local businesses and communities were essential components to the success of the most stable franchises.

Wrigley ended his involvement in the league prior to the start of the 1945 season, but after two successful years it was well established and able to continue without his sponsorship. The league executives learned a valuable lesson from the 1944 season, doing away with the franchises in the circuit's largest cities of Milwaukee and Minnesota, replacing them with the smaller cities of Fort Wayne, Indiana, and Grand Rapids, Michigan. The women garnered more local support in the smaller communities where they had less competition for the sports fan's money, and attendance nearly doubled to 450,313, an average of 1,364 fans per game. The Rockford Peaches finished the 110-game season in first place and also won the post-season championship.

The end of World War II did not spell the end for the AAGPBL, and the league benefited from the same post-war popularity of baseball that drove the growth in the men's professional leagues. It reached the peak of its popularity in 1948, the same year the women began pitching overhand, with over 900,000 fans turning out to see them play. From that point on, however, the league's popularity waned, and after the conclusion of the 1954 season it folded, ending women's professional baseball for the foreseeable future.

* * *

The most consistent impact of the war years on baseball was the ever-increasing struggle to find talented players and keep them on the field. All of the male leagues found themselves scrambling just to put teams on the field as the war progressed. From an attendance standpoint, white and black baseball had different experiences. Whereas Organized Baseball saw three out of every four minor leagues go dormant during the war and attendance drop dramatically in 1942 and 1943, the Negro Leagues entered a new era of popularity, stability, and financial gain. What all the leagues had in common was the desire to put the best product possible on the field, and despite the challenges they generally succeeded in maintaining baseball's popularity and image as the National Pastime.

CHAPTER 5

Baseball in the Military

Thinking about the American military during World War II conjures up countless images, from the burning ships at Pearl Harbor to soldiers and Marines waist-deep in water wading to shore from landing craft. The war produced countless iconic images of American men who left their homes, families, and lives, traveling far away to fight. The images that stick out most in our minds were taken in the thick of combat, or of the immediate aftermath. But a war as long as World War II (which even at close to four years was much shorter for the United States than it was for the other belligerents) could not be continuous combat. There were also countless hours, days, weeks, and months of tedious boredom. Training, building, healing, trying to stay dry/warm/cool, eating the same food over and over again, and doing all this in often very cramped quarters with hundreds or thousands of other men who do not want to be there any more than you do, constitutes much of the wartime experience. Countless photos exist of these experiences too, but those are not the images or experiences we tend to recall. Consider also the massive logistical support required to supply those fighting men. Millions of Americans served in support roles, both at home and overseas, and they faced dangers too — not only air raids and surprise offensives, but also the type of accidents that are bound to happen when men are doing dangerous things with machines and explosives. One of the common elements that appeared wherever there were American servicemen was baseball. Areas were cleared near camps and airfields so that at least for a while the men could relieve themselves of oppressive boredom and enjoy a fleeting taste of home. Baseball and baseball news from the home front were important ties to their pre-war lives.

America's military men operated in different spheres based on their duties and responsibilities. Some faced constant danger; some served in support roles near the combat zones; some worked in overseas locations relatively safe from the immediate threat of attack; and some served at home. Former professional baseball players were found in all of these spheres and in all branches, both as officers and enlisted men. Sometimes, however, their roles were directly tied to their position in society as professional athletes in America's National Pastime. Society, both civilian and military, struggled with the sometimes seemingly preferential treatment received by some ballplayers and other celebrities during the war, and it was impossible to find a common ground. Should they be treated differently from "ordinary" men because their talents could be used to entertain thousands or even millions, or should they face the same dangers as other men in the service? Did it make sense to hand an entertainer a rifle or a wrench, or could he actually better serve his fellow servicemen and Americans with a bat, glove, or microphone? There is no right answer. But it is indisputable that the military experience of professional ballplayers during World War II shows that all men were not, in fact, treated equally by the military, and that their skills on the diamond were sometimes more important than their fitness for combat.

Baseball as Training

During the 1920s the military evaluated the World War I experience of its soldiers and officers to see what lessons could be learned and used in future conflicts. One of the frequent assertions by men who served overseas was that the most physically capable men made the best soldiers and leaders. Organized sports and recreation represented not only an excellent means of physical fitness, but also provided the added benefits of promoting teamwork and competitiveness. They occupied men's free time, kept them out of trouble, and boosted morale.[1] This view of sports extended to the highest levels of the military and was a core philosophical belief at West Point. Speaking in 1922, while serving as the Superintendent of the United States Military Academy, General Douglas MacArthur stated, "Nothing more quickly than competitive athletics brings out the qualities of leadership, quickness of decision, promptness of action, mental and muscle coordination, aggressiveness, and courage. And nothing so readily and so firmly establishes the indefinable spirit of group interests and pride which we know as morale."[2] Sports not only created physically strong soldiers, it also developed in them the characteristics deemed necessary for success on the battlefield.

The initial rounds of the draft in 1940 and 1941 resulted in high rejection rates of men deemed physically unsuitable for service. The draft boards were very selective, which they could afford to be during this period before the nation entered the war, though the frequency of rejections set off alarms in Washington. Roosevelt's National Physical Fitness Director, John B. "Jack" Kelly, told the president that the country needed a national physical fitness program that emphasized both sport and exercise to better prepare men for military service, an idea that found support with many military leaders. Though Roosevelt agreed with Kelly in principle and continued to support funding for Kelly's department, he stopped well short of agreeing to any type of national program.[3]

Baseball was one of the most popular sports in the country at the time, and in many ways ideal for the military purposes. Its popularity ensured that most men knew the rules, large groups could play at the same time, and it was easily organized with a relative minimum of equipment. Physically it incorporated running, throwing, and hand-eye coordination, plus it had a strong teamwork component, especially when playing defense. Because the game was not timed, it could easily be shortened by playing fewer innings, or proceed at a more leisurely pace if time was not an issue. Perhaps just as importantly from a military perspective, baseball involved limited physical contact between players, reducing the risk, frequency, and severity of injuries that could keep men away from their normal duties.

The familiarity of the game to the general population resulted in other tangible benefits. Baseball was seen as the National Pastime and America's Game, so immigrants were often drawn to it as part of their integration into American culture. Those who served during the World War II era reported that the game brought together men from different ethnic and sometimes even racial groups — they all knew the game and enjoyed it, and playing together was a way to build bonds and attachments that might otherwise not have formed without the shared recreational interest. Further, as a shared experience baseball was a safe common ground for conversation, a topic that two men who found themselves together could discuss and use to relate to one another.[4]

Military and political leaders seized upon this national familiarity with baseball and its terminology, making a conscious decision to use baseball metaphors to explain political and military news. This was nothing new, of course; sports metaphors abounded then just as they do today, in large part because they successfully communicate messages. Sociologist Donald Mrozek put it succinctly in writing about the use of sports metaphors during the 1940s, concluding, "The purpose of using sports metaphors was simple: to make easily comprehensible to the masses of people those policies which leaders sought to advance. The metaphors translated into the common language of mass spectator sports the complications and implications of far-reaching military programs."[5] This was true in communicating with both servicemen and the civilian population.

While baseball was not an official part of the military training program, it was used in both organized and impromptu fashions to promote physical fitness and build *esprit de corps*. Major League Baseball and the National Association ensured that baseball remained in the forefront of servicemen's minds by providing equipment via the Ball-and-Bat Fund throughout the war, just as they had during World War I. *The Sporting News* allowed readers to purchase subscriptions to the paper that were sent to troops serving overseas, and even made arrangements for previously read copies to be donated and shipped out. Newsreels and films of important events and games were sent to camps, and players past and present visited bases both at home and overseas to play and talk baseball with the troops. All in all, Organized Baseball did an excellent job in integrating itself with the military to ensure the continuing popularity of the game among millions of servicemen, all of who represented potential customers when they returned from the war.

Players in the Line of Fire

Many ballplayers found themselves in harm's way during the war, while others served in relatively safe roles at home or at "secure" bases overseas. This was not unusual, as a military comprised of millions required considerable logistical support. Not everyone was given a rifle and sent to the front. Logistical specialists managed the supplies; drivers and pilots moved men and materials where they needed to go; engineers rebuilt destroyed infrastructure. Communications, construction, and mechanical repair were all things that happened at the front, but also to the rear of the action. In the European Theater of Operations (ETO) the American Army deployed 45 percent of its combat soldiers in purely logistical roles,[6] and this does not even include specialized logistical units or those located outside the theater but still supporting it. It is estimated that an overall ratio of support to combat elements was roughly 2.5:1 in the Army during World War II.

When men enter the military during a time of war, whether as volunteers or draftees, they do so with different objectives in mind. Some specifically request combat roles, while others try to put themselves into the safest position possible. Many go through their training and follow their orders without pursuing any specific goal. There is no evidence in the historical record of ballplayers requesting special treatment or safer assignments once they were in the military, nor of owners trying to use influence to protect their stars from danger. Some, like Bob Feller, made it a point to insist publicly on combat service, but most remained quiet, at the most offering a quote about just wanting to do their part. However, it is clear from the existence of full-time, U.S.-based service teams that at least some skilled ballplayers had options for safe duty that were not available to ordinary new recruits.

Gary Bedingfield has done the most extensive research on baseball players who served in the military during World War II, and he has identified 4,549 former professional baseball players who served in the armed forces during the war, 4,076 minor leaguers and 473 major leaguers.[7] Determining how many of these men served in combat roles is problematic. An examination of the units in which they served would quickly identify those who were in purely non-combat units or units that did not ship overseas, but even those who were in deployed combat units may have served in non-combat roles or remained behind the front. So is there a way to determine the level of risk faced by baseball players in the military to determine if they received preferential treatment that kept them safer than the average soldier?

In 1941 a total of 582 players appeared in at least one major league game, with an average age of 27.8 years.[8] As professional athletes, one can also assume that the typical major leaguer was in above average physical health and condition compared to the whole population. Of course, some professional athletes still found themselves excluded from the draft for medical reasons that did not impact their ability to play sports at the highest level. Punctured ear drums, blood conditions, ulcers, and even bad teeth could make a man ineligible for service, yet still capable of suiting up most days to play ball. For these purposes, however, we are concerned with those players who were deemed suitable for service and were inducted into the military. Most major leaguers were in excellent physical health and, based on their average age (at least in 1941), near or at the peak of their physical abilities. As such one would assume they were better than average candidates, or certainly no worse than average, for physically demanding combat roles. There are no indications that major leaguers had a higher than average level of education or specialized skills that would have made them more valuable in non-combat positions.

What of the minors? The average age of minor league players was highest at the top classifications and decreased as the classifications dropped to the lower levels. A sampling of four leagues classified A and AA in 1941 yields an average age of 26.9 years, slightly lower than the majors, with the notable exception of the Pacific Coast League, which had an average player age of 28.2 years.[9] At the B level the average age was 24.2 years,[10] dropping to 23.5 at the C level,[11] and 22.0 years in Class D ball.[12] Every level of professional baseball was populated with men in good physical condition who fell within the most desirable age ranges for the military. Professional baseball represented an ideal pool of military talent.

One way to determine the level of risk faced by ballplayers is to look at American military casualty figures for the war. The total military force mobilized by the United States during World War II was approximately 14.9 million men and women, with 292,100 reported killed (combat and non-combat deaths) and 571,822 wounded. This yields ratios of 1.96 percent of military personal killed and 3.84 percent wounded over the course of the war, ratios far below those of any of the other major combatants with the exception of Italy. By comparison the United Kingdom experienced a ratio of 6.42 percent killed, Germany and Japan saw over 20 percent fatalities in their militaries, and the Soviet Union lost roughly 30 percent of its troops.[13] It was certainly safer to be in the American military than any other. In evaluating the level of risk experienced by professional ballplayers compared to those of the military as a whole, we can look to the casualty ratios between the two groups. Doing such comparisons with wounded servicemen is difficult, primarily because while the sporting press and local newspapers ran stories on men who were killed, players who were injured or wounded were not as widely or consistently reported. It is easier to provide accurate fatality ratios than to do so for men who were injured or wounded.

Of the 473 former major leaguers in the military, two were killed during the war: Elmer Gedeon and Harry O'Neill. Gedeon was 22 years old when he made his major league debut with the Washington Senators in September 1939, appearing in five games as an outfielder and batting .200 with one RBI in 15 at-bats. He played 131 games with the Class B Charlotte Hornets of the Piedmont League in 1940 before being drafted into the Army in early 1941, eventually being assigned to the Army Air Corps as a navigator for B-25 bombers. As if to emphasize the dangers of military service even for those not in combat, Gedeon was badly injured when his plane crashed during a training exercise in North Carolina in 1942. He later became a B-26 Marauder pilot and was shipped to England in early 1944. On April 20 of that year his B-26 was shot down while on a bombing raid over France, killing Gedeon and all but one member of the crew.[14] Like Gedeon, O'Neill made his major league debut in 1939 as a 22-year-old, playing in one game as a catcher for the Philadelphia Athletics and making no plate appearances. He remained with the Athletics as a third-string catcher for the rest of the year, and was later assigned to the Interstate League for the 1940 season. By 1941 he traded his baseball uniform for that of the United States Marines. He participated in a number of brutal amphibious landings in the Pacific, eventually rising to the rank of first lieutenant. O'Neill was killed in action during the fighting on Iwo Jima on March 16, 1945, just five months before the end of the war.[15]

Gedeon and O'Neill shared many things in common. Both graduated from college in 1939, Gedeon from the University of Michigan and O'Neill from Gettysburg College, and they made their major league debuts that same year. Both were multi-sport athletes in school and large of stature (Gedeon at 6-foot-4, O'Neill at 6-foot-3). Even their military careers were similar, with both men entering the service in 1941, rising to the rank of lieutenant, and shipping overseas in 1944. From a major league baseball standpoint, they also had something important in common — neither was an established or well-known major league player, both having appeared in the majors only for a "cup of coffee." In addition, neither had extensive minor league experience, making them relatively anonymous with respect to their athletic prowess.

Based on two men killed out of 473 who served, major leaguers experienced a fatality rate of 0.42 percent during the war, almost five times lower than the rate of the military as a whole. That was a sharp contrast from the experience of the minor leaguers. Perhaps the most notable minor leaguer killed was Joe Pinder, a man better known for his actions on the battlefield than on the baseball diamond. Pinder pitched in five minor league seasons between 1935 and 1941, never advancing beyond Class D. He entered the Army in 1942, where he served as a radio operator in an era when a "portable" field radio weighed in at 86 pounds. Pinder was part of the D-Day landings on June 6, 1944, making three trips under fire from the shore back to various landing craft to salvage more radio equipment for the troops fighting for survival on the beach, and it was on his third such trip that he was killed by German machine gun fire. For his selfless acts of bravery under enemy fire Pinder received the nation's highest award, the Congressional Medal of Honor.[16] Pinder was not the only professional player to earn the Congressional Medal of Honor; so did Jack Lummus, who played for the Wichita Spudders of the Class D West Texas–New Mexico League in 1941 before joining the Marines in early 1942. He rose to the rank of first lieutenant and, like O'Neill, was killed on Iwo Jima in 1945.[17] Pinder and Lummus were among the approximately 140 former minor leaguers identified by Bedingfield as having been killed during the war, a number that continues to increase as biographical research continues. Based on those figures, approximately 3.43 percent of career minor leaguers who entered the service were killed, a rate higher than the overall average and considerably greater than that of major leaguers.

To recap, 1.96 percent of all American military personnel were killed during World War II. The rate for those with major league experience was 0.42 percent, nearly five times less than that of the military as a whole. Minor leaguers experienced a fatality rate of 3.43 percent, more than 1.5 times that of the average serviceman, and incredibly more than eight times that of former major leaguers. Why were these disparities so great?

In addition to being athletes, major leaguers were also regional if not national celebrities known to sports fans and in many cases to the public at large, and their celebrity was a key factor in the roles they played in the military. Like celebrities in other fields, they often found themselves being sheltered by the nation's political and military decision makers. As noted by historian Steven Bullock, "It seemed to be an unwritten rule during World

War II that Major League stars and other celebrities were to be exempted from exposure to dangerous situations."[18]

Initially the public response to this perceived special treatment was mild, but as the war progressed and casualties mounted, the issue evolved. Many if not most in the public were willing to accept the fact that celebrities in the military were often given relatively safe assignments, so long as they in fact served like everyone else and were not excluded from the military or released early due to their status. Chairman of the House Military Affairs Committee Andrew May more or less admitted as much in 1945, stating, "Any man who is able to play baseball is able to fight or work in a war plant. And the morale value of baseball? If baseball has a morale value it can be just as great played in the Army."[19] Even the common soldier was generally not upset about the type of duties assigned to celebrities, so long as they remained in the service.[20] As Pfc. Joseph Wynne wrote to the *New York Times* in 1945 in response to an editorial that suggested some celebrities should be released form the service to return to their former occupations,

> The Army's policy on discharges is that if a man can do any kind of work he is not to be discharged. Every one of the athletes and movie actors who are released can hold down desk jobs even though they have bad feet, back injuries and the like which would prevent them from marching. The average guy with these infirmities is given light duties, but not discharged.
>
> Yes, sir, very many men are much worse off physically than these discharged stars, and nothing is done to release them. Consequently we disagree with you heartily when you try to justify the release of the glamour boys who seem to be able to come and go out of the services at will.
>
> Many a fellow comes back after a year or two in the service, is kicked around, but not discharged. So if you want to crusade, you might take up the cause of our less fortunate buddies who have much less to look forward to than the glamour boys.[21]

Regardless of whether or not it was part of an unwritten policy, or simply that the decision makers recognized that the death of popular celebrities would look bad splashed all over the front pages of the newspapers, it is undeniable that celebrities on the whole received a certain level of special treatment and often protection. They may not have asked for it, but they received it, and the fatality rate among major league servicemen bears it out.

The career minor leaguers were the opposite side of the celebrity coin from their major league counterparts. Certainly some of them got opportunities to play ball in the service and hold down relatively safe assignments, but the majority did not. Those not good enough to play military baseball lacked the celebrity necessary to find themselves assigned to non-combat roles solely due to who they were. This, combined with their better than average physical abilities, made them even more likely to end up in more demanding and dangerous roles, and the data supports this conclusion. The minor leaguers with the most recognizable names and best baseball skills received treatment similar to that afforded major leaguers, but the vast majority followed the same paths as other recruits with no special considerations. Their fitness and athleticism contributed directly to their higher than average fatality rate by making them more likely to find themselves in harm's way.

Often overlooked were the estimated 119 black ballplayers who served during the war.[22] Their military experience was considerably different from that of white soldiers, as they usually served in segregated all-black units under the leadership and supervision of white officers. The black units were mostly relegated to support functions, though there were a number of notable exceptions such as the famous Tuskegee Airmen, who gained distinction as fighter pilots escorting Allied bombers in Europe. Among those black players who served was future Hall of Famer Monte Irvin, who shipped out to England in early 1944 and later went to France a few months after D-Day. Irvin's all-black unit spent most of its time guarding prisoners, building roads, and doing "menial jobs," and even in Europe they experienced discrimination. "The Army was segregated. And everything was, you know, unequal, and we weren't treated very well. Not by the Army itself, but by our own soldiers. Here we are in a place where we're trying to fight against the, you know, the brutal situation in Germany and our own soldiers and fellows treated us as if we were the enemy. That was hard to understand. But somehow we survived it," he recounted in an interview more than six decades after the war.[23] At least one black ballplayer was killed in combat, when Nazi soldiers murdered Sergeant James Stewart and other members of his artillery support unit after capturing them on December 17, 1944. Stewart never played in the organized Negro Leagues, but he did play for the black Piedmont Giants prior to joining the service at age 36.[24] If black ballplayers found themselves in safer roles in the military, it was not due to preferential treatment, but instead due to prejudice and discrimination that kept them out of most types of units.

While being a major leaguer conferred certain advantages with regards to the type of duty a man was assigned while in the military, with respect to the draft itself it actually became a detriment, at least later in the war. Prior to Pearl Harbor service deferments were available for a wide range of reasons, from seemingly benign medical conditions to having a family to support, but as the war progressed and the manpower needs increased, so too did the range of men considered eligible for service. By late 1944 many players previously labeled 4-F by the draft boards were required to reappear before them due to some very public and political backlash against professional athletes who were not in the service. Many men previously declared medically ineligible were now deemed fit for service, at least in some capacity, an experience that was not shared by all 4-Fs but limited to those who worked in very public and visible jobs such as professional athletes. Despite the uproar and the subsequent reclassification of some ballplayers, there was never any evidence that the draft boards showed them favoritism during their initial reviews earlier in the war. They were simply victims of politics and public perceptions.

Regardless of the branch of the military they served in, major league ballplayers were considerably more likely to find themselves in safer jobs exclusively due to their celebrity status and baseball skills. The same cannot be said for their minor league brethren, who due to their better than average physical condition and lack of celebrity were more likely to serve in dangerous roles and locations. The fatality rates of the two groups emphasize the divide that existed between those at the pinnacle of the baseball world and those who excelled but lacked the notoriety and popularity that came with a major league uniform. Society treated major leaguers differently than minor leaguers, and those differences continued when they walked off the diamond and onto the parade grounds, just as black ballplayers found their roles in society reflected in their placement and treatment in the military. The military mirrored the society it served.

Service Teams

Prior to World War II there was already a baseball subculture that existed within the military, with many of the larger camps and bases supporting their own leagues and teams. With the advent of the draft in 1940, however, some enterprising (and arguably egocentric) commanders saw an opportunity to improve the talent level on their base teams significantly and thus increase the prestige of their units. Professional ballplayers entering the military were quickly identified and funneled to specific locations to begin their enlistments, locations that not so coincidentally were run by commanders who had an interest in improving the caliber of their teams. The successes of base and service branch clubs were portrayed as morale builders by military leaders, but in many ways the teams were nothing more than a source of pride for the men who put them together. Teams were often built using questionable means, sometimes even resorting to recruiting men who were not yet in the service. Major league prospect Frank Baumholtz alleged that officers of the Great Lakes Naval Training Station actively recruited him to volunteer for the Navy, promising that he would be sent to their base and given a special assignment that would basically allow him to focus all his energy on playing for the base's baseball and basketball teams.[25]

Early in the war, the majors and the military worked together for a common cause, agreeing to put on a second All-Star Game in 1942 featuring the winner of the regular All-Star Game against a ballclub made up of active duty servicemen, with all the proceeds going to the Army and Navy Relief Funds. Staged on July 7, 1942, in Cleveland, the pre-game festivities featured parades of military vehicles, including tanks driving around the warning track and precision drill by the Marines. Over 62,000 fans turned out to watch the American League all-stars defeat the military squad led by hometown favorite Bob Feller by a score of 5–0.[26] It was still early in the war and most of the big-name players had yet to enter the service, so while the service team was stocked with major league level talent, it was not of the caliber of the teams that took the field later in the war.

By 1942 the race to build the best service teams was under way in earnest, with the Navy at the forefront. This was due primarily to the limited number of large training facilities employed by the Navy, which meant that a significant portion of new sailors passed through only a few bases, whereas the Army had considerably more intake facilities for new soldiers. Naval officers took advan-

Military service baseball teams began to take on added prominence after the draft got under way in 1940 and professional ballplayers found themselves in the military. The 1941 Navy Norfolk Training Station team shown here won 33 consecutive games that season, but was nothing compared to the powerhouse clubs the base fielded starting in 1942 when the draft was under way in earnest (author's collection).

tage of these concentrations of baseball talent and built some exceptional teams.

Arguably the two most noteworthy service teams were those from the Great Lakes Naval Training Station in Illinois and the Norfolk Naval Training Station in Virginia. The Great Lakes Bluejackets amassed a 163–26–1 record between 1942 and 1944 with rosters that consisted almost exclusively of major league players. Of their 26 losses, 12 came against actual major league teams in exhibitions, though the Bluejackets held a winning record overall against major league teams, going 17–12 during that three-year stretch. They had the added advantage of having veteran major league manager Mickey Cochrane on the bench, coaching and leading the team. The Norfolk Sailors were built under the watchful eye of Captain Harry McClure, who admittedly knew little to nothing about the game but was savvy enough to surround himself with people who did. McClure believed that the team provided value to the Navy as a recruiting tool while also creating a sense of unity among the men under his command. At the opening of the 1943 season he told the crowd of sailors at the ballpark,

> In welcoming you to the opening of another baseball season, I remind you that this team belongs to all of you as a service team as much as it belongs to the officers and men connected with it in official capacities. You, as they, share in its victories and its defeats. Nothing typifies the American spirit more than a baseball game and the crowds attending these games. The continuation of games like this of today is pointblank proof to our enemies that they cannot succeed in overhauling our way of life. Play ball![27]

The Sailors relied more heavily on high-level minor leaguers than did the Bluejackets, and though strong they did not compete against major league teams. That being said, their 92–8 record in 1943 was impressive, and the question as to which of the two Navy teams was the best was a hot discussion topic that unfortunately was never resolved, as the teams did not meet head-to-head that season.[28]

Until relatively late in the war, service teams remained racially segregated. However, with an increasing number of black men joining the military it became important to provide them with the same type of recreational opportunities as their white counterparts. Great Lakes was a leader in this regard, putting together its first all-black team, a basketball squad that played in 1943–1944. The success of that club led to the creation of the Great Lakes Negro Varsity baseball team in the spring of 1944, a club that drew from an impressive roster of experienced Negro Leagues talent, including Larry Doby. The club went 32–10 as part of the Midwest Servicemen's League, a league that included white teams, and perhaps more importantly seven members appeared on the integrated league all-star squad that played a game against the white Great Lakes Bluejackets on June 17, 1944. This was an important step towards integration, and by 1945 some service teams were racially mixed.[29]

In 1944 and 1945 various service team "World Series" and all-star games took place. In the Pacific these events were concentrated in Hawaii, where all service branches regularly shipped men on their way to or from their forward postings. There was certainly some gamesmanship involved, with players often finding that their military skills were mysteriously needed in Hawaii at around the same time that important games or series were scheduled. In Europe early series were played in England, but in 1945 the European Theater championship took place in newly conquered Germany. These series were well attended by war-weary and baseball-hungry servicemen, and represented the pinnacle of military baseball.

Other Roles

One of the more frequent roles played by professional athletes in the military was that of training or recreation officer, either as commissioned or non-commissioned officers. Boxer Joe Louis was the most prominent athlete in this role, putting on boxing clinics and exhibition tours at home and overseas, while also appearing in military films designed to break down the barriers between white and black soldiers. Even though the military remained segregated throughout the war, black athletes were sometimes given opportunities to compete alongside whites, most notably for baseball at the European Theater of Operations World Series in 1945, when Negro Leaguers Willard Brown and Leon Day played on a team alongside white players.[30]

Baseball had its share of recreation officers, though due to the racially segregated nature of the game they generally were not able to reach across the color line as did Louis. Perhaps the most notable was Henry "Zeke" Bonura, a former first baseman and veteran of seven major league seasons who ended his career with the Chicago Cubs in 1940. After building a service team at Camp Shelby, Mississippi, early in the war, Bonura was sent to North Africa, where he was involved in providing recreational opportunities for the troops, which of course included the laying of baseball diamonds and creation of leagues. Bonura continued to promote baseball in Italy and France as he followed the Allied troops into Europe,[31] where he was tremendously popular with the GIs for being able to use his status as a ballplayer to get what he wanted from the officers so that the men could continue to have baseball. According to *Baseball Magazine*, his ability to rub elbows with generals and have them treat him as an equal was not only good for the troops in terms of recreation, but it also gave them something to laugh about. "Next to vanilla cupcakes like Sherry Britton and Ginger Rogers, Master Sergeant Zeke Bonura is the most popular of all characters to sold[i]ers in North Africa and Italy."[32] Anecdotes of his exploits made the rounds among the enlisted men and further increased his reputation.

These positions were not limited to active players, but also extended to former players, managers, and executives. Mickey Cochrane, the Hall of Fame catcher and player-manager who played 13 seasons with the Athletics and Tigers before retiring due in large part to a beaning he suffered in 1937, entered the Navy and attained the rank of lieutenant. After improving an already strong Great Lakes Bluejackets club in 1942, he found "off-season" work as a battalion commander for new recruits at the Great Lakes base, with eight companies and 960 sailors-in-training under his command.[33] Brooklyn Dodgers executive Larry MacPhail, a veteran of World War I, re-entered the Army in 1942 at the age of 52, and though he did not specifically work in training and recreation, he was involved in trying to get "reinforcements" for the Army team that was being drubbed by the Navy in an inter-service series in Hawaii in 1944.[34]

Those not eligible for military service for whatever reason often still made efforts to support the troops. Boston Red Sox manager Joe Cronin was involved with the Red Cross and participated in tours to visit servicemen, where he found them anxious to talk baseball. According to Cronin, "The boys would hand around copies of the *Baseball Magazine* until they literally fell apart. No doubt they discussed other sports, but baseball appeared to be the universal language whenever more than two get together."[35] Another Red Cross contributor was Walter "Red" Barber, the radio play-by-play voice of the Brooklyn Dodgers, who in 1945 became the chairman of the organization's war fund efforts in New York City.[36]

In addition to the Red Cross, active and retired players, managers, and umpires toured the world with the United Service Organization (USO) to provide entertainment to the troops overseas. Various groups were put together during the war and sent out to as many theaters as possible, including areas like the Middle East and Southeast Asia. During the 1944–1945 off-season the USO created five touring groups that consisted of 23 baseball notables, including future Hall of Famers Mel Ott, Frankie Frisch, Harry Heilmann, Carl Hubbell, Leo Durocher, Paul Waner, and Joe Medwick. The groups were spread out over the corners of the world for roughly seven weeks, making over a thousand stops as they traveled to large bases and far-flung outposts. Efforts were made to bring the groups close to the front, and in both Europe and Asia they got to within a couple of miles of the fighting, sometimes a little too close for comfort. The European group was actually forced to make a hasty evacuation from its location in Belgium in December when the Nazis broke through the Allied lines at the start of the offensive that became known as the Battle of the Bulge. Everywhere the baseball men appeared they were warmly received by the troops, talking baseball with them and playing scheduled and impromptu exhibitions.[37]

* * *

The contributions made by individual players to the war effort are irrefutable. Players from every level of baseball entered the military or aided the war effort in other ways, from the youngest minor league rookies to the most established major league stars. A review of the historical record, however, reveals that while almost everyone did their part, their military experiences were not always equal, and that those with the best diamond skills or most recognizable names often found themselves facing considerably less risk to life and limb than did their less talented and popular counterparts. This point is driven home by the significantly greater fatality rate experienced by minor leaguers when compared to their major league brethren. The fact that minor leaguers were actually more likely to be killed when compared to the military as a whole further establishes that it was not simply being a professional athlete that made one more likely to receive special treatment in the military, but that such treatment was reserved for only the elite.

This should not diminish our perception of the risks faced by many major leaguers while in the military. Many served in combat roles, and even those in non-combat areas and positions experienced the dangers that come simply from being part of a military at war. But even then, they could still get some special consideration because of who they were. By 1945, with the war moving toward what appeared to be an inevitable conclusion, servicemen were being released and sent home if they met certain qualifications, one of which was the amassing of a specific number of "points" based on their length and type of service. Combat veteran Bob Feller had more than enough points to be released by the Navy and he wanted to get out in time to pitch for at least a part of the 1945 season, but even though he had been returned to the Great Lakes Training Station he could not speed up his release. His commander told him that he would just need to wait out the process. Most men had no recourse other than to hurry up and wait for the slow military system to run its course. But when you are Bob Feller, a famous baseball player, you have other avenues available to you. According to Feller, "Who did I call? The Secretary of the Navy. So he sent out a radiogram: 'Release Feller and 19 others tomorrow.' Other guys who had enough points to get out; not ballplayers."[38] The vast majority of servicemen could not simply pick up the phone and talk to the Secretary of the Navy, but Bob Feller could because of his notoriety, and that allowed him and 19 other men to speed up their discharges.

Whether they saw combat or played for service teams, professional ballplayers proved willing and able to contribute to the war effort. When deferments were sought or granted, they were on the same basis as those available to all American men eligible for the draft. Certainly those who were placed in non-combat roles could have insisted on combat duty as did Feller and others, but like everyone in the military they ultimately had to follow their orders and accept the assignments they were given. Regardless of the roles they were assigned, they did what was asked by the nation's military.

CHAPTER 6

The Business of Baseball

Owners of professional sports franchises have always been very tight-lipped about the financial records of their teams, a trend that continues into the present day when player's unions routinely ask leagues to open their books during labor negotiations, something they steadfastly refuse to do. If anything, the financial workings of professional sports were shrouded in even more mystery in earlier decades. Today members of the sports press are often the best source for inside information on the business of sports, but in the past they had less objective relationships with the players and owners they wrote about, at times even burying stories that could be embarrassing, including the business aspects of the game.

Uncertainty surrounded the finances of professional baseball more or less from its inception through the World War II era, but the veil was lifted somewhat in 1951 when the House of Representatives Committee on the Judiciary held a series of hearings on professional sports in response to three bills that proposed exempting them from the federal antitrust laws under the Sherman Act. Between July and October, 33 men associated with baseball testified before the committee, including former and current players, owners, and executives, both from the minor and major leagues. In 1952 the House Committee released two publications related to the baseball portions of the hearings, the all-inclusive 1,643 page *Hearings Before the Subcommittee on Study of Monopoly Power of the Committee on the Judiciary, Serial 1 Part 6, Organized Baseball* (hereafter referred to as *Hearings*) and the shorter, consolidated *Organized Baseball — Report of the Subcommittee on Study of Monopoly Power of the Committee on the Judiciary* (hereafter referred to as *Report*), a 232-page summary of the hearings that omitted much of the detail while offering editorial comment and analysis from the committee. In addition to over 1,000 pages of direct testimony and relevant exhibits, the *Hearings* includes more than 500 pages of documentation in its appendix, including some very detailed financial data for all levels of professional baseball. It is a treasure trove of information that provides considerable details that the owners and executives surely would not have made public had it not been necessary as part of Congressional hearings. The 1951 Hearings were far from the last government investigations baseball had to withstand, with further hearings in front of both the House and Senate taking place throughout the 1950s and into the 1960s.

At the time of the Hearings, baseball faced eight lawsuits brought against it that alleged antitrust violations, many of which were aimed specifically at the game's sacrosanct reserve clause, the linchpin that allowed the owners to control the players. Fortunately for the owners, they had a few things working in their favor. For one, they had successfully built a mythology around the game in the preceding decades that changed baseball from a game to the "National Pastime," a fact that was not lost on the House Committee. In the part of the introduction to the *Hearings* that discussed the pending lawsuits, Committee chairman Representative Emanuel Celler of New York stated:

> In this connection it should be clear that, in the event any of the plaintiffs are successful and the cases result in an injunction against the operation of the various rules and regulations of baseball, it is not unlikely that this sudden change would have a marked effect on the game. Thus there would be endangered the livelihood and the investment of the thousands of people who are presently dependent on organized baseball. This, in turn, might also effect the general public which looks upon baseball, and properly so, as our national pastime.[1]

Baseball was important as a business, but it was even more important for its place in society according to this view, and therefore potentially entitled to special privileges and protections. The game also had some strong political allies, most notably United States Senator Edward C. Johnson of Colorado who, in addition to authoring one of the bills designed to formally legalize antitrust exemption for professional sports, also happened to be the president of the Class A Western League. Instead of raising a possible conflict of interest in the eyes of the Committee, this relationship with Organized Baseball appeared to give Johnson even more credibility with them as an expert. Baseball certainly had some things stacked in its favor.

The 1951 Hearings represent an excellent starting point for an evaluation of the business of baseball during World War II, not because the hearings themselves were in any way specifically concerned with the war years, but because they establish a history of the baseball business leading up to and moving through the war, making them a valuable resource in reviewing the validity of claims made by the owners. Baseball's antitrust exemption gave tremendous power and leverage to the owners in their negotiations with players, and also stacked the playing field heavily against any interlopers who wanted to establish rival leagues. It is against this background that professional baseball operated during World War II.

In addition to the *Hearings* and *Report* that came out of the 1951 Congressional hearings, there is another document of arguably equal importance, the *Report of Major League Steering Committee* published in August 1946 (hereafter referred to as the *Steering Committee Report*). On July 8, 1946, the American and National Leagues held meetings in Boston that coincided with the All-Star Game. At those meetings both leagues approved identical resolutions to create a steering committee charged with evaluating those issues facing the game. The National League resolution read:

> RESOLVED; that the President of the National League appoint a Steering Committee of two Club representatives, the League President to be a member and Chairman of said Committee. The Committee is directed to employ counsel and to consider and test all matters of Major League interest and report its conclusions and recommendations not later than August 15, 1946. The said Committee is also authorized to represent the National League in conference with a similar Steering Committee of the American League. Said Committee is to function until the next annual meeting of the National League.[2]

The National League committee members were league president Ford Frick, St. Louis Cardinals owner Sam Breadon, and Chicago Cubs owner Philip Wrigley. On the American League side were president William Harridge, Boston Red Sox owner Tom Yawkey, and Larry MacPhail, one of the owners of the New York Yankees.

Two versions of the *Steering Committee Report* were published by the committee, which in many ways is as telling as the contents of the *Steering Committee Report* itself. In 1951 the House Committee on the Judiciary requested a copy of the *Steering Committee Report* as part of its hearings. Initially the attorney for Major League Baseball advised the House Committee that the documents had been destroyed and were no longer available. However, a copy was eventually tracked down from an undisclosed source, and when the owners found out about this they asked to see it. Shortly thereafter representatives from baseball "found" a copy of the *Steering Committee Report*, but noted that it was indeed quite different from the version uncovered by the House Committee. According to baseball the House Committee version was the initial draft of the document presented to the owners for discussion, but it was not the final version that was ultimately approved.[3] According to Louis F. Carroll, the secretary of the Steering Committee, "the material in Mr. MacPhail's draft, I repeat, was not acceptable to the committee as a whole, was not adopted by them, was not satisfactory to counsel in its characterization of legal opinions and was not the report on which the major leagues acted in 1946."[4] It becomes clear after reviewing the two versions side-by-side that the portions of the original draft eliminated from the final version were those that would be the most controversial and damaging if they were ever leaked to the public.

So what was so potentially damaging to baseball that it needed to be expunged from the final copy of the report? Much of the detail originally included in the Foreword that addressed the nature of baseball as a business was eliminated. More telling were the categories listed in the section of the document titled "Problems." Both versions of the *Steering Committee Report* included categories for Organization, Player Relationships, and Operational Problems. The original draft, however, further included categories for Legality of Structure, Public Relations Problems, and Race Questions.[5] Just based on the category titles alone, one can imagine why the owners would be hesitant to address these issues in writing, both for legal and public relations reasons.

While the *Hearings* provides valuable insight into the economic details of the business of baseball, the *Steering Committee Report* pulls back the curtain even further and gives us insight into the actual thoughts of baseball's owners, those they shared among themselves in private and which often differed from their public statements. Coming as it did immediately after the war years, it provided a sort of "state of the union" of the professional game, especially at the major league level, one that helps us better understand the years that immediately preceded its publication. Unless otherwise noted, moving forward any references to the *Steering Committee Report* refer to the original draft version and not the final, approved version, as the draft both addresses a greater number of topics and provides more detail. Given that the Steering Committee included both league presidents as well as four of the 16 owners, men chosen by their peers to represent them, one can be confident that the opinions expressed in the draft do not vary considerably from those of Major League Baseball as an organization.

Baseball as a Legal Monopoly and the Reserve Clause

Baseball's antitrust exemption and status as a legal monopoly has long been a topic of discussion and debate, one widely covered in depth in a variety of sources. The same is true of the reserve clause that bound player to team and could be renewed annually at the team's discretion. Neither was unique to baseball during the World War II era, but a brief overview of both will help set the stage for how the business operated during the war years.

The founding of the National League (NL) in 1876 represented the beginning of what we know as Major League Baseball. Professional teams and leagues existed prior to the National League, but it took over the position as the premier professional baseball league in the nation upon its foundation, a position it continues to occupy as half of Major League Baseball into the present day. The new league's owners did not waste any time in consolidating their power, establishing a League Alliance with other professional leagues whereby teams in the member leagues agreed to respect one another's contracts, territories, and player blacklists.[6] This not only ensured roster stability by reducing the risk of raids from rivals, it also helped the member leagues keep player salaries lower by stymieing competition in the marketplace.

In 1879 the National League owners made what was likely the most pivotal decision in the history of the business of baseball by establishing a version of what would later be known as the "reserve clause." The 1879 version of the reserve clause allowed each team to "reserve" five players from the prior year's roster, in effect making those players off-limits to other clubs and the property of the team holding them in reserve. This ensured that clubs could maintain their most desirable players by eliminating the ability of those players to negotiate with not only other National League teams, but also other teams that were part of the League Alliance. Because teams were most likely to exercise their reserve options on their top players, the reserve clause eliminated bidding wars and curbed salary increases. By 1883 the reserve list expanded from five players per team to 11, which was usually a team's entire active roster. Clubs could now completely control the movement of players and salaries within and across leagues, though they still faced raiding threats from other professional leagues that operated outside the alliance.[7]

The NL worked towards solidifying its position as the premier professional baseball league, though it continued to face challenges from rivals such as the American Association. The champions of the two leagues met in a postseason series from 1884 to 1890 in a precursor to the World Series, but they were still in financial competition. Both leagues faced significant challenges from a third "major" league with the establishment of the Players' League in 1890, a circuit formed by the players in direct response to the draconian reserve system that limited their movement and ability to negotiate salaries effectively. After a bitter fight that financially damaged all involved, the Players' League folded after just one season and the rebel players were allowed back into the fold. The American Association disbanded a year later and some of its member clubs joined the National League, leaving it at the top of the baseball world in 1892, having survived challenges from rivals and a revolt by the players.

The American League emerged as a new rival in 1901, and roster raiding threatened the stability of both leagues. Later that year the National Association of Professional Baseball Leagues was founded by a group of minor leagues to formalize their relationships, establish operating territories, and protect contracts, similar to the earlier League Alliance. In 1903 the American League, National League and National Association entered into what became known as the National Agreement, to a large extent ending the baseball wars by establishing control over territories and making the reserve clause a standard feature in all player contracts. It also established the primacy of the American and National Leagues in the baseball world. The agreement established four objectives:

(1) Perpetuation of base ball [*sic*] as the national pastime of America, by surrounding it with such safeguards as will warrant absolute public confidence in its integrity and methods, and by maintaining a high standard of skill and sportsmanship in its players.
(2) Protection of the property rights of those engaged in base ball [*sic*] as a business without sacrificing the spirit of competition in the conduct of the clubs.
(3) Promotion of the welfare of ball players as a class by developing and perfecting them in their profession and enabling them to secure adequate compensation for expertness.
(4) Adoption of a uniform code of rules for playing base ball [*sic*].[8]

The goal of establishing baseball as America's National Pastime was clearly outlined in the first objective, and baseball's success in that goal can be seen in the introductory comments from the chairman of the House Hearings in 1951. The second objective outlined the business purpose of the agreement, the "protection of property rights." In the world of baseball there were two basic types of property, though neither was property in a traditional sense. The first was territorial rights, and the protection from infringement on those rights without financial compensation. The second was the players themselves, equating men with property and solidifying those rights via the reserve clause. The agreement created a three-man National Commission to handle disputes, with the American and National League presidents holding two of the three seats and naming a mutually agreeable third member. A cartel had been formed with members agreeing to respect the rights of one another in order to keep out competition and maintain strict control over labor.

Following the establishment of the National Agreement, the majors only faced one real challenge to their hegemony, which came with the formation of the rival Federal League in 1914. The Federal League competed with the majors for both playing talent and consumer dollars, and though the two-year war was short, it was costly. Not only did major league clubs lose players to the rival league, but in many cases they were forced to increase salaries and contract lengths to prevent players from jumping to the Federals. The leagues found themselves in the court system as they battled over player rights, and the Federals eventually escalated matters with a federal suit against the majors that alleged antitrust violations in their control over the player market, both through the reserve clause and the National Agreement itself. In an interesting twist, the case ended up in the courtroom of Judge Kenesaw Mountain Landis a handful of years before the major league owners made him the game's first commissioner. Landis intentionally dragged his feet and delayed ruling on the injunction request, and by the end of 1915 it was obvious the Federals could not go on. The league folded, but not before entering into agreements with the majors that allowed some Federal League owners to gain partial or full ownership of major league clubs, along with some financial considerations. It appeared another rival was crushed, and the owners quickly went about lowering salaries and doing away with the more generous contracts they had offered players to prevent them from jumping to the Federals.[9]

Not all the former Federal League owners walked away happy, however. The Baltimore club chose to pursue its own litigation on the antitrust issue, and after six years in the court system the case of *Federal Baseball Club of Baltimore, Inc. v. National League of Professional Baseball Clubs, et al.* reached the Supreme Court. The Baltimore club argued that the major league owners conspired to monopolize the business of baseball through their purchase and dissolution of the rival Federal League, in effect shutting out the owners of the Baltimore franchise from participating in professional baseball. Associate Justice Oliver Wendell Holmes wrote the decision on behalf of the court and made it very clear that professional baseball was in fact a business, and one that involved the crossing of state lines:

> The clubs composing the Leagues are in different cities and for the most part in different States. The end of the elaborate organizations and sub-organizations that are described in the pleadings and evidence is that these clubs shall play against one another in public exhibitions for money, one or the other club crossing a state line in order to make the meeting possible.[10]

Based on those criteria, one would assume the court considered professional baseball to be interstate commerce, but that was not the case.

> The business is giving exhibitions of base ball [*sic*], which are purely state affairs. It is true that, in order to attain for these exhibitions the great popularity that they have achieved, competitions must be arranged between clubs from different cities and States. But the fact that in order to give the exhibitions the Leagues must induce free persons to cross state lines and must arrange and pay for their doing so is not enough to change the character of the business. According to the distinction insisted upon in *Hooper v. California, 155 U.S. 648, 655,* the transport is a mere incident, not the essential thing. That to which it is incident, the exhibition, although made for money would not be called trade or commerce in the commonly accepted use of those words.[11]

According to the court, the playing of a baseball game did not represent production since the game itself was simply personal effort and in fact produced nothing. Baseball was not commerce, so the movement of players across state lines to play in games, even when those games were held to generate revenue, was not interstate commerce, meaning that baseball was not subject to the Sherman Act.

Baseball had gained an invaluable antitrust exemption from the highest court in the land, and in the years that followed the owners took full advantage of their legal monopoly to control the players and keep costs down, using the reserve clause as their weapon of choice. If a man wanted to pursue a career in professional baseball with the intention of making it to the majors, his only recourse was to enter into a contract with a club, something that almost always resulted in his assignment to the minors (a few players, notably those who played baseball in college, signed their first professional contracts and went straight to the majors). A player might sign with an independent minor league club or, as became more and more frequent with the growth and expansion of the farm system, he signed into the minor league system operated by a specific major league club. Either way, his fate was now sealed with regards to his professional career within Organized Baseball, which controlled the vast majority of minor leagues and represented the only real path to the majors. Once he signed that first contract with its reserve clause, his rights became the team's property for eternity, as it could continue to renew the terms of the contract every year without the player's agreement. Certainly it was possible for a player to obtain his release from the team that held his rights, and in some circumstances the commissioner declared a given player a free agent, but for the vast majority of players the signing of that first contract set them on a path over which they had limited to no control, with clubs trading, selling, or reassigning their rights to other teams with no input from the player, nor usually with any direct financial gain on his part.

The reserve clause was one of the major topics of investigation by the House Committee in 1951. National League President Ford Frick testified regarding the reserve clause in front of the House Committee on July 30, 1951, roughly seven weeks before becoming baseball's new commissioner. "In brief, the reserve clause simply reflects the fact that the ballplayer offers a unique and unusual service and that each individual club must be able to depend upon the availability of qualified personnel from season to season so that the competitive balance essential to the survival of organized baseball may be maintained," explained Frick. He went on to compare a baseball contract with its reserve clause to a long-term contract between a movie studio and a performer, in that both contracts tied the service of the performer or player to the contracting company while prohibiting him from selling his services to competitors.[12] Frick conveniently overlooked the facts that failed to support his comparison. An entertainer entered into a contract with a specified term and for a specific rate of pay, while a ballplayer's rights were held by the team forever, with the team able to modify his pay, within certain limitations, at its discretion, from year to year. Under questioning from the House Committee, Frick later acknowledged that if a ballplayer left his contracting team to play for a league outside of Organized Baseball he would be placed on the ineligible list, effectively blacklisting him from all teams and leagues within Organized Baseball. This type of punishment was only available because the reserve clause gave the player no way to get out of a contract on his own, and the National Agreement ensured other teams would not sign him if he tried.[13]

Baseball's antitrust exemption and the reserve clause combined to make Organized Baseball a force with which to be reckoned. Certainly there were no legal hurdles preventing a group of businessmen from forming their own league outside of Organized Baseball, and some such leagues existed. They fell into two basic categories: independent and outlaw. Independent leagues were not members of the National Agreement, but agreed to honor the contracts of their competitors and as such behaved in a manner very similar to member leagues while remaining outside of the organizational structure, and, just as importantly, outside the Major-Minor League Agreement. Outlaw leagues, however, did not respect the contracts of other leagues and freely signed any players they could entice to play for them. Organized Baseball tolerated independent leagues, and so long as a player had not broken a contract when he signed with an independent, he was still able to play within Organized Baseball. Outlaw leagues presented a different problem. If a player broke his contract with a member club under the National Agreement, not only was the player himself placed on the ineligible list, but so too was anyone who played on a team with or against the ineligible player. This was a savvy way for Organized Baseball to make playing in an outlaw league, even under a legitimate contract, a dangerous proposition, as it could ruin a player's chances of moving into Organized Baseball in the future simply because he played on the same field as someone it had declared ineligible. Organized Baseball thus exerted its influence even outside of its own organization.

How the Owners Viewed the Business of Baseball

The business model of professional sports leagues was and is unusual. Leagues are comprised of a number of teams that are usually independently owned and operated, while remaining subject to a specific set of rules of conduct. On the surface the teams are competitors, in that they stage competitions against one another with each attempting to defeat the other. Yet at the same time the teams depend upon their direct competitors to ensure that they themselves can continue with their business — they need others to compete against. In professional sports, if your competitors fail on the field that is a good thing, but if they fail from a business standpoint it is a bad thing, and failure on the field, especially if it is consistent and long-term, will in most cases lead to an overall economic failure of a team. In a way the goal is to win more often then your competition, but not so frequently that your competition disappears completely.

Baseball's owners were acutely aware of this fact, and it was one of the areas outlined in the Foreword of the *Steering Committee Report*. The first portion of the below appeared in both versions of the report, but the italicized section was deleted from the final approved draft.

> Baseball, as a game, provides pleasure and relaxation to millions who see it played and to countless millions who follow it through the printed page and radio. The time is not far distant when millions will relax at home or in the theatre and see and hear the games wherever it may be being played [*sic*].
>
> Professional Baseball, however, is more than a game. It is Big Business — a one hundred million dollar industry — actively engaged in providing the American public with its greatest and, next to the movies, its cheapest entertainment to buy.
>
> Professional Baseball is a peculiar and complicated industry. Most of us like to think that we run our own organizations and that it is our initiative, experience and ability that have been responsible for success. This is true, of course, to some extent. But, to a greater extent, we are in business with seven (and sometimes fifteen) active partners. *This partnership, and the agreement among the partners to cooperate in the business of baseball, constitute a monopoly. Our counsel do not believe we are an illegal monopoly (because our partnership arrangement and cooperative agreement are necessary in the promotion of fair competition and are therefore for the best interests of the public) but we are a combination, and as such, the policies and rules and regulations adopted control every one of us in the operation of our individual businesses.*[14]

These three paragraphs clearly outline how the owners viewed baseball during the war years. The game was an extremely inexpensive recreation for the public, one it indulged in frequently and with great ongoing interest, and thus of great intrinsic value to society. In fact it was the nation's "greatest" entertainment. However, it was also "Big Business," in capital letters, an actual "industry" that controlled vast revenues. Finally, it was indeed a monopoly, though one protected by the law at the present and not "illegal." The owners' understanding of why their monopoly was not illegal is odd, however, in that it completely missed the reason established in *Federal Baseball Club of Baltimore v. National League*, that the act of putting on baseball exhibitions for money did not constitute interstate commerce. The Supreme Court's ruling had nothing to do with the necessity of acting as a monopoly being an essential part of baseball's business model, nor did the Court assert that the baseball monopoly was in any way good for the public. This represents exactly the type of self-delusion that often characterized the way the owners thought and talked about the game. If you keep telling yourself over and over again that your questionable business practices are for the good of the game and the public, you eventually come to believe that your own misrepresentations are in fact true, similar to how the owners described the game's morale value and contributions to the war effort during World War II.

The exclusion of the last two sentences from the final version of the report was very telling in that they clearly acknowledged that Organized Baseball in 1946, and specifically Major League Baseball, was indeed a monopoly. The draft was prepared by the two league presidents (one of who would go on to become commissioner in 1951) and four owners who had extensive baseball experience and some impressive business credentials — Wrigley owned and operated an enormous chewing gum empire, while MacPhail was an attorney. These were baseball men and businessmen who were smart and experienced enough to know that they were a monopoly, and firm enough in their convictions on the matter to commit it to print. The removal of these sentences was, of course, very wise from a business perspective, as they could potentially be seen as the admission of wrongdoing despite the Supreme Court's ruling that baseball was not interstate commerce. In all likelihood the editing was done in an attempt to avoid the very embarrassment that arose when the draft version of the report made its way into the hands of the House Committee. While at the end of the day this admission in print did not negatively impact baseball before the House Committee, it looked bad and had the potential to cause problems in the future.

In addition to touching on the questionable legality of baseball's monopoly status, the Steering Committee also examined the reserve clause in a section titled Legality of Structure, which appeared in the draft but was completely eliminated from the final version for reasons that will be readily apparent. The members of the committee deemed the reserve clause to be the absolute foundation upon which professional baseball rested.

> The reserve clause, which gives Clubs in Professional Baseball, under certain conditions, continuing options upon the services of players, is, in the opinion of your Committee, the fundamental upon which the entire structure of Professional Baseball is based, and it must be maintained if the structure and competition of Baseball are to be preserved.

The reserve rules are not only necessary but they are for the benefit of all parties concerned — Club owners, players, and the public. They create jobs for the players in an industry which probably could not survive if the basis of fair competition between Clubs and between Leagues, built around the basic fundamental of the reserve clause, is not maintained.

In the well-considered opinion of counsel for both Major Leagues, *the present reserve clause could not be enforced in an equity court* in a suit for specific performance, nor as the basis for a restraining order to prevent a player from playing elsewhere, or to prevent outsiders from inducing a player to breach his contract[15] [emphasis added].

The Steering Committee correctly recognized the importance of the reserve clause, but even more importantly that it likely would not hold up in court. While they stopped short of advancing their own argument and admitting that the reserve clause was therefore in fact illegal, such a clear admission that the entire business of baseball was built upon an unenforceable contract element would create a troubling image of an ownership group that ruled their teams using a bluff. The Steering Committee further noted that "Any form of option in a uniform contract may be [attacked] as inequitable on the grounds that the player is deprived of bargaining power on the option and the option is a perpetual one for the player's life and amounts to 'peonage.'"[16]

Much in the same way that the owners eventually convinced themselves that their monopoly was allowed to exist because it served the public good and not due to a legal technicality in how interstate commerce was defined, they sold their message about the reserve clause to the players and convinced most of them that the clause was indeed necessary for baseball and therefore, in a way, in the best interests of the players themselves. Hall of Famer Ty Cobb was one of the former players asked to testify before the House Committee, and when asked if he thought the elimination of the reserve clause was in the best interest of the individual player he replied, "It would be in his interest, yes, the baseball player, but it certainly wouldn't be in the interest of baseball as an organization."[17] Cobb was convinced that without the reserve clause the wealthiest few teams would control all of the top talent, effectively toppling the entire baseball system. Even active players like Pee Wee Reese, who was a strong proponent of the players having a voice in how baseball was run and the selection of the commissioner, were convinced that the reserve clause was necessary. Reese echoed Cobb's sentiments that without it the wealthiest teams would sign all the best players, so he too favored the reserve clause. As for ballplayers in general:

MR. LANE: Mr. Reese, do you know of any ballplayers that are opposed to the reserve clause?
MR. REESE: No, sir; I do not.

> Mr. Lane: To your own knowledge?
>
> Mr. Reese: No, sir.
>
> Mr. Lane: It seems to be unanimous among the ballplayers that they are in favor of retaining the reserve clause in their contracts?
>
> Mr. Reese: Yes, sir; I think so. Now, some of the players that have been kicked around in the minor leagues and sent up and sent down, they may feel differently toward it, but I am sure that the fellows in the major leagues are all in favor of it.
>
> Mr. Lane: All in all, they are in favor of it?
>
> Mr. Reese: Yes, sir.[18]

By holding to the message consistently and repeating it over and over, baseball's power brokers convinced nearly everyone, including themselves, that the reserve clause was essential to maintaining competitive balance by keeping the rich teams from buying all the talent. This was despite the fact that this was already happening, and specifically that the reserve clause *allowed* wealthy teams to purchase player contracts from their poorer competitors in what became a sort of farm system within the majors itself, one that continued to exist well into the 1960s. The poor major league clubs were often forced to sell players to the wealthier teams, either because they could not afford the salaries or because they simply needed the money to stay afloat. The only difference was that the reserve clause kept the decision-making and profits with the owners, not the players.

Baseball certainly was a big business, one that used its monopoly power to smother competition and keep the players in line through the reserve clause. It was a ruthless business model, and one that put the power in the hands of a small group of men who were both competitors and business partners, men who had to work together and trust one another in order to ensure the survival of their joint enterprise. Yet despite the fact that their competitors were essential to their own success and therefore in many ways not competitors at all, it is apparent that the owners did not entirely trust one another, and they believed rules like the reserve clause were necessary to protect them from each other and to some extent from themselves. Ford Frick admitted this in front of the House Committee:

> Mr. Rodino: Would you say that without the reserve clause the richer clubs might buy off the better players so that competition would undoubtedly die off?
>
> Mr. Frick: That is true.
>
> Mr. Rodino: Again, do you think it would be prudent for the richer clubs, knowing that would be the ultimate result, to do that?
>
> Mr. Frick: I do not think it would be prudent at all, but I haven't any doubt in my mind they would do it.
>
> Mr. Rodino: Despite the fact it would kill off competition?

MR. FRICK: Yes. Because you must remember that these men fundamentally — I want to emphasize to you — these men owning ball clubs today fundamentally want a winner, and if the rules are off they are going to get a winner as best they can. It is not prudent certainly. It would be unwise. It would be hurtful, but they want to win.[19]

Frick was not the only member of the baseball elite to hold this view regarding the emphasis on winning. Philip Wrigley, the wealthiest major league owner and one who certainly did not need his team to turn a profit, agreed.

Baseball, as an institution that has existed for 75 years, has evolved itself. It just sort of grew, and the things that come into it and so forth. I think it is very remarkable that it has developed the way it has, but it has its own — I don't know just how to describe it — balances within itself. The principle thing is that you've got everybody that is in baseball trying to get a winning team: First, because you have to have it in order to exist and, secondly, for the pride and prestige that you have. So you've got an organization of partners who are violent competitors, and that apparently is what gives us checks and balances that keep it pretty well balanced off.[20]

Winning was one of the most important keys to financial success. The more a team won, the more fans it drew; the more fans it drew, the more money it made; the more money it made, the more money it had

Albert B. "Happy" Chandler had a distinguished political career before becoming Commissioner of Baseball, having served as the Governor of Kentucky and a United States Senator. He quickly learned that the commissioner's role was no less political than his previous positions, and his unwillingness to support the owners consistently resulted in him serving just one term in that role. His testimony before the House of Representatives in 1951 was often critical of the major league owners and their practices (Transcendental Graphics).

to spend on players, especially if there was no reserve clause; the better caliber of players acquired, the more the team would win. The owners convinced themselves that this was true, and thus the reserve clause served the dual purpose of keeping salaries down and restraining the impulses of the owners, all for the good of the business as a whole.

Happy Chandler, who succeeded the late Landis as commissioner in 1945, quickly became disillusioned by the cutthroat nature of the business of baseball, and he pulled no punches in front of the House Committee when he testified soon after the end of his first and only term as commissioner.

> As long as the American people have confidence in the playing of the game, that is the most important thing. If they ever lose that, [the owners] do not have anything; and I repeat what I said: These fellows are very fortunate that they own franchises — the 16 major-league club owners — and some of them think they own the game. They do control it. They think they own it, you understand, and they sometimes get delusions of grandeur and power.[21]

Chandler was even more blunt in his assessment of the owners as time went on, indicating that some would do anything necessary to make money. In his 1989 autobiography he questioned their integrity as they focused on the bottom line.

> Sadly, I found that there were a lot of cheaters. Not the true benefactors of the game, the great grass-roots types like Mack and Griffith, but corporate raiders like Del Webb, Lou Perini, Dan Topping, and Fred Saigh. More about them later.
> There was such an overabundance of avarice that the majority of owners didn't want to let any stray dimes slip out of their grasp.[22]

Chandler came to the commissioner's office as a fan of the game, but found himself at odds with the owners almost immediately following his election. He departed after serving only one five-year term, embittered and disillusioned by the nature of the business that went on behind closed doors.

World War II

Throughout World War II professional baseball consistently stuck to the message about how much the game was doing in support of the war effort, but cracks showed from time to time as the owners grumbled publicly about their economic struggles and travel restrictions. Were their concerns legitimate, or simply another example of the owners believing their own story even when facts failed to support it? What was the true impact of the war on the business of baseball?

Attendance

By far the biggest revenue generator for professional baseball during this era was ballpark attendance. At the major league level, the receipts for each game played were divided between the two clubs involved and the league offices, though the home team retained the largest portion. According to Frick, the National League operated under a model that split the first 50 cents of admission for each ticket purchased, with 10 percent ($0.05) going to the league and the other 90 percent ($0.45) split evenly between the two teams. Any amount over 50 cents charged on a ticket, such as for box seats, was kept entirely by the home team.[23]

During the 1939 major league season, 79.9 percent of all gross revenue was generated through admissions. Radio and television was a distant second at 7.3 percent, with ballpark concessions accounting for another 7.0 percent. Prior to 1933 attendance accounted for an even larger portion of revenue, as radio and television income was minimal or non-existent. By 1943 major league attendance bottomed out, reaching its lowest level since the Depression, though the shift in revenue streams was only slight with attendance still generating 76.0 percent of gross revenue, concessions jumping to 10.0 percent, and radio and television dropping to 6.7 percent.[24] Attendance was still the primary driver of revenue, and considering that concessions were directly tied to those fans who came out to the park, bodies coming through the turnstiles were responsible for roughly 86 percent of the money that went into the major league coffers (it should be noted the visiting teams did not share in the concessions, only a portion of the ticket sales). The business model of baseball was all about getting more fans out to the ballparks.

The sharing of admissions between the home and visiting teams was such that the home team on average earned 2.5 to three times more money from ticket sales (excluding concessions) than did the visitor. There is of course a certain logic to this, since the home club was responsible for all of the non-team expenses involved in hosting the game, such as stadium rent and maintenance, taxes, and the cost of the employees necessary to serve the customers. The breakdown rewarded those teams that consistently drew well in their home markets more than those that did not. Despite the inequity in the division of admissions, this component of the business model remained essential to the continued financial stability of the league's weakest teams. Clubs that regularly drew below the league average depended not only on the increase in home attendance they experienced when more popular teams played in their cities, but also from the visitors' portion they received when they traveled to cities that regularly drew well. Teams like the St. Louis Browns benefited when a good draw like the Yankees came to St. Louis, but also from their visitor's share of gate when they traveled to New York, which generally drew well for home games. It was an early form of revenue sharing that showed the owners recognized they were dependent on the continued financially stability of their opponents to keep their own teams solvent. No matter how popular a team was in its own home town, it could not bring fans to the ballpark if there were not other teams to play against, and those other teams had to be profitable if they were to continue to operate.

Attendance figures can be sliced and diced in various ways to look for trends, but three of the most practical are league attendance, team attendance, and attendance by city. The first two are commonly reported, while the third is often ignored, though in some ways it is just as important. From 1903 through the end of World War II, the same sixteen teams comprised the majors with no franchise movement, and the teams were spread out over ten cities. Boston, Chicago, Philadelphia, and St. Louis all had two major league teams each (one National League and one American League), while New York boasted three teams (two National League and one American League). These multi-team cities allow one to consider the role of team success as well as the impact of population changes on attendance.

Table 1 — Major League Attendance by Team and League, 1940–1945[25]

National League

	1940	1941	1942	1943	1944	1945
Boston	241,616	263,680	285,332	271,289	208,691	374,178
Brooklyn	975,978	1,214,910	1,037,765	661,739	605,905	1,059,220
Chicago	534,878	545,159	590,972	508,247	640,110	1,036,386
Cincinnati	850,180	643,513	427,031	379,122	409,567	290,070
New York	747,852	763,098	779,621	466,095	674,483	1,016,468
Philadelphia	207,177	231,401	230,183	466,975	369,586	285,057
Pittsburgh	507,934	482,241	448,897	498,740	604,278	604,694
St. Louis	324,078	633,645	553,552	517,135	461,968	594,630
TOTAL	4,389,693	4,777,647	4,353,353	3,769,342	3,974,588	5,260,703

American League

	1940	1941	1942	1943	1944	1945
Boston	716,234	718,497	730,340	358,275	506,975	603,794
Chicago	660,336	677,077	425,734	508,962	563,539	657,981
Cleveland	902,576	745,948	459,447	438,894	475,272	558,182
Detroit	1,112,693	684,915	580,087	606,287	923,176	1,280,341
New York	988,975	964,722	922,011	618,330	789,995	881,845
Philadelphia	432,145	528,894	423,487	376,735	505,322	462,631
St. Louis	239,591	176,240	255,617	214,392	508,644	482,986
Washington	381,241	415,663	403,493	574,694	525,235	652,660
TOTAL	5,433,791	4,911,956	4,200,216	3,696,569	4,798,158	5,580,420

ALL MAJORS	9,823,484	9,689,603	8,553,569	7,465,911	8,772,746	10,841,123
CHANGE		-1.36%	-11.72%	-12.72%	17.50%	23.58%

Major League Baseball experienced some significant swings in attendance during the course of the war. The drop from 1940 to 1941 was relatively minimal, and even with the introduction of the draft there was little difference in the quality of play on the field. While the shadow of a possible war hung over the country like a cloud in 1941, baseball fans were treated to two amazing storylines as Joe DiMaggio chased and then destroyed the all-time consecutive game hitting streak, while in Boston young slugger Ted Williams pursued the elusive .400 batting average all season. The country was out of the Depression, and even with war looming fans still came to the ballpark in near record numbers (the single season attendance record at the time was 10,132,262, set in 1930), with ten teams experiencing attendance increases and six decreasing. Cincinnati and Detroit, adversaries in the 1940 World Series, had the greatest dips, attributed in large part to the falls from grace those teams experienced in 1941. Cincinnati dropped to third in the National League and finished 12 games out, while Detroit sank to fifth in the American League and ended the season with a record under .500. The biggest gains in 1941 were seen in the National League, as the Dodgers and Cardinals battled for the league crown and both franchises benefited with attendance increases. The Philadelphia Athletics also had an impressive increase at the gate due in part to improving their record by ten more wins in 1941, though they still finished in the cellar both seasons.

The drop in attendance experienced in 1942 was a blow to the financial standing of the majors. Another double-digit percentage drop in 1943 hit even harder, though the decreases were not across the board. In the National League, Boston, Philadelphia, and St. Louis all saw attendance go up from the pre-war levels through 1943, while Pittsburgh was relatively unchanged. The biggest losers were the two New York clubs and Cincinnati, three teams that actually fared consistently better in the standings than the perennial cellar-dwelling Phillies and Braves. Of the roughly one million fewer fans that turned out for National League games in 1943, more than half abandoned the Brooklyn Dodgers, the hardest hit club in the circuit. The American League witnessed a more consistent drop in attendance, with only the Washington Senators and St. Louis Browns showing increased turnouts during the first two years of the war. The Senators undoubtedly benefited from the massive buildup of men working in the Washington D.C. area in support of the military, while the Browns put together a pair of respectable seasons on their way to their first and only American League crown in 1944. Of the American League clubs that experienced attendance drops, no one team accounted for a disproportionate amount of the loss in the same way the Dodgers did in the National League, though if we choose 1940 as our starting point, both Cleveland and Detroit had their attendances halved by 1943.

Table 2 — Major League Attendance by City, 1940–1945

Major Leagues

	1940	1941	1942	1943	1944	1945
Boston	957,850	982,177	1,015,672	629,564	715,666	977,972
Chicago	1,195,214	1,222,236	1,016,706	1,017,209	1,203,649	1,694,367
Cincinnati	850,180	643,513	427,031	379,122	409,567	290,070
Cleveland	902,576	745,948	459,447	438,894	475,272	558,182
Detroit	1,112,693	684,915	580,087	606,287	923,176	1,280,341
New York	2,712,805	2,942,730	2,739,397	1,746,164	2,070,383	2,957,533
Philadelphia	639,322	760,295	653,670	843,710	874,908	747,688
Pittsburgh	507,934	482,241	448,897	498,740	604,278	604,694
St. Louis	563,669	809,885	809,169	731,527	970,612	1,077,616
Washington	381,241	415,663	403,493	574,694	525,235	652,660
TOTAL	9,823,484	9,689,603	8,553,569	7,465,911	8,772,746	10,841,123

In considering major league attendance by city, it becomes even more apparent that the shifts were uneven. The majors as a whole drew 2.2 million fewer fans in 1943 than they had in 1941, with over half of this drop caused by the three New York teams. Of the cities that had two major league teams, Boston and Chicago both experienced significant declines, St. Louis was down but not as sharply, and Philadelphia actually improved (it should be noted that in 1943 the St. Louis clubs drew more fans than they had in 1940, but not 1941). The House Committee explored the theory that attendance was directly correlated to on-field performance, and *Hearings* includes four charts that graphically show their results. The Committee projected the percentage of overall league (examining the National and American Leagues separately, not the entire major leagues combined) attendance a team would expect to account for given its on-field performance, as measured by win percentage. The results appeared to indicate that winning percentage was positively correlated to attendance. When they graphed the results at the team level, they found that their theory held up for some teams and cities, but not others. The three New York teams, though all suffering from drops in attendance through 1943, each accounted for a higher than projected percentage of the overall draw for their leagues, while the St. Louis clubs both regularly drew a lower than expected percentage. In Chicago the results were split, with the White Sox generally drawing at a level near the projections while the Cubs consistently accounted for a larger percentage of fans than would be expected based on their record.[26] What was going on?

Well, the House Committee failed to take into account some very relevant factors in their projections. The two most obvious were city populations and stadium sizes. Reliable population figures are available for each decade thanks to the United States Census, but estimating population for non–Census years is more challenging, especially during the war years when many cities in the industrial north experienced massive growth as workers swarmed to them for war industry work.

Table 3 — Population by City, 1940 and 1950[27]

	1940	1950
Boston	1,175,000	1,177,000
Chicago	2,250,000	2,738,000
Cincinnati	789,000	898,000
Cleveland	1,215,000	1,454,000
Detroit	2,296,000	2,973,000
New York	3,897,000	4,277,000
Philadelphia	1,449,000	1,830,000
Pittsburgh	1,994,000	2,206,000
St. Louis	684,000	857,000
Washington	908,000	1,458,000

New York had by far the largest population base from which to draw, so it is logical that the Dodgers, Giants, and Yankees routinely accounted for a larger percentage of the overall league turnout. The opposite was true for St. Louis, the smallest city in the majors and one that still hosted two clubs. With its small population base it was almost impossible for the Browns and Cardinals to compete with the New York teams in attendance, or the teams from most other cities for that matter.

Even if the people of St. Louis went baseball crazy and packed Sportsman's Park, the home of both the Cardinals and Browns, they still could not compete with many of their rivals. Sportsman's Park had a seating capacity of slightly more than 30,000 fans during the 1940s. Meanwhile, in New York, the Dodgers played in the cozy confines of Ebbets Field, which was slightly larger than Sportsman's Park, holding just over 34,000 fans in 1940, while the Giants and Yankees had massive parks. The Polo Grounds, home of the Giants, held 56,000 fans in 1940, while Yankee Stadium dwarfed even that with a capacity of 70,000 fans by 1942.[28] Cities like Cleveland, Detroit, and New York not only had large population bases, but also cavernous ballparks. While Ebbets Field and Sportsman's Park were roughly the same size, the Cardinals and Browns were still not on an even footing with the Dodgers, who drew from a massively larger pool of potential baseball fans. The attendance playing field was unbalanced and conveyed considerable advantages to some clubs.

Attendance in the majors resurged in 1944, regaining all the losses from the previous year as well as chipping away at some of the 1942 decrease. Eleven teams improved at the gate, with the improbable American League champion Browns more than doubling their 1943 draw. Of the five clubs that lost ground at the gate, four finished at the bottom of their league standings with Boston, Brooklyn, and Philadelphia holding down the last three spots in the National League, and Washington in the cellar in the American. Surprisingly the other attendance losers were the St. Louis Cardinals, who won 105 games and the National League pennant. One suspects that the shocking success of their intra-city rivals, the Browns, who gained massively at the gate, probably took away fans who might otherwise have gone out to see the successful Cardinals had the Browns been at the bottom of the standings, where they normally resided. In fact St. Louis fans came out to Sportsman's Park in much greater numbers than they had in 1943, since both clubs were in the pennant race, and the teams combined to draw considerably more fans than they had even prior to the war.

What contributed to the gains of 1944? Certainly the war news was more favorable. In Europe the Allies successfully invaded Italy in 1943, and the D-Day landings on June 6, 1944, established the Allied forces in France, while the Russians defeated the Nazis at Stalingrad and Kursk and were steadily advancing towards Germany. The tide also turned in the Pacific, where the Allied island-hopping campaign was shrinking the Japanese sphere of influence, though at frightful costs in lives. By the middle of 1944, military victory appeared likely, though no one thought that it would happen quickly or without continued loss of life.

Another contributor to the attendance increase was the expansion of night baseball, something most teams in the majors had consistently resisted even in the face of President Roosevelt's request for more night games in his "Green Light Letter." Prior to the war teams were limited to hosting no more than seven night games per season, and with five teams lacking lights at their stadiums (both Boston clubs plus the Cubs, Tigers, and Yankees) that meant a maximum of 77 evening contests were possible in 1941. Roosevelt's letter forced the owners to increase the number of night games, and they doubled the maximum number of games allowed per team to 14 with the Senators allowed 21, much to the pleasure of Clark Griffith, a recently converted supporter of night ball. This set the potential for 161 regular season night games in 1942, though there were limitations, such as the blackout rule in New York City that prevented the Dodgers and Giants from playing at night for much of the war. Even with the increased number of games permitted, there were still those who doubted the success of an expanded night schedule, including the man responsible for the first night game in major league history, Larry MacPhail. In discussing night ball prior to the start of the 1942 season, MacPhail said:

When [critics] said night baseball wasn't really baseball they were absolutely correct. It isn't. But because of its novelty it has helped serve a valuable purpose by providing clubs with a financial stimulus they badly needed. But for this success to remain, the novelty must continue. Increase the number of games indiscriminately and the novelty wears off. In the meantime daylight baseball must suffer as you increase the night games and by that time baseball will have arrived at its saturation point. For should night baseball suddenly pall on the fans because of an overabundance of it, where next could you go to stimulate new interest?[29]

Ed Barrow of the Yankees made it clear he did not believe the expense in installing a lighting system would be economical for his club, though under new ownership the Yankees wasted no time in installing lights in 1946.

Even with the request from the President and the fact that night games drew larger crowds on average than day games, the owners remained stubborn in expanding the night schedule. Griffith was forced to get creative to skirt the limitations placed on the clubs in 1942 by starting many of the Senators' weekday games very late in the afternoon. These so-called twilight games began in the fading daylight with the stadium lights turned off, but within a few innings the lights came on and the teams played into the evening.[30] At the 1942 winter meetings, a resolution was proposed to increase the night schedule, but it was voted down by the owners and the majors went into 1943 with the same maximum allotment of 161 games it had in 1942.[31] A total of 156 regular season night games were played in 1943, showing that most teams sought to take maximum advantage of the games they had been allocated. Griffith took his support of night baseball on the road as well, with the Senators participating in 45 evening contests, 21 at home and another 24 on the road.[32] This allowed his club to earn $131,500 as its portion of the gate at away games in 1943,[33] the second-best total in the American League behind the Yankees, who were not only America's most popular team but also league champs that season. In 1944 the owners finally accepted the fact that night games regularly drew better than day games, and allowed unlimited night games so long as the visiting team agreed to the start time.[34] By 1945 there were 210 night games played in the majors, with the two small market St. Louis clubs leading the way with 40 night home games for the Cardinals and 37 for the Browns, leaving Griffith's Senators a distant third with 29.[35] The era of night baseball had begun, and the owners had to be dragged into it kicking and screaming until they themselves literally saw the light and recognized that evening baseball was good for the bottom line.

By the start of the 1945 season, military victory was in sight and baseball experienced a massive attendance boom, increasing 23.6 percent from 1944. However, even with such a large overall increase not every team shared in the success. Both Philadelphia clubs lost fans, as did Cincinnati and the St. Louis Browns. The Philadelphia and Cincinnati franchises had the three lowest winning percentages in the majors, so their poor turnouts are not surprising. The Browns finished a respectable third in the American League, six games out of first, but still a far cry from their first-place finish in 1944. Their attendance decrease was actually relatively small, and turnout remained much higher than the club average over the previous two decades, but it was still a drop. For the league as a whole the turnout increase was the largest seen since the 1919–1920 era, foreshadowing an even greater jump in 1946 as America emerged from the war and baseball entered its golden era.

Profits

Attendance was clearly the primary revenue generator for major league clubs during the World War II era, just as it had always been, so certainly the declines in attendance during 1942 and 1943 had an impact on team finances. But how much of an impact?

In 1939 major league attendance was 8,977,779, compared to the 7,465,911 fans drawn in 1943 when attendance bottomed out. Even with that nearly 17 percent decrease, half the National League clubs generated *more* revenue off home game ticket sales in 1943 than they had in 1939, as did three others in the American League. Of those seven teams with higher home game revenues, the Boston Braves and Philadelphia Athletics did so despite drawing *fewer* fans in 1943, and six of the seven showed increases in their overall gross operating income. At the league level, both leagues had overall drops in all income streams with the exception of concessions, which showed healthy increases in 1943, helping to explain why the owners fought so hard against the Congressional proposal that same year to abolish concessions at sporting events.[36] With attendance down, the teams needed to take maximum advantage of every fan coming through the doors, and the best way to do that was by selling food and drinks in an era of shortages, when people might be more likely to splurge since they were attending a game.

Table 4 — Gross Operating Income, Major League Teams, 1939[37]

	Home	Road	National League Exhibition	Radio	Concessions
Boston	$190,779	$129,303	$15,314	$45,000	$22,889
Brooklyn	$752,523	$134,353	$43,068	$87,500	$73,899
Chicago	$562,201	$143,656	$50,457	$41,000	$76,564
Cincinnati	$915,238	$182,879	$109,819	$27,500	$109,001

New York	$542,453	$142,029	$24,744 $110,000	$91,169
Philadelphia	$185,240	$96,867	$7,941 $46,500	$10,935
Pittsburgh	$350,224	$138,204	$5,812 $66,000	$77,237
St. Louis	$301,386	$151,315	$24,561 $33,000	$71,955
TOTAL	$3,800,044	$1,118,606	$281,716 $456,500	$533,649

American League

	Home	Road	Exhibition	Radio	Concessions
Boston	$363,432	$151,477	$25,160	$45,000	$41,470
Chicago	$415,755	$138,687	$51,155	$41,000	$39,205
Cleveland	$424,788	$175,754	$19,339	$44,500	$27,700
Detroit	$658,633	$148,569	$-	$70,000	$68,212
New York	$563,281	$267,499	$104,609	$110,000	$105,944
Philadelphia	$249,796	$95,189	$6,806	$45,000	$5,000
St. Louis	$75,618	$108,023	$17,001	$42,500	$8,788
Washington	$215,292	$116,422	$9,961	$30,000	$20,429
TOTAL	$2,966,595	$1,201,620	$234,031	$428,000	$316,748

Table 5 — Gross Operating Income, Major League Teams, 1943[38]

National League

	Home	Road	Exhibition	Radio	Concessions
Boston	$198,844	$94,441	$6,587	$40,000	$37,202
Brooklyn	$598,907	$138,049	$5,264	$150,000	$93,348
Chicago	$386,272	$102,680	$11,695	$41,000	$121,145
Cincinnati	$372,920	$115,610	$5,755	$45,000	$61,501
New York	$384,452	$96,873	$2,680	$65,000	$100,223
Philadelphia	$348,530	$78,988	$10,090	$32,800	$43,842
Pittsburgh	$484,319	$110,034	$9,265	$32,000	$72,644
St. Louis	$438,537	$155,435	$94,242	$39,200	$108,287
TOTAL	$3,212,781	$892,110	$145,578	$445,000	$638,192

American League

	Home	Road	Exhibition	Radio	Concessions
Boston	$245,566	$128,188	$11,116	$40,000	$47,376
Chicago	$372,569	$109,033	$8,032	$41,000	$71,205
Cleveland	$378,748	$119,093	$4,318	$37,500	$29,066
Detroit	$506,131	$118,987	$5,572	$60,000	$76,808
New York	$463,568	$208,794	$82,242	$-	$131,022
Philadelphia	$254,845	$119,426	$4,682	$40,000	$5,500
St. Louis	$154,473	$117,601	$12,219	$39,200	$38,892
Washington	$402,622	$131,500	$41,216	$22,500	$41,856
TOTAL	$2,778,522	$1,052,622	$169,397	$280,200	$441,725

One of the charitable efforts by the majors was the donation of the total (home and road shares) receipts from one home game per team to war charities, which certainly ate into the income generated in 1943. There was some negative publicity around poorly attended charity games and rumors that some teams intentionally chose less desirable dates and opponents in order to reduce the impact on the bottom line. There were many contrary examples, too, such as the games between the cross-town rival Dodgers and Giants that drew exceedingly well. Regardless, the charity games still represented roughly 1.4 percent of a team's home and road revenue in a given year, and with attendance already down those were ticket sales teams could ill afford to lose. It is difficult to get a handle on the exact amounts professional baseball contributed to relief charities during the war, and even more challenging to get an accurate breakdown of where the money came from. In early 1945 Earl Hilligan of the American League Service Bureau indicated that the majors had raised $2,630,460 between 1942 and 1944,[39] while Ford Frick provided a figure of $2,128,698.58 when he testified in front of the House Committee.[40] Regardless of the actual final figure, it is clear that the majors contributed over $2 million during the war years, with roughly half of that amount coming from receipts from the All-Star Game and World Series. Even with the war on, the total World Series receipts exceeded $1 million per year, despite the 1942 and 1943 Series both being relatively short at five games each.[41] These contributions meant the owners received reduced shares of World Series money from 1942 to 1944, further stressing their finances.

Another revenue stream that took a hit during the war years was exhibition games. One driver of this decrease was a patriotic one — professional teams, both in the majors and minors, frequently played exhibition games against military teams with all the proceeds going to charities, or played on bases in front of non-paying audiences made up entirely of servicemen. Frick informed the House Committee that major league clubs participated in 61 exhibitions on military bases for exclusively military audiences during the war,[42] a good number of which occurred during the spring training or postseason periods. The other contributing factor to the lowering of exhibition revenue was Commissioner Landis' unilateral decision to end the traditional spring training held in warmer southern states or California, instead requiring teams to remain in the north to cut back on travel. The so-called "Landis-Eastman Line," named after Landis and Office of Defense Transportation Joseph B. Eastman, went into effect in 1943 and limited teams to spring training locations north of the Potomac River and east of the Mississippi River. Landis made this decision without consulting the owners and without being asked to do so by any government agency, and while the owners went along with it quietly in 1943, a repeat decree in 1944 caught them by surprise. Sportswriter John Drebinger, writing about the announcement that spring training would once again be held in the cold north in 1944, noted, "Neither were the majority of owners for it. A survey had just been taken revealing that at least twelve had committed themselves to returning to the South, assured that it was the sensible thing to do with no need for doing anything else."[43] Certainly teams drew fewer fans in the colder northern climates than they would in the warmer south and west, and training so close to their home bases eliminated the normal procedure of playing exhibition games as the teams traveled back to their home cities to start the season. Once again Landis showed his willingness to exercise dictatorial power independent of the owners, hurting their pocketbooks and souring their feelings towards him. Memories like these made them cautious when it came time to select his successor.

While the owners complained about the dwindling attendance and Landis' insistence on continuing heavy donations to war charities, their financial picture was hardly bleak. For one thing, salaries were down. The average major league salary (including players, managers, and coaches) in 1939 was $7,306, but this dropped to $6,423 by 1943 as most of the game's pre-war stars were in the service, replaced by less experienced and therefore less expensive players. However, Philadelphia, St. Louis, and Washington in the American League carried higher payrolls in 1943, as did Brooklyn, Pittsburgh, and St. Louis in the National League.[44] The clubs also supported fewer farm teams, with only 46 farm clubs operating in 1943 compared to 173 such teams in 1939. It is difficult to pin down precise major league expenses for this period since the *Hearings* only provides very high-level figures and lacks detail in many areas, but it is clear that the expense situation was not particularly unfavorable.

So, were the majors profitable during the war years? One would not think so based on Frick's testimony in 1951, when he described the majors' contributions to the war effort by stating, "These represent a total in cash contributions from baseball's coffers of $2,128,698.58 *made in years in which baseball on the whole finished in the red*"[45] (emphasis added). Owners complained privately, and sometimes not so privately, during the war about the financial burdens faced by their teams, and the reduced World Series pool only further dampened their spirits. As early as 1942 Powell Crosley of the Reds told the press that his franchise suffered a net loss of $451 for the recently concluded season, although to ensure this announcement was not perceived as complaining he noted "we must forget profits for the duration."[46] Based on the comments from baseball's leaders, one would conclude that most if not all clubs actually lost money during the war years, or at the very least during the low attendance years of 1942 and 1943.

The fact of the matter is that major league baseball did not finish in the red during the war years, but was actually profitable overall at levels similar to those experienced in the decade prior to the war. During the 1920s (1920–

1929) the major league clubs combined for an average annual profit margin of 18.2 percent, with a low of 10.0 percent in 1928 and a high of 23.7 percent in 1920. The Depression hurt baseball just as it did the entire country, and from 1932 to 1934 the majors suffered three consecutive years of losses, culminating with a dismal 23.9 percent deficit in 1933. Starting in 1935 the game was back on solid footing and remained profitable every year until after the start of the war, though annual profits remained below the heady figures posted in the 1920s, averaging 5.7 percent between 1935 and 1941.

Table 6 — Major League Profit Margins, 1941–1945[47]

Year	Profit Margin
1941	3.6%
1942	2.9%
1943	(2.7%)
1944	7.8%
1945	8.0%

When the House Committee calculated the profits of the majors they relied on a number of different data sources, as they were only provided with complete, detailed financial statements for a few seasons. For the war era, only the 1943 results can be considered "actual," while the other years are estimated based on other data available to the committee. Regardless, their report paints a very different picture from that portrayed by Frick during his testimony. Profits were certainly below average during the 1941–1943 period, but 1943 was the only wartime season during which the major leagues lost money. Frick's statements appear to be another example of owners and executives telling themselves a story enough times that eventually they came to believe it, even thought it was not true.

At the team level, results varied. Between 1920 and 1945 the majors as a whole registered financial losses in four seasons, but only once during that period was every club profitable (1921) and no individual team earned a profit in every single season. Even during the Depression a small number of teams managed to finish in the black. So regardless of how the league as a whole did on the balance sheet, every season there were financial winners and losers. In the seven seasons between 1935 and 1941, the years following the worst of the Depression and before the start of the war, between eight and 11 teams turned a profit in any given season, meaning that in most years more than half the clubs were profitable. Cleveland and Cincinnati finished in the black all seven seasons, and every team made money at least once, with the Boston Braves barely breaking even in 1941 to end a financial losing streak that went back to 1931. Were the war years any different?

Table 7 — Number of Major League Teams Profitable/Not Profitable, 1935–1945[48]

Year	Profit	Loss
1935	11	5
1936	10	6
1937	9	7
1938	8	8
1939	9	7
1940	10	6
1941	10	6
1942	10	6
1943	10	6
1944	12	4
1945	11	5

The answer appears to be no, at least with respect to the overall profitability of the majors and the number of teams that were profitable each season. Even in 1943, when the majors lost money, the majority of the teams actually reported net gains, though generally small ones. Eight of the ten teams finishing in the black that year had profits of under $100,000, including the Philadelphia Phillies, who barely scraped by with a $6,076 gain. Remember Powell Crosley indicating that the Reds lost $451 in 1943? The *Hearings* show the club generated a slight profit that year of $4,916, and in fact the franchise made money every year during the war with the surprising exception of the generally profitable 1945 season.

Table 8 — Major League Team Profits/Losses, 1942–1945[49]

	National League				
	1942	*1943*	*1944*	*1945*	*Total*
Boston	$(57,941)	$(41,166)	$(133,022)	$(137,142)	$(369,271)
Brooklyn	$155,451	$(62,719)	$3,923	$252,721	$349,376
Chicago	$(7,188)	$33,009	$69,660	$45,554	$141,035
Cincinnati	$4,916	$16,503	$30,611	$(33,224)	$18,806
New York	$54,151	$(248,973)	$53,489	$339,079	$197,746
Philadelphia	$(56,251)	$6,076	$(136,669)	$(202,923)	$(389,767)
Pittsburgh	$(33,735)	$56,160	$111,112	$43,943	$177,480
St. Louis	$63,553	$105,791	$146,417	$94,826	$410,587
TOTAL	$122,956	$(135,319)	$145,521	$402,834	$535,992

	American League				
	1942	*1943*	*1944*	*1945*	*Total*
Boston	$28,343	$(264,277)	$(43,131)	$(30,287)	$(309,352)
Chicago	$(55,251)	$24,423	$61,295	$102,327	$132,794
Cleveland	$35,775	$27,873	$86,803	$108,737	$259,188

Detroit	$1,966	$132,046	$207,043	$191,755	$532,810
New York	$136,567	$(88,521)	$151,043	$200,959	$400,048
Philadelphia	$(44,198)	$(28,255)	$(6,133)	$(17,026)	$(95,612)
St. Louis	$80,855	$45,375	$285,034	$30,452	$441,716
Washington	$42,526	$46,631	$90,429	$222,473	$402,059
TOTAL	$226,583	$(104,705)	$832,383	$809,390	$1,763,651

A detailed examination of the profits/losses for the individual clubs during the war shows over that four-year period, 12 of the 16 major league franchises were profitable. Five clubs managed to come through the war earning profits every single year, while only two were in the red all four seasons. The two consistent losers (the Philadelphia Athletics and Boston Braves), both had long histories of financial failure prior to the start of the war. Not only were many of the teams making money, seven of them even issued dividends to shareholders at various times during the war, with Cleveland, Cincinnati, Pittsburgh, and the St. Louis Cardinals paying out dividends every single year, including years when those clubs lost money (Brooklyn also paid a dividend in 1943, a year in which the Dodgers lost money).[50]

There was much concern among the owners going into the 1943 season, and their fears appear to have been reasonable. Profits were down slightly in 1942 and it was much harder to find players to put on the field. Meanwhile, Landis continued to push them to contribute and donate more to the war effort. Many owners feared that 1943 would be an economic disaster and wanted to pull the plug on the game for the duration of the war. Their concerns, of course, were entirely selfish, as indicated by a "reliable source" to the Associated Press in early 1943:

> A reliable source who cannot be named said some baseball men want [War Manpower Commission Chairman] McNutt to tell them not to operate on the ground that this would force Commissioner Kenesaw Mountain Landis to "freeze" all player contracts. If the leagues quit without such orders, this informant asserted, the players would become free agents.[51]

This truly gets to the crux of the thought process of the owners, and even though the source was not named, one can infer it was an insider with direct knowledge of the situation. The owners publicly proclaimed the morale value of the game to the American people, but when their profits appeared threatened they wanted to shut the game down despite its alleged importance to society, something they trumpeted to support its continuation in 1941 and early 1942. However, they did not want to shut the game down themselves — they wanted the government to order the stoppage, both for the obvious public relations reasons and the much more important economic considerations surrounding the sacred reserve clause. The owners feared that a self-imposed shutdown could result in the players becoming free agents due to the failure by teams to exercise their reserve clause options and offer new contracts for the following year. Ultimately the government did not order a professional baseball shutdown and the owners opted to continue on, not because of the value baseball provided to Americans, but because financially it was better for them to face short-term losses and keep the reserve clause intact than it might be to experience the free agency of every player on their wartime reserve lists if they shut down the game themselves.

One team did fail during the war years. The woeful Philadelphia Phillies managed to come through the Depression in relatively good shape, even registering a six-figure profit of $100,716 in 1932, the best result in the majors and one of only three teams in the black that year. The next four seasons found them slightly better than break-even, before 1937 ushered in a run of six consecutive seasons of financial losses. Gerald Nugent was the majority owner of the franchise during this period, having taken over ownership in 1932, and though he promised upon taking control of the club that he would not fall into the trap of selling his players to generate revenue, the team's financial situation quickly forced him to change his stance.[52] Between 1932 and 1942 the Phillies had the lowest home attendance in the National League each season, and Nugent's player deals were the only thing that kept the debtors away. Nugent was forced to borrow more and more to keep the team afloat, and by the start of the 1940s he was even taking loans from the league, which had a vested interest in keeping the club solvent. By 1942 it was clear that Nugent could not hold out any longer with the Phillies carrying a debt reported to be at $330,000, and he let the league know that if an owner could be found who was acceptable to the other clubs he would sell. With no buyers readily available, the National League itself purchased the team in February 1943, paying only $26,000 to the various shareholders while also assuming all the club's debt. Less than a week later the league "found" a buyer in a group led by William D. Cox, allegedly selling the Phillies to this group for roughly ten times the price for which it was purchased from Nugent.[53] Even when dealing with their own struggling peers, the owners were financially ruthless. Cox lasted less than a year before a gambling scandal that involved him placing bets on his own team led to his ouster, and the Phillies had their third owner of 1943 when Robert R. M. Carpenter, Sr. bought the club. The Carpenters finally brought some stability to the franchise and operated it successfully for decades thereafter.

Overall the war years were financially successfully for the majors and the teams were only forced to weather a few difficult years. Those that struggled most, like the Phillies, were the same ones that had financial problems well before the war and found themselves hit even harder by the downturn of 1942–1943. Despite the complaints and the selective memories about the financial losses allegedly suffered throughout the war, once baseball turned the corner following the 1943 season, attendance and revenues grew quickly, returning to pre-war levels by 1945 and breaking records just a year later. In many ways the war was good for the business of baseball.

The Spink Letter

For decades *The Sporting News* operated as a sort of unofficial official publication of Organized Baseball. The weekly sports newspaper was devoted exclusively to baseball — no other sports graced its pages, even during the off-season. Publisher J. G. Taylor Spink, who took over the paper from his father, carried the torch in support of professional baseball and defended it against all comers. Generally he toed the "company line" laid down by the major league owners, but sometimes stood up and pointed his finger at perceived injustices. During the war Spink filled *The Sporting News'* pages with messages about the patriotic and morale value of baseball both at home and to the servicemen overseas, regularly publishing stories about how much the game meant to the men in uniform. He took steps to make *The Sporting News* accessible to men serving overseas by allowing readers to buy subscriptions for servicemen, and even arranging for the collection of previously read issues that were then shipped to the four corners of the globe. Certainly Spink's actions were not entirely altruistic — not only was selling subscriptions and getting *The Sporting News* into the hands of servicemen good for business, but so too was his continued support for the professional game, since he relied in part on his relationship with the major league owners to ensure the continued success of his paper. His long-standing relationship with Landis, however, was often strained, and a pair of 1942 articles in the national press that dubbed Spink "Mr. Baseball" caused it to deteriorate further as Landis believed *he* was "Mr. Baseball," though the two retained a certain amount of professional respect for one another.[54]

However, Spink could be a loose cannon at times. On January 28, 1944, he wrote a letter to President Roosevelt and asked the president to once again publicly support the continuation of baseball. Writing the president during wartime as the editor of a sports newspaper and asking him to comment on baseball can be viewed as an act of vanity and self-importance, and those charges are probably accurate given Spink's personality and his thoughts about his personal stature in the world of baseball. But it also speaks to his passionate belief in the role of baseball in American society, even when this was at odds with what the owners wanted. As Spink noted in the pages of *The Sporting News* when controversy erupted surrounding his letter to the president, "The club owners owe an obligation both to the game and to the nation to carry on, even at a loss, the coming season. So do the players, without whom there could be no competition. All should consider themselves highly privileged to be able to pursue their diamond activities in 1944, the third year of the war."[55] Strong words from a man who not only relied upon, but also reveled in, the support he had from baseball's elite.

At 11 paragraphs Spink's letter is considerably longer than the very succinct one Landis sent Roosevelt in early 1942, and his self-importance comes through with phrases like "As publisher of THE SPORTING NEWS, baseball weekly published since 1886..." Most of the letter was a summary of Roosevelt's own 1942 "Green Light Letter" and a reiteration of the basic premise that professional baseball required a small number of men to entertain a population of millions — something Roosevelt himself indicated in 1942 and Spink simply repeated as if it was his own idea. The concluding two paragraphs got to the root of the matter of why it was important for baseball to continue, and why it again needed the president's support.

> This belief not only is based upon your statement two years ago, but has been strengthened by the hundreds of letters we have received from servicemen in this country and all over the world, telling of their great interest in baseball. This interest in the game among the armed forces also has been emphasized by returning war correspondents, such as Quentin Reynolds, Cy Peterman, and others.
>   I realize you have many more pressing problems to solve and that you fully covered the situation at the time in your previous splendid indorsement [sic] of the game as a morale factor. However, an expression from you on baseball's place in the war effort alongside that of industry, undoubtedly would furnish valuable guidance now and your consideration would be greatly appreciated.[56]

Spink did not receive a response from the president, but he did get a reply from the president's secretary, Stephen Early, who wrote in part:

> I am not sure, however, that it would be in the best interests of the war effort for the President to make a supplemental statement at this time. We have traveled a long way since the President wrote Judge Landis more than two years ago. It might well be that the President would prefer to leave the matter from now on for determination under the regulations laid down under the Selective Service Act and the regulations governing the manpower situation generally.[57]

While polite in tone, Early's letter clearly implied this was an issue that did not require the president's attention, one that could be handled more effectively within the framework of the various manpower and labor organizations already in place.

Landis and the owners were appalled by Spink's letter, and they immediately took steps to distance themselves from it publicly. Clark Griffith noted that Spink "was not talking for baseball when he wrote President Roosevelt," and Landis took it ever further, stating, "Mr. Spink is not a member of the baseball organization and does not speak for anybody but himself."[58] After surviving a 1943 season in which the majors as a whole lost money (but most teams still turned a small profit), and with improved news coming from the war front, the last thing the owners wanted was to have government attention focused back on baseball. It was clear now that the owners would survive and they wanted to continue, unlike at the start of the 1943 season when the situation was much less certain, so publicly calling attention to the manpower issue was not in their best interest. In fact Landis privately wrote General Lewis Hershey, Director of Selective Service, the month prior to Spink's letter to make baseball's stance on any type of preferential treatment for its players very clear:

> Arguments that preferential treatment would serve "morale" can have only the effect of making that word odious. Furthermore, favored treatment in any way or to any extent of professional athletes not only would be harmful to their interests and the interests of the organizations with which they are connected, but also would inevitably and justifiably arouse bitter public resentment.[59]

Landis seemingly had no intention of ever releasing this letter to the public because dredging up the issue of perceived favoritism to athletes once again, even to declaim it, was not beneficial to baseball. Spink's letter forced his hand, however, and fortunately for Landis he had this earlier letter available to use in an effort to distance baseball completely from Spink's comments that, while relatively benign, had the potential to reopen debate on a topic that baseball was content to let rest.

The Spink letter stands as a strange footnote to the overall experience of professional baseball during the war, one that shows the tenuous back-and-forth nature of the game's struggle to find its place as both an industry and part of American society. Spink was so passionate about the importance of the game that he felt the need to seek reassurance from the one man whose words carried the most weight, but in so doing alienated himself from the allies he relied upon for the success of his business and opened up a can of worms that baseball had done everything in its power to close and bury. Even asking for clarification could be seen as asking for favors or special consideration, something baseball sought to avoid at all costs. The game could survive government involvement, and even a government ordered shutdown; but no one was sure it could survive if it lost the respect and support of the population.

Internal Struggles

There is no question that Landis ruled baseball with an iron hand, often to the chagrin of the owners who hired him. Unlike many men whose roles and influence only become known after their deaths, Landis' power was clearly on display throughout his tenure as commissioner. Just months before Landis' death, sportswriter John Drebinger noted that while owners were willing to share their opinions on issues the game faced during the war,

> What they say is strictly "off the record" and "don't quote me" stuff and they are taking all these precautionary methods with good reason. For up to now one Commissioner K. M. Landis has not yet spoken and until he does you can rest assured none of the magnates will speak, either in or out of turn. It is positively amazing the way the good commissioner is held in awe and reverence by the men who pay him.[60]

Landis took charge of baseball's public proclamations related to the war and early on made it clear to the owners that they were to follow his lead. Immediately following Pearl Harbor he made the initial contribution to the Ball and Bat Fund out of the major league coffers and exchanged his famous letters with Roosevelt. Even in those early days, however, the owners were resistant to committing too much financially. Larry MacPhail of the Dodgers tried to get the other teams on board with each donating the receipts from one regular season game to war relief, but even at the winter meetings immediately following Pearl Harbor he found little support from the owners (though the plan eventually came to fruition in time for the 1942 season). According to MacPhail, "I probably will be criticized for this move, but I can take it. At the league meetings earlier this month (February 1942) I advocated adoption of this uniform plan for going all-out for the war, but without success."[61] Eventually the other owners came around to support MacPhail's proposal, and in April Landis announced that not only would there be two All-Star Games in 1942, but that the receipts from both would be donated to war relief charities.

Landis' support of the military had its roots in World War I when his son served as a pilot in France and Landis was still a federal judge. At the start of the new war he was quick in throwing baseball's support behind the war effort to prevent a replay of the public backlash it experienced due to its own missteps during the previous conflict. Under his leadership the majors contributed the total receipts (including the visitors share) from one home game for each team, the All-Star Game revenues, and a significant portion of the World Series receipts from 1942 to 1944, to service charities. These decisions, especially with regards to the World Series, were not embraced by all the owners, and there was grumbling that the commissioner had extended his reach too far. His creation of the Landis-Eastman Line for spring training added insult to injury, as now the judge was directly interfering with how teams ran their businesses, even though Landis used it as a means to get positive publicity for baseball in the national press.

When Landis passed away on November 25, 1944, the recollections of him in the press were uniformly positive. The *New York Times* referred to him both as the "guiding genius" of baseball and also its "czar,"[62] a fitting moniker that described how he ruled over the game. For the owners his passing, which came shortly before the annual winter meetings, gave them the opportunity to take stock and reflect on their goals for 1945 now that the war and the baseball economy had both turned the corner and were once again on solid footing. They were in no hurry to select another absolute ruler for baseball and wanted to take advantage of the opportunity afforded by Landis' passing to clarify the existing off-the-field rules of the game. According to one owner, who tellingly commented under the promise of anonymity, in the years following Landis' hiring, "There have been, since then, numerous amendments and new rules adopted, not to mention the interpretations Landis placed upon the rules as a precedent. We therefore merely plan to clarify the code for the benefit of both the clubs and the new commissioner."[63]

During the winter of 1944–1945, baseball faced its last great challenge of the war in the work-or-fight edict that came down from the War Manpower Commission. Baseball's leaders adroitly navigated the situation without a commissioner and came out the other side with government support for a 1945 baseball season, a significant accomplishment. During this period the game received both support and criticisms, from many within government and the military. One notable advocate was a Democrat Senator from Kentucky who was also a member of the Senate Military Committee. The *New York Times* noted that the senator "thinks baseball is worth continuing and that he will go to bat for the game."[64] The senator's name was Albert B. "Happy" Chandler, and a little more than two months later he would be selected as Landis' successor.

Chandler was the opposite of what the owners publicly said they were looking for in a commissioner. He was not a "baseball man" from a business perspective, lacking experience in team ownership or management, though he had been a talented ballplayer in his own right, good enough to play in college and have a brief stint in the minors. While he did not meet their stated criteria, Chandler gave the owners what they really wanted — a nationally recognizable name with strong political connections who would champion their plans, unlike the unpredictable Landis. To be on the safe side they adjusted the commissioner's role and eliminated his authority to override a rule as being detrimental to baseball, solidifying their control over the game.[65] It turned out the owners were wrong about Chandler, and after he took over as commissioner on a full-time basis in late 1945 he frequently found himself at odds with them. They hired Landis because they knew at the time they needed a strong, decisive individual whom the public perceived as fair and righteous to lead baseball out of the gambling scandals of the era, and ended up with man who ruled based on his own convictions. They hired Chandler because they wanted someone who was the opposite of Landis, who would go along with them and allow them to run the game their way, but once again got more than they bargained for. Chandler was no patsy, as they came to discover in the post-war era.

Race

When Brooklyn Dodgers manager Leo Durocher commented in the press in 1942 that there were a number of black ballplayers who were capable of playing at the major league level whom he would sign if allowed to, he brought down Landis' wrath. "There is no rule, formal or informal, or any under-standing — unwritten, subterranean or sub-anything — against the hiring of Negro players by the teams of Organized Ball," said Landis. "I told Durocher that he could hire one Negro ball player, or 25 Negro ball players, just the same as whites."[66] The story received considerable attention in the New York press. Meanwhile, *The Sporting News* ran it as part of a small three-paragraph blurb on the bottom corner of page 11, a section of the paper primarily devoted to box scores.

The minor leagues offered similar public statements when confronted with questions about race. The U.S. Student Assembly sent a telegram to the members of the National Association during their annual winter meetings in December 1943, protesting the continued racial segregation of professional baseball. The telegram was addressed at the meeting, and "President [William] Bramham was authorized to reply there was no present practice of discrimination, and that it was not a matter for consideration by the Association, since it was up to the individual clubs, who had the right to employ whoever they desired, without any restriction."[67]

It is certainly true that there is no evidence of any formal, written rule that prohibited Organized Baseball's member clubs from signing blacks to their rosters. It is also true, however, that no black player had appeared in Organized Baseball in decades. A few situations occurred in which a team tried to pass off a black player as Cuban or Native American only to be "found out" and forced to quietly drop him, but even these were rare. Even without a formal rule it is clear that the "Gentleman's Agreement" was a form of peer pressure that kept black players out of Organized Baseball. In reality there were likely very few if any owners who were even interested in signing black players for their teams in the segregated America of the era. Landis receives a considerable amount of the blame for the continued segregation of professional baseball, and surely as the commissioner for such a lengthy period he likely had the power to force the issue had he chosen to do so. The fact remains that there really was very little pressure being exerted from within baseball to integrate the game, and in fact there was even some opposition to it from within the black community and the Negro Leagues.

Roosevelt's Executive Order 8802 in June 1941 barred racial discrimination in war industries, and many hoped it would open the door to further integration in America. It was a starting point, but American society remained segregated and so did the military. While blacks were accepted into the military's ranks, they were generally kept in segregated units, limiting their interactions with their white counterparts. Here professional baseball mirrored society, allowing other racial and ethnic groups to play, but keeping black athletes segregated in their own leagues.

The World War II era actually presented Organized Baseball with its best and most compelling reasons to integrate. Blacks joined the industrial workforce in record numbers and were part of the nation's military in a time of war. Black athletes from other sports, such as boxing champion Joe Louis, were in the military, doing their part to break down racial stereotypes and move integration forward. Meanwhile, the baseball owners faced an acute shortage of quality players as more and more men entered the armed forces. The Negro Leagues seemed to offer a fantastic source of previously untapped talent that could be used to supplement major league rosters. Not only would signing black players have improved the quality of play on the field, it would have expanded the fan base, as black fans would certainly come out to major league parks in greater numbers if black players were in the two leagues. Some other amateur and professional sports were already integrated, so this was not a new concept to the sporting public. Certainly there would have been backlash from some quarters, but the facts that the nation was at war and that blacks were serving in the military would likely have muted opposition, while at the same time improving the game and stabilizing rosters.

To some extent the reasons behind baseball's failure to take advantage of the wartime environment and integrate remain cloudy. We can look to what the owners and executives said at the time, but in many cases we are left wondering if they legitimately believed their statements or if it was all merely window dressing that covered deeper issues. In most cases we cannot be certain, but their words, both public and private, do provide some clues.

While Spink apparently tried to bury the 1942 Durocher-Landis story in the back pages of *The Sporting News*, it simply refused to die, and in August

Spink wrote an editorial regarding race and baseball. Spink opened by conceding that some sports were indeed integrated, noting that "Other sports had their Joe Louis, Fritz Pollard, and like notables, respected and honored by all races, but they competed under different circumstances from those dominating in baseball." One of those different circumstances, according to Spink, was the propensity of baseball fans to heckle players in unflattering terms. Though left unspecified in the editorial, these barbs often included ethnic slurs. "Clear-minded men of tolerance of both races realize the tragic possibilities and have steered clear of such complications, because they realize it is to the benefit of each and also of the game." Spink rationalized that because some people would use racial slurs against black ballplayers, that in itself was reason enough for the game not to integrate. He felt that this environment was somehow different from that experienced by Joe Louis in boxing and Fritz Pollard in football, a position both men would certainly have refuted. Spink went on to explain the business impacts of integration, most notably the perceived detrimental impact on the Negro Leagues. "Organized Negro baseball has become a million-dollar business annually and is beginning to emerge from the red-ink stage into the profit column. It would be a staggering blow should its leading players be drawn into the majors and with them, its fan support," he wrote. "It is doubtful if the colored game could survive."

Spink believed that those who spoke out in favor of integration actually did so to promote their own personal agendas. "However, there are agitators, ever ready to seize an issue that will rebound to their profit or self aggrandizement, who have sought to force Negro players on the big leagues, not because it would help the game, but because it gives them a chance to thrust themselves into the limelight as great crusaders in the guise of democracy," he opined. That being said, Spink indicated he understood that some in the black community legitimately sought integration and equality, though he personally disagreed with their views.

> Of course, there are some colored people who take a different view, and they are entitled to their opinions, but in doing so they are not looking at the question from the broader point of view, or for the ultimate good of either race or the individuals in it. They ought to concede their own people are now protected and that nothing is served by allowing agitators to make an issue of a question on which both sides would prefer to be let alone.[68]

There are so many holes in Spink's position that pointing them out almost seems unnecessary. Spink conceded that there were some in the black community who wanted integration, yet then stated that "both sides" preferred to leave as the status quo, obviously contradicting himself. He also held to the idea that segregation was not a bad thing at all, but in fact served to protect the black community. While his earlier point about the potentially negative impact on the business of the Negro Leagues was valid, and in later years proved to be true, the idea that segregation should continue because it was good for some business owners is to modern readers repugnant. Spink also provided some quotes from the black press and from Negro Leagues manager Jim Taylor that indicated their support for continued separation of the races on the baseball diamond. The essence of his argument was that both blacks and whites preferred segregation, and therefore it should continue.

Landis was quick to point out that Spink did not speak for Organized Baseball during the affair surrounding the editor's 1944 letter to Roosevelt, so the lack of any public refutation of Spink's views on this issue implied that the commissioner and owners did not disagree with them. Certainly any number of owners, executives, and players offered quotes on the topic of integration over the years, and those made publicly often mirrored those shown above from Landis and Spink, concluding that it was simply better to have segregation and that it was supported by both races. Every now and again, however, someone provided a more direct response to the question of baseball integration, as Larry MacPhail did when he was contacted by sociology professor Dr. Dan Dodson, who at the time was working as the Executive Director of the Mayor's Committee on Unity of New York City. "You d — d professional dogooders know nothing about baseball," MacPhail said. "It is a business. Our organization rented our parks to the Negro Leagues last year for about $100,000. That is about return we made on our investment. The investment of Negro Clubs is also legitimate. *I will not jeopardize my income nor their investment* until some way can be worked out whereby it will not hurt the Negro Leagues for major leagues to take an occasional player of theirs"[69] (emphasis added). Like Spink, MacPhail focused on the business reasons for continued segregation. Segregated baseball was good for the bottom line, at least for MacPhail and the Yankees.

The 1946 *Steering Committee Report* is also notable for what it said, and then later failed to say, about the issue of race. The initial draft submitted to the owners, league presidents, and commissioner, included a 2.5-page section titled "Race Question" that outlined the views of the committee (including MacPhail) on the Negro Leagues and integration. Following an introductory paragraph that noted the black community held great interest in baseball and supported the game, the committee made a surprising admission: "The American people are primarily concerned with the excellence of performance in sport rather than the color, race or creed of the performer." The report appeared to acknowledge that sports fans, and therefore baseball fans as well, were not concerned with race but with the quality of play. If that was indeed true, then why were blacks kept out of Organized Baseball? The issue, of course, was money.

Larry MacPhail (left) and Branch Rickey (right) worked together in the Brooklyn Dodgers organization prior to MacPhail re-joining the military in 1942. In 1945 MacPhail became a part-owner of the New York Yankees. Both men were known as baseball innovators, but they found themselves on opposite sides of the race issue, with Rickey seeking to end segregation in baseball and MacPhail making comments in support of its continuation (Transcendental Graphics).

In 1946 Jackie Robinson broke the color line in Organized Baseball when he played with the Montreal Royals of the AAA International League, so at the time the *Steering Committee Report* was written, Robinson had already proven that he could be successful in the minors. This fact was not lost on the committee, nor was the impact of Robinson on the bottom line. "The employment of a Negro on one AAA League Club in 1946 resulted in a tremendous increase in Negro attendance at all games in which the player appeared. The percentage of Negro attendance at some games in Newark and Baltimore was in excess of 50 percent." This sounds like a good thing—a black player on the Montreal roster improved attendance throughout the league by bringing more black fans to the ballparks. However, the report quickly followed by noting, "A situation might be presented, if Negroes participate in Major League games, in which the preponderance of Negro attendance in parks such as Yankee Stadium, the Polo Grounds and Comiskey

Park could conceivably threaten the value of the Major League franchises owned by these clubs." So while having black players would increase the number of black fans through the gates, that increase could actually have a detrimental impact on the value of the clubs, presumably because an increase in black fans would result in a decrease in white fans and therefore overall admissions, an extrapolation that was left unsaid.

Following a discussion of the negative financial impact the signing of black players by major league clubs would have on the Negro League franchises, the *Steering Committee Report* returned to major league economics.

> The Negro leagues rent their parks in many cities from clubs in Organized Baseball. Many major and [m]inor league clubs derive substantial revenue from these rentals. (The Yankee Organization, for instance, nets nearly $100,000 a year from rentals and concessions in connection with Negro league games at the Yankee Stadium in New York — and in Newark, Kansas City and Norfolk). Club owners in the major leagues are reluctant to give up revenues amounting to hundreds of thousands of dollars every year. They naturally want the Negro leagues to continue. They do not sign, and cannot properly sign, players under contract to Negro clubs. This is not racial discrimination. It's simply respecting the contractual relationships between the Negro leagues and their players.

Once again the owners returned to the idea that segregation was good for business, and with the description of the impact on the Yankees in particular we see MacPhail's hand, along with confirmation of the exact same comments he previously made to Dodson regarding this issue. The discussion about respecting the contracts of the Negro League teams is interesting in what it overlooks, specifically that the Negro Leagues at that time were not part of Organized Baseball and therefore its player contracts were not binding on major league clubs. It also ignored the fact that the majors could simply purchase player contracts from the Negro League clubs if they chose, exactly as they did with unaffiliated minor league teams that were members of the National Association or independent teams (and each other). There were perfectly ethical ways for major league clubs to obtain the rights to Negro League players if they chose to pursue them and the Negro League franchises were willing to deal. These were nothing more than excuses made in an attempt to show that the owners were taking the moral high road when in fact they really believed it was in their economic best interests to maintain the status quo of segregation.

In addition to the focus on the business impacts of integration, the Spink editorial and the *Steering Committee Report* have other elements in common. Like Spink, the *Steering Committee Report* denigrated those who favored integration through name-calling. "Certain groups in this country including political and social-minded drum-beaters, are conducting pressure campaigns in an attempt to force major league clubs to sign Negro players," it read, contending these groups used baseball as their target for the publicity value. The *Steering Committee Report* also used a quote from a black baseball insider, citing Sam Lacy, a sports writer and editor who played a role in the signing of Jackie Robinson, to support the contention that the Negro Leagues did not have any players who could excel at all aspects of the game at the major league level.

The section on race concluded by acknowledging that the issue of integration was a serious one, one that required the ownership group to work together towards a solution.

> There are many factors in this problem and many difficulties which will have to be solved before any generally satisfactory solution can be worked out. The individual action of any one Club may exert tremendous pressures upon the whole structure of Professional Baseball, and could conceivably result in lessening the value of several Major League franchises.
>
> Your Committee does not desire to question the motives of any organization or individual who is sincerely opposed to segregation or who believes that such a policy is detrimental in the best interests of Professional Baseball.
>
> Your Committee wishes to go on record as feeling that this is an overall problem which vitally affects each and every one of us — and that effort should be made to arrive at a fair and just solution — compatible with good business judgment and the principles of good sportsmanship.[70]

This conclusion was written in such a way as not to cast aspersions on those taking either side of the issue and asked everyone to consider the impact on the group as a whole, particularly the potential financial ramifications. That being said, at no point did the report indicate that integration could actually have a beneficial impact on revenues, even going so far as to use the attendance increases associated with Robinson's play in Montreal to cast a negative light on the subject. While "Race Question" was written in a way that implied all sides of the issue were under consideration, everything was spun to support the unstated conclusion that segregation was good for business and should continue.

We must be careful when considering the *Steering Committee Report* as a source regarding the stance of the owners regarding race during the war, since the document was prepared in 1946, a year after the end of World War II. However, the opinions expressed in the report appear to match the comments made before and during the war by various baseball insiders, supporting its relevance. It is one of the few documents about this issue written by members of the major league inner circle (including both league presidents) and intended only for distribution within that group. Particularly telling is the fact that the section on the "Race Question" was omitted from the final draft of the report approved by the owners, league presidents, and commissioner. Was its exclusion due to the owners' disagreement with the position the committee took on the issue, or because they preferred that topic not to be committed to writing to prevent it from being disseminated? Either way, the *Steering Committee Report* has some relevance as to the thoughts of those in power on the issue of race and integration.

One man claimed to have plans to integrate the majors during the war and to do so in a big way, though these have proven difficult if not impossible to verify. Bill Veeck already had a lifetime of experience in baseball when the war broke out, working for the Cubs when his father owned them before later purchasing the American Association Milwaukee Brewers in 1941. Even early in his baseball career Veeck had the reputation of being a bit of a radical among the normally conservative owners, and his antics over the years became legendary. In his autobiography Veeck describes his plan to buy the struggling Phillies from Gerry Nugent in 1943 and "stock it with Negro players."[71] He was sure that by being the first to tap the talent in the Negro Leagues he could quickly turn the Phillies around and make them a contender, especially given the depleted level of major league talent at the time. Veeck made it clear that his plan was not driven by any type of altruism or morality, but simply a matter of good business since he could acquire better talent at a lower price than what he would pay for white ballplayers. He alleged that when Landis learned of the plan, the commissioner arranged for the quick sale of the Phillies to Cox, preventing Veeck from buying the team. While Veeck's story was long accepted as true, in the late 1990s a group of baseball historians failed to find any validation for it in the primary sources of the period, including the black press. Despite Veeck's claims to have been working closely with members of the black press to identify potential players, there were no mentions of his plans found in print in either the black or the mainstream media. Nugent too denied having any conversations with Veeck in which he even hinted at an interested in purchasing the team. It is possible that the conspirators did an excellent job of keeping their plan quiet, and it certainly sounds plausible of Veeck, but one suspects that Veeck would have gone public with the story after baseball made moves to shut him out instead of waiting more than 15 years to publicize it for the first time.[72]

The story of Jackie Robinson's breaking baseball's color barrier has been widely told and reveals much about hardship, courage, and the human spirit. Robinson, a gifted athlete, was selected by Branch Rickey to integrate baseball in part due to his intelligence, maturity, and mental toughness, and history shows that the choice was a smart one. The changes to the nation's social fabric during the war contributed to the creation of the environment that

Rickey and Robinson used to their advantage, but given the seemingly continued resistance to integration within the ranks of baseball's owners, one wonders if the color barrier could have been broken earlier had they thought that it would be profitable. It is possible that even then Landis might have stood in the way because of his views on race, but we cannot be sure. Certainly Rickey and Robinson benefited from having Chandler as commissioner, as he was much more receptive to such a change. When asked why he supported Robinson's move to Organized Baseball, Chandler replied, "I don't have to answer that question. You have to answer instead, 'Why shouldn't I?' He was good enough to wear Uncle Sam's uniform. He is a qualified ball player. Why shouldn't I?"[73]

The owners had the perfect opportunity to integrate during the war years but failed to do so. Not only was the social situation advantageous, it was an economic advantage for them to bring in more talented players to improve the quality of play on the field, stabilize their rosters, and increase the draw at the gate, though they failed to recognize it. For a group of men who often used economic and financial explanations for their actions (or inactions), they appear to have overlooked the obvious in this case. Unless, of course, there is another reason for their stance — perhaps the majority of them simply did not want black players on their teams, or a large number of black fans in their stadiums. It is difficult to believe that the owners were truly concerned for the future of Negro League ball clubs or the black ballplayers. Keeping baseball white was safe, easy, and predictable, as is typically true of maintaining the status quo.

Gender

Women had their own niche in the baseball world prior to the war, though generally limited to all-female barnstorming teams. Occasionally women played on a men's semi-pro or industrial league club, and a few women were good enough to actually participate in exhibitions against major league players and/or teams, most notably Lizzie Murphy in the 1920s and Olympic athlete and golfer Babe Didrikson in 1934. But it was not until the advent of the All-American Girls Softball League (later the All-American Girls Professional Baseball League) that women had their first real opportunity to play the game professionally in their own established league.

Founded by Cubs owner Philip Wrigley in 1943, the AAGPBL (for simplicity the league will be referred to with this acronym regardless of its actual name used during any given year) was created to be, as he later described it before Congress, "an idealistic, nonprofit corporation"[74] intended to provide wholesome entertainment to people in towns that did not have professional baseball. During Wrigley's two-year involvement, the league controlled the players and assigned them to the various clubs, though the uniform player contracts omitted the reserve clause deemed so essential to men's professional baseball. When Wrigley ended his affiliation with the league in 1944 it was operated by the new ownership group as a for-profit enterprise, and by 1947 "the directors due to problems that were developing, felt it necessary to include a reserve clause in the contract."[75]

The AAGPBL was little more than a small offshoot of the majors during World War II, a noble idea that received a little support but was never intended to represent a step towards the gender integration of professional baseball. It was, however, an important vehicle in the expansion of the role of women in society, a role that grew rapidly during the war as women took over many of the jobs and roles men left behind when they went off to war. Even though the AAGPBL was a professional sport league, it was still of paramount importance to the league that the women ballplayers acted in ways deemed appropriate for their gender by society, resulting in the inclusion of contract clauses that required that a player "pledges herself to the American public to conform to high standards of personal conduct, fair play, and good sportsmanship."[76] Women could play professional baseball, but they had to remain women first and foremost, both on and off the field. Much as the independence women gained during the war receded upon its conclusion, so too did the AAGPBL struggle to maintain its place in society following the war, and it eventually folded at the end of the 1954 season.

The Minor Leagues

The general plight of the minor leagues during World War II has been touched upon, primarily the sharp decrease in the number of leagues that remained in operation due to the lack of available players as the war progressed, especially at the lowest classifications. At the highest levels most leagues were able to ride out the war, with five of the six Class A and higher minor leagues operating throughout the conflict (the only exception was the Class A1 Texas League that folded following the 1942 season). So how did the leagues that remained fare, and were their experiences similar in any ways to those of the majors?

The three highest classification minor leagues in 1941 were the American Association, the International League, and the Pacific Coast League. All three circuits remained in operation throughout the war and retained the same roster of cities and teams. They exhibited similar attendance trends over the period from 1941 to 1945, reporting increased attendance in 1942, a decrease in 1943, and then consecutive increases in 1944 and 1945.

Table 9 — Class AA Minor League Attendance, 1940–1945[77]

| | High Level Minor Leagues | | | | | |
	1940	1941	1942	1943	1944	1945
AA	1,055,879	1,057,060	1,136,320	1,107,886	1,153,900	1,380,942
IL	1,117,803	1,203,393	1,222,186	1,121,369	1,429,187	1,430,241
PCL	1,482,016	1,476,652	1,513,277	1,117,209	2,343,266	2,918,966

While the leagues all had similar overall trends, the magnitudes of the swings varied. In comparing these leagues to the majors, the primary difference was in 1942, when the majors saw an attendance drop of 11.7 percent while the high level minors all improved slightly over their 1941 totals. What was consistent across the majors and all the high level minors was that the low point in attendance came in 1943, and that by 1945 it improved to levels considerably higher than the immediate pre-war era. The key to success for these leagues lay in large part to the relatively small decreases in fan turnout, with only the Pacific Coast League experiencing a notable attendance drop in 1943, and that was due in large part to the shortening of the league schedule from 178 games per team in 1942 to 155 games in 1943. The Pacific Coast League expanded the schedule to 169 games in 1944 and to 183 games in 1945, accounting for much of the increased attendance in those years.

All minor league clubs that were part of the National Association had some type of relationship with the majors, either directly through ownership or working agreements, or indirectly through the drafting and sale of players. The Major-Minor League Agreement formalized the relationship between the majors and the National Association, one that was supposed to provide adequate representation for the minors but actually stacked the deck against them, as was described by *Milwaukee Journal* sports editor R. G. Lynch before the House Committee in 1951:

> The National Association was created by the minor leagues to present a united front in dealing with the majors. The majors made their own agreement — the major league agreement — between the two leagues for their own benefit, but then they had to deal with the minor leagues and they had to make what they called the major-minor league agreement. And when that comes up in the national convention of the National Association, each league has one vote, and the vote of the league is determined by the majority of the clubs within that league. In Mr. Halligan's [six-team Class A Central] league, for instance, the vote would be determined by the four clubs owned by the major leagues, because they have the dominant voice. Then the league would have one vote when they went to the National Association convention.
> So when they vote down there now, and it has been true for the last few years, the rules that they make and the policies they adopt are no longer for

the benefit or protection of the minor leagues, but are for the benefit of the operation of the major leagues.

That has permitted the major leagues to operate in the minors as they see fit. And from my observation it is a completely self-serving operation. They are not operating the minor leagues for the good of baseball or for the good of competition in the minors. They are operating only to produce baseball players for themselves.[78]

In 1941 of the 41 minor leagues operating under the National Association, 22 had at least half their teams under the ownership of or in some type of farm relationship with a major league franchise. By 1943 the influence of the majors increased further as seven of the ten remaining minor leagues had at least half their teams in arrangements with the majors, and in 1944 and 1945 just the Pacific Coast League could claim to be operating somewhat independently, with only three of its eight teams tied in some way to the majors. Needless to say, the majors exhibited considerable influence over the minors, further strengthening their monopoly power and control of the market.

A major league parent club could afford to operate some minor league teams at break-even or even at a loss, so long as the minors continued to produce and develop talent that eventually reached the majors or could be sold to another team for a profit. The success of the conglomerate headed by the parent organization supported some minor league clubs despite their individual economic losses, conferring a great economic advantage to farm teams when competing against independents. Ross Horning, a former minor league player and World War II veteran who was a graduate student studying foreign affairs at George Washington University at the time of the Hearings, described baseball as a mercantile economic system,

> whereby each major league club has little colonies all over the United States, and the primary purpose of these colonies or minor league clubs is to produce baseball players for the parent club. That is the primary interest. They are secondarily concerned with the baseball fans of the minor league club, or with the outcome of the local baseball owners, who have absolutely no control over their baseball club under a working agreement.[79]

The same was true during the war years. While the majors were forced to shut down a significant number of farm teams, decreasing from 148 farm teams in 1941 to only 46 by 1943, those that remained accounted for an even greater proportion of all minor league clubs. In 1941 just over half (50.8 percent) of minor league teams were under some level major league influence or control as farm clubs; by 1943 the majors controlled 74.2 percent of the minor league teams still in operation. The loss of players to the military forced the majors to consolidate their remaining players into a smaller number of teams, but it devastated the independent owners who lacked the scouting and support network to locate replacement players for those lost to military service and war industries.

While Lynch and Horning were baseball "insiders" of sorts due to their involvement with the sport and business aspects of the game, they were not privy to the conversations that went on behind closed doors, raising questions as to the validity of their assertions. However, at least one member of baseball's inner circle shared his views on the relationship between the majors and minors — Happy Chandler. At the 1951 House Hearings, Chandler was asked if it was true that there were a "good many" independent minor league franchises. "Very few," Chandler replied. "*The majors control the minors.* All the legislation, if you don't know, originates in the minors because that is where the farm directors control. They control the operation largely in the minors, there is no question in my mind they control the minors, and no question in the mind of anybody else who knows the way things operate"[80] (emphasis added). Chandler may have had an axe to grind when he testified at the end of his one-term reign as commissioner, but he unquestionably had exposure to the inner workings of the business of baseball at both the major and minor league levels, and therefore spoke from experience.

Not everyone agreed with this view, of course. George Trautman was the president of the National Association at the time of the House Hearings, and he testified that independent minor league clubs could successfully compete against those owned and operated as major league farms. "Some of our most successful operators in the lower classifications are independent operators," he said. "I think there is a place in baseball for the farm system and the independent operator."[81] Upon further questioning, however, Trautman was forced to admit that a major league club that owned a number of minor league franchises could transfer players among them to improve the competitiveness of some, an advantage that an independent minor league team with no major league affiliation did not have. Trautman later acknowledged that it was very difficult to run a minor league franchise profitably, describing the lower classification clubs as "civic enterprises," not traditional businesses. "The operation of a minor league club is most assuredly no bonanza," stated Trautman. "In fact with a great many of them it is rather a case of keeping losses to a minimum rather than making or expecting to make a profit."[82]

In late 1943 a group of minor league owners attempted a coup of sorts when they sought to replace the incumbent National Association president, William G. Bramham, with Frank J. Shaughnessy, the president of the International League and an opponent of the Major-Minor League Agreement in place at the time. The potential ramifications on the majors of the agreement's cancellation or forced re-negotiation were serious. It established player draft rules and purchase prices, and enabled the system that allowed Landis and the majors to impose their will on the minors. The irony of the situation was that one of Bramham's own heavy-handed rulings almost did him in.

In September 1943, Bramham issued a bulletin in which he indicated that only those teams and leagues that actually participated in and completed the 1943 baseball season would be permitted to vote on matters at the National Association winter meetings. On the surface this appeared to be a relatively straightforward decision. However, there were 15 minor leagues that had ceased operations for the duration of the war with the blessing of the National Association, but still continued to pay their annual dues under an agreement that guaranteed their territorial rights and re-entry into the Association following the war. Bramham advised the inactive leagues that they could appeal this decision to the executive council, but since that group was comprised solely of the leagues currently active, it was obvious that the council would not support allowing voting rights for the inactive circuits.

The failure of the Class E Twin Ports League to complete the 1943 season left nine active minor leagues with voting rights going into the winter meetings. Five of the nine remaining leagues were ready for a change, including the three largest circuits: the American Association, the International League, and the Pacific Coast League. Aligned with them were the Piedmont and PONY leagues, and given the voting structure that resulted from Bramham's September ruling, this block had the ability to replace him with a new president and dissolve the current Major-Minor League Agreement. They intended on nominating Shaughnessy as the new president when the meetings opened, but Bramham caught wind of their plans and had a surprise of his own waiting for them on December 1, the first day of the meetings. Bramham's first order of business was to call the roll, during which he included representatives or proxies of the 15 inactive leagues despite the objections of many of the active leagues. Then he gave the floor to James Boyd from the Jacksonville club of the inactive Sally League. Boyd acted as the attorney for the 15 inactive leagues and laid out their case to the meeting, citing various articles within the National Association rules that his group felt supported their continued voting rights. Bramham announced that he had also done some further review of the rules and determined that Article 25 of the agreement gave the dues-paying inactive leagues the right to vote on league business. This did not sit well with many of the active leagues, particularly those who intended on replacing Bramham with a new president. To them it appeared that the president's reversal was self-serving, since Bramham knew he needed the votes of the inactive leagues to retain his presidency. To add further insult to injury, unlike his September decision that took away the voting rights of the inactive leagues and offered them an appeal only to the active leagues that retained their voting rights, this time he stated that any appeal would be put up before a vote of all 24 leagues identified during the roll call — and one certainly would not expect any of the inactive leagues to vote to eliminate their own voting rights.[83] It was political maneuvering at its worst, but highly successful.

The five leagues that sought Bramham's ouster appealed to Landis, but not surprisingly he ruled in favor of the National Association president. There were further arguments about the proxies alleged to represent some of the leagues when it came to light that in most situations the team owners in those leagues were never polled about their views, but instead had a proxy selected solely at the discretion of their league presidents. Despite the continued protests, Bramham's consolidation of power was a *fait accompli* and he easily moved forward with his agenda. Faced with an impossible task, the group attempting to oust Bramham did not even bother to nominate their candidate. Those five leagues abstained from the voting, which gave Bramham unanimous support for another five-year term as president. The National Association now found itself in an unusual position, as the 15 inactive leagues formed a larger voting block than the nine active ones, meaning they could in fact alter rules and requirements to the detriment of those teams still in operation while they just sat on the sidelines and watched, a fact that was not lost on Milwaukee Brewers owner Bill Veeck, who railed against the inequity to no avail.

Bramham made his opinion of the opposition group clear. "I despise the man who says he is in my corner and then find out he is conniving against me," he said. "I do not want the support of them."[84] Landis went so far as to describe the behavior of the opposition camp in allegedly attempting to deprive their fellow leagues of their voting rights as "conduct detrimental to baseball,"[85] ironic given that he had offered no opinion on Bramham's unilateral decision to strip the inactive leagues of their rights three months earlier. Spink was somewhat more practical in editorializing about the political fight. "The public is not interested in either the causes or results of administrative conflicts; its most vital concern is the continuation of baseball and the game's rehabilitation after the war," he wrote. "It is up to the rebellious group to close ranks with the others."[86] The harsh words issued in the press by the victors did nothing to help the game's image in the wake of this political squabble during a time of war, but they did reinforce the fact that baseball, to the owners, was first and foremost a business.

The 1943 National Association winter meetings cast some doubt on the allegations Lynch and Horning made before Congress. If the majors exercised total control over their farm teams as alleged, then the political wrangling that took place likely would have never occurred. While the Pacific Coast League had only two clubs operating as major league farm clubs in 1943, the other four breakaway leagues all had more than half of their teams tied in some way to the majors. If the majors truly controlled these leagues, it does not make sense that the parent organizations would have allowed them to try to oust Bramham and dissolve the Major-Minor League Agreement. Of the four active leagues that supported Bramham, the Southern Association stood out as having a minority (three of its eight) of its teams involved in some kind of working relationship. The majors certainly wielded tremendous influence over the National Association due to their participation on the executive council and their direct involvement with many minor league teams, but that did not prevent some minor league clubs from pursuing their own individual best interests regardless of their affiliations with the majors.

Though the war years saw the minor leagues shrink in size by roughly 75 percent, the attendance figures show that at least for the largest leagues the financial impact of the war was not overwhelming. Those leagues continued to procure enough players to put a decent product on the field, and many of their cities were industrial centers that grew in population during the era. The season following the war's end saw the minors explode in size, actually surpassing pre-war levels by fielding 43 leagues in 1946. Returning veterans sought to resume their baseball careers, even if just for a short period of time, while youngsters were free from the specter of the draft, and quality players were readily available. The majors quickly re-established their wide-reaching farm systems and baseball was once again booming, with total minor league attendance reaching 32.7 million fans in 1946, completely destroying the old record of 18.6 million established in 1939.[87] Baseball was back and reaping the benefits of the post-war economic boom.

* * *

An examination of the business side of professional baseball shows that contrary to the public complaints by major league owners, baseball was in fact a profitable business during the war years as a whole. The 1942–1943 period was essentially a wash, with the combined net income of roughly $110,000 for the 16 teams still impressive given that these were the two years of largest war relief contributions. Profits in 1944 and 1945 jumped to levels not seen since 1930, yet the majors chose to curtail their contributions even though the war continued. Based on the financial data it certainly appears they had more to give had they chosen to do so, but instead the owners were more concerned with getting back to turning a profit on the national pastime. Baseball was big business, as the game's leaders acknowledged both in the *Steering Committee Report* and the *Hearings*, and they intended to make money at it, war or no war. The political infighting in the minors in 1943 and the attempt to replace Landis with a more controllable commissioner in 1944–1945 underscore the importance of the business side of the professional game — there was a tremendous amount of money at stake, and exploiting baseball's antitrust exemption along with the use of the reserve clause allowed the cabal of major league owners to exercise their monopoly powers to their fullest extent.

Though money remained the primary driver, major league owners were also very conservative and set in their ways, even at times to their own financial detriment. The failure to embrace night baseball with its higher attendance more fully is one such example, though it appears that the majority of the owners who opposed it truly believed that the financial gains would be short-lived once the perceived "novelty factor" wore off. The unwillingness to consider racial integration also had an economic component as Larry MacPhail pointed out in interviews and in the *Steering Committee Report*, but that was little more than window dressing to cover up the fact that the owners simply did not want black players in Organized Baseball nor large number of black fans in their ballparks attending major league games. The war offered the perfect opportunity for integration, with the nation taking steps to eliminate discrimination in war industries and the military (though with only limited success), and the draft siphoning off the best available talent. Signing black players would have improved the quality of play on the field, boosted attendance, and shown support for the social changes Roosevelt's administration tried to start in motion. Baseball's conservative nature caused it to miss this social and financial opportunity until after Landis' death and the end of the war.

Chandler perhaps put it most succinctly in 1962 after a decade to reflect on his stint as commissioner. "I thought baseball was a sport when I became commissioner," he said. "I was mistaken. The semibandits own it."[88]

CHAPTER 7

The Players Come
Marching Home

Tony Lupien was ready to get back onto the baseball diamond. Unlike many returning vets, Lupien actually spent most of the war years playing in the majors, so his skills had not grown stagnant. After graduating from Harvard in 1939, he spent most of the 1940 season in the minors before being called up to make his major league debut and play ten games with the Boston Red Sox, hitting an impressive .474. He spent the following season in the minors before making it back to the majors as the starting first baseman for Boston in 1942 and 1943, then moved to Philadelphia to fill the same role for the Phillies in 1944. He was 27 years old at the end of that season, and as the sole supporter of his wife and two children he had up to that time been exempt from the military draft. Lupien found himself draft-eligible in January 1945 when the draft parameters broadened, and became a member of the United States Navy. He was fortunate, however, in that the war was rapidly drawing to a close, and by September of that same year he was released from the service and returned to the Phillies in time to play 15 games and hit .315. He was ready to regain his starting spot at first base for the 1946 season, but the Phillies had other plans, and those plans did not include Tony Lupien.

Lupien was shocked when he received a call from Phillies general manager Herb Pennock informing him that he was being placed on waivers with the intent of selling his contract to the Hollywood Stars of the Pacific Coast League. Perhaps even more surprising was the player the Phillies picked up to replace him — 34-year-old Mike McCormick, the starting first baseman of the Cincinnati Reds for the past eight seasons. Not only was McCormick six years older than Lupien, but he was not even a returning military veteran and had in fact played full seasons throughout the war years. Lupien believed that as a returning veteran he was legally entitled to get his job back as outlined in the Selective Training and Service Act of 1940 (and the subsequent additions and alterations to this act during the course of the war). An appeal letter to Commissioner Happy Chandler was returned unopened, leaving Lupien with three choices: file suit against the Phillies and Major League Baseball for violating the Selective Training and Service Act, accept the transfer to the PCL and try to work his way back to the majors, or quit the game he loved. Faced with the prospect of lengthy and costly litigation, along with the very real fear of being blacklisted from baseball if he filed suit, Lupien packed his bags, loaded his family in the car, and headed to Southern California. The Stars agreed to pay him the same $8,000 he had earned in his last full season in the majors, though he suspected that the Phillies were secretly contributing to part of what was a high minor league salary in an effort to keep him quiet.[1]

Though the situation didn't sit well with Lupien, his plan of playing his

way back to the majors worked. He played two long PCL seasons with the Stars in 1946 and 1947, appearing in 356 games and hitting a solid .319. Perhaps just as importantly he showed he could hit with power, slamming 21 home runs in 1947 and putting to rest the knock against him as a "no power" hitter, something that surely contributed to his demotion to the minors in this era of power-hitting first basemen. His performance on the West Coast was good enough to earn him one more season in the majors as the starting first baseman for the Chicago White Sox in 1948.

The last thing the owners wanted with the war finally over was a negative publicity over how they were treating returning military veterans, which explains why the Phillies were willing to pay some money to make the Tony Lupien problem go away. Little did they know, however, that trouble was exactly what they would get. It was not Tony Lupien who eventually challenged them, though his

Tony Lupien was demoted to the Pacific Coast League upon his return from the military, and though he chose not to challenge the move legally, his chance meeting with fellow minor leaguer Al Niemiec in 1946 gave Niemiec the confidence to pursue his case through the courts (courtesy Dave Eskenazi collection).

assignment to the PCL played a small but important part in their most public battle over the issue of returning veterans.

The Rights of Returning Veterans

The primary purpose of the Selective Training and Service Act of 1940 (54 Stat. 885, 50 U.S.C. App. § 301) was to establish a military draft to build the strength of the American armed forces as the country faced the very real possibility of being dragged into World War II. One of the key provisions guaranteed returning servicemen the right to regain the jobs they left prior to entering the military. Section 8 of the Act read in part:

> (a) Any person inducted into the land or naval forces under this Act for training and service, who, in the judgment of those in authority over him, satisfactorily completes his period of training and service under section 3 (b) shall be entitled to a certificate to that effect upon the completion of such period of training and service, which shall include a record of any special proficiency or merit attained...
>
> (b) In the case of any such person who, in order to perform such training and service, has left or leaves a position, other than a temporary position, in the employ of any employer and who (1) receives such certificate, (2) is still qualified to perform the duties of such position, and (3) makes application for reemployment within forty days after he is relieved from such training and service —
>
> (A) if such position was in the employ of the United States Government, its Territories or possessions, or the District of Columbia, such person shall be restored to such position or to a position of like seniority, status, and pay;
>
> (B) if such position was in the employ of a private employer, such employer shall restore such person to such position or to a position of like seniority, status, and pay unless the employer's circumstances have so changed as to make it impossible or unreasonable to do so; ...
>
> (c) Any person who is restored to a position in accordance with the provisions of paragraph (A) or (B) of subsection (b) shall be considered as having been on furlough or leave of absence during his period of training and service in the land or naval forces, shall be so restored without loss of seniority, shall be entitled to participate in insurance or other benefits offered by the employer pursuant to established rules and practices relating to employees on furlough or leave of absence in effect with the employer at the time such person was inducted into such forces, and shall not be discharged from such position without cause within one year after such restoration.

In 1944 Section 8 (b) was amended, changing the third point to read "(3) makes application for reemployment within ninety days after he is relieved from such training and service or from hospitalization continuing after discharge for a period of not more than one year."[2] In essence a returning veteran had 90 days to ask to return to his old job, and unless the employer's situation had changed to the point that it was impossible to bring the veteran back into its employ, he was guaranteed his former position at his prior level of pay and seniority for a period of one year.

It didn't take long following the war's end for litigation to ensue as returning veterans attempted to secure their pre-enlistment positions. One early non-baseball case, *Fishgold v. Sullivan Drydock* (1946), made it all the way to the Supreme Court, and in their decision the justices weighed in on the purpose of the protections provided to returning veterans:

> The Act was designed to protect the veteran in several ways. He who was called to the colors was not to be penalized on his return by reason of his absence from his civilian job. He was, moreover, to gain by his service for his country an advantage which the law withheld from those who stayed behind.[3]

It is easy to see how the Act could create hardship on employers, especially those in the private sector. In many cases it forced businesses to release their war year employees and replace them with returning veterans. For some businesses, like Major League Baseball, the Act provided an additional challenge. The teams continuously cycled players through their rosters during the war years, and many of these players were drafted by the military, so there were hundreds of players returning from the service who potentially could demand their baseball jobs back for one year. Would baseball find itself in a position in which teams did not field the best and most talented teams possible in 1946, but simply teams of returning veterans, some of whom had been away from the game for up to five years? And if they did bring back all the returning veterans, would there be any room left on the rosters for any non-veterans at all?

The owners did not believe this presented a problem, because in their eyes the job guarantees of the Act did not apply to baseball. Chandler worked with Organized Baseball to establish a different set of rules to apply to professional ballplayers, eventually promising returning players thirty days of training time (spring training or at some other point in the season) and a minimum of two weeks' pay before the player could be sold, traded, farmed out, or released. The owners felt they were being quite magnanimous in even offering this much, according to Washington Senators owner Clark Griffith, who made the following statement in 1946 when the issue of Organized Baseball's treatment of returning veterans was in the courts:

> The intent of the law as I understand it, was to protect the returning veteran for a fair trial on his old job. The veteran, however, has to show that

he is qualified to hold down that position. [...] I don't think the law ever was intended to cover professional people who are highly paid in highly competitive fields like baseball.[4]

With the reserve clause still alive and well, players could not shop their skills to other teams or leagues as the owners retained complete control over where and even if a man could play. If the team opted to sell or transfer his contract to another team, he had to accept it or leave Organized Baseball, and if the move was to a lower classification he could usually expect an accompanying cut in pay. With the number of minor leagues exploding from only 12 active leagues in 1945 to 43 at the start of the 1946 season, there were plenty of places for owners to off-load surplus players who in their eyes could no longer cut it in the majors. Most eventually accepted their situations and moved on with their lives and careers, either taking what their teams offered or leaving the game behind, but a few stood up to the owners and fought against what they believed was a trampling of their rights as veterans.

The Vets Fight for Their Jobs

Arguably the most famous case of a returning baseball player challenging Organized Baseball did not happen at the major league level, but instead in the Pacific Coast League. Tony Lupien, still bitter over his treatment by the Phillies, came back to haunt the major league owners as a small but important part of a minor league lawsuit with major league implications.

Al Niemiec was born on May 19, 1911, in Meriden, Connecticut, and like Lupien he played college baseball in New England, starring at Holy Cross from 1931–1933 where he appeared alongside a number of other future major leaguers, including Bob Friedrichs, Hank Garrity, Ed Moriarty, and Joe Mulligan. Niemiec moved on to professional ball with the Class A Reading Red Sox in 1933, hitting .306 in 62 games, primarily as a third baseman. A promotion to the American Association Kansas City Blues followed in 1934, and his play was good enough to earn him a late-season call-up to the Boston Red Sox, where he made his major league debut on September 19, eventually appearing in nine games at second base that year and hitting .219. After that it was back to the American Association for a successful season with the Syracuse Chiefs, generating enough interest to be included in a trade that sent him and Hank Johnson to the Philadelphia Athletics for Doc Cramer and Eric McNair. Niemiec got his second and final shot at the majors with the A's in 1936, appearing in 69 games as a middle infielder and hitting a woeful .197. He was demoted to the Southern Association in 1937, and there got his hitting back up to a respectable .313.

The San Diego Padres of the PCL acquired Niemiec's rights for the 1938 season, which marked the start of a successful five-year stint on the west coast. Following two seasons with the Padres, he was shipped north to Seattle where he became the starting second baseman for the Rainiers on their three consecutive PCL championship clubs from 1940 through 1942. Niemiec was a fixture for the Rainiers, playing in 509 games and hitting .280 during that period, and earning honors as the league's top second baseman in 1941. He was a popular player in the city, and when he was called up to active duty with the Navy in October 1942, he fully expected to return to Seattle after the war to resume his baseball career.

Lieutenant Niemiec earned his release from the Navy on January 5, 1946, and contacted the Rainiers about his old job, signing a contract with the club on February 11 at the salary of $720 per month. He struggled to reacquire his old form and did not hit well at the start of the season, during which he was only used as a utility infielder, and he was worried about his job. On a train ride back north to Seattle for a home stand, Niemiec ran into Tony Lupien, who was heading north with the Hollywood Stars for a series in Portland. The players got

Al Niemiec sued the Seattle Rainiers in 1946 after the team cut the recently returned military veteran. Niemiec won his suit and established that baseball players were entitled to the same rights as other returning veterans, though not all courts followed the Niemiec ruling (courtesy Dave Eskenazi collection).

to talking and when Niemiec expressed his concerns, Lupien told him what he learned about veterans' rights while deciding what course of action to take during his dispute with the Phillies. It was a fortuitous meeting for Niemiec, who was released by the Rainiers shortly thereafter on April 21, having appeared in only 11 games with 18 at-bats.

The Rainiers believed they treated Niemiec fairly. They signed him to a contract, allowed him to attend spring training to get back into shape, and kept him on the active roster for the first few weeks of the season. Though the team chose to give him his outright release, manager Bill Skiff and team vice president Roscoe "Torchy" Torrance wrote a letter of introduction for their former second baseman that outlined his past achievements with the club and gave some insight as to why the Rainiers chose to release him:

> Al has just returned from more than three years in the United States Navy and returned to our roster this year. The surplus of talent and the fact that we have had to make room for some younger ball players has made it necessary for us to dispose of Mr. Niemiec's services. Al still has a lot of fine baseball left we are sure and is the type who would be a credit to the game in years to come as a manager of some club. The loyalty and integrity of this ball player has always been away above average and we would not hesitate a moment in recommending his services to anyone in the baseball business.[5]

These words would come back to haunt the Rainiers when in later court proceedings they tried to portray Niemiec as past his prime and unable to play effectively.

Niemiec approached the Selective Service Board, which wasted no time in arguing his case in a letter to club president Emil Sick on April 24. In the two-page letter, Lieutenant B. V. Vercuski outlined the facts, as well as the team's obligations under the Selective Training and Service Act of 1940. Vercuski wrote that Niemiec's dismissal was "without cause" and that he was still capable of playing baseball at an acceptable level. "There is nothing in the record to reflect that he does not have the ability or background to continue in his former position," wrote Vercuski. He took the argument even further and pointed out that the minor league player's contract the Rainiers tendered to Niemiec for the 1946 season, which he signed, explicitly stated "this contract is subject to Federal or State Legislative regulations, executive or other official orders," clearly making it subordinate to the Act.[6]

Representatives of the Rainiers met with the Selective Service Board and discussed the situation on May 2, but failed to reach a resolution as both sides stood firm. The Board forwarded the matter to the United States District Attorney's office, which sent a letter to the club dated May 6, reiterating the government's demand that Niemiec be rehired per the requirements of the Act. Once again the Rainiers refused to budge, as was explained in a letter written by the team's attorney.

> We replied by letter dated May 9, but delivered May 12, declined to reemploy upon the ground that we had reemployed, *he had been accorded the time prescribed as a reasonable minimum by National Association rules*, and had demonstrated his inability to comply with the accepted standards of work performance and professional skill and proficiency required of our players and by clubs with which we were in competition, and accordingly had been given his unconditional release and had accepted transportation to his home[7] [emphasis added].

The Rainiers recognized the seriousness of the situation. This was not the only such case involving the team, as Leonard Gabrielson, who played with the club in 1943, also sought to regain his old job. The Gabrielson situation was further complicated by the fact that he was a wartime replacement for another player, Earl Torgeson, who entered the service after playing 147 games with Seattle in 1942 and who had been reemployed by the team in 1946. Other cases were popping up throughout baseball, and the result of any judicial ruling could have a far-reaching impact at every level of the baseball world. As the Niemiec case appeared to be headed to court, the Rainiers prudently informed the baseball "powers" what they faced, sending letters to Pacific Coast League President Clarence Rowland, National Association President William G. Bramham, and Major League Baseball Commissioner Happy Chandler.

The group facing off against Niemiec consisted of four main adversaries: Emil Sick, Roscoe "Torchy" Torrance, Stephen Chadwick, and Happy Chandler. The first three were affiliated with the Rainiers, while Chandler represented the interests of Major League Baseball, and in many ways professional baseball as a whole. Surprisingly, all four had strong ties to the military, and in many ways they did not seem like men who would normally take sides against veterans' rights.

Emil Sick made his fortune in the beer brewing business, and it was through that industry that he became friends with fellow beer magnate Col. Jacob Ruppert, who just happened to own the New York Yankees. Ruppert encouraged Sick to get into baseball, and in 1937 he purchased the Pacific Coast League's struggling Seattle Indians. Sick's first order of business was to rename the franchise the Rainiers, the name of his signature beer brand, followed by building a brand new stadium. He hired talent on the field and, just as importantly, in the front office, and the formerly hapless Indians quickly became one of the most successful and profitable franchises in the league. Though the team struggled at the gate during much of the war, Sick had a soft spot in his heart for players who had been called up to serve, and continued to pay Rainiers players who joined the military a portion of their pre-service salaries.[8]

Roscoe "Torchy" Torrance was the vice president of the Rainiers, brought on board by Sick when he purchased the team in 1937. Torrance had a long history of military involvement, volunteering for the Student Army Training Corps while attending the University of Washington in 1918 and later serving as a member of the Marine Corps Reserve from 1926 to 1936. At the outbreak of World War II the 42-year-old father of three volunteered for active duty, serving in the Pacific Theater where he remained heavily involved in baseball, organizing leagues and building diamonds on various islands. He did not stop there, though, and even used his connections to scout talent while deployed, signing a number of players to contracts to play with the Rainiers after the war.[9] He returned home with the rank of major and wearing a bronze star.

Emil Sick retained the law firm Chadwick, Chadwick, and Mills to represent his brewery businesses, and the same firm also oversaw legal matters for the ballclub. Partner Stephen Chadwick took the lead on the Niemiec case. Chadwick too was a veteran, and served in the Russian Civil War, one of the little-known conflicts related to the First World War. While the Bolshevik rise to power in the 1917 Revolution is well documented, often neglected by popular history is the attempt by the anti–Bolshevik "White" forces to overthrow the new communist government. A number of foreign powers participated on both sides of this conflict, and Chadwick served with U.S. forces in support of the Whites from August 1918 to May 1919. Chadwick was also heavily involved in leadership roles in various veterans'-rights organizations, serving as the National Commander of the American Legion in 1938–1939 and in leadership roles with the United Service Organization and the Civilian Military Training Camps.

Chandler had a distinguished political career prior to becoming commissioner in 1945, including stints as the governor of Kentucky and as United States Senator, where he also served on the Committee for Military Affairs. As a Democrat he often had the support of organized labor, and he had taken a pro-baseball stance at various points during the war. However, as commissioner he served different masters, and he needed to look out for their best interests. Chandler pledged his support and that of Major League Baseball to the Rainiers, writing to Torrance that "every possible assistance will be rendered to you"[10] with respect to the Niemiec case.

On the surface all four men had backgrounds that should have led them to support the rights of returning veterans. They were also businessmen, however, and they could also see the potential financial ramifications of providing contracts to all the returning veterans who sought to resume their baseball careers. Though money was certainly a factor, there was also the practical issue of where all these men would actually play. Even with the massive expansion of the minor leagues in 1946, there were not enough roster spots for all the men talented enough to play professional baseball and all the returning veterans, many if not most of whom would only end up playing for the one year they were guaranteed under the Act. Torrance understood this situation, and even suggested in a letter to Chandler that it might make sense to option the unwanted returning players to the upstart Mexican League.

> Just as an after-thought, don't you think it would be a good idea to let the Mexican League have about 200 ball players so that they could set up a real baseball program and take care of some of our surplus talent? It might be better to have a good league down there and make more room for the extra ball players than to continue having trouble.[11]

The Mexican League was already attempting to persuade major league ballplayers to jump their contracts and head south to play in Mexico, and the situation was starting to put pressure on Organized Baseball. Torrance could see how providing the Mexican League with a pool of experienced players might put an end to the raiding from south of the border, while allowing the best talent to remain in the United States.

As the legal wrangling continued, Niemiec signed with Providence of the New England League on May 17 for $150 a month. Back in Seattle the two sides prepared to present their cases in front of federal judge Lloyd L. Black on June 15, and Niemiec returned from Providence to participate. Further complicating matters for the Rainiers was that the club fired manager Bill Skiff on June 11, though they still needed him to testify on their behalf at the hearing. In fact, the pending Niemiec litigation was one of the factors considered by the club in its discussions regarding Skiff's termination. When the Rainiers' board of directors met on June 10, Torrance "advised the Board of the case re Al Niemiec, who had applied for reinstatement in his position under the G. I. Bill of Rights, after having been released by Manager Skiff, and which case is scheduled for hearing on June 15, 1946, and that the Board should take this matter into consideration in determining when and if action should be taken in changing managers."[12] Despite his termination, Skiff toed the company line and testified that Niemiec was too old and slow to play in the Pacific Coast League. Niemiec's representatives pounced on the former manager, impeaching his judgment in baseball matters by discussing his recent termination and showing that Skiff himself had still been an active player when he was older than Niemiec.[13]

Judge Black announced his decision in favor of Niemiec on Friday, June 21, and brought the parties back to the courtroom on June 24 to elaborate on his ruling. Black specifically addressed three arguments made by the Rainiers — that baseball was "a quasi public institution not operated primarily for profit,"[14] that Niemiec's skills eroded and he was no longer capable of playing at an acceptable level, and that by signing a contract that gave the club the right to cut him, Niemiec waived his rights under the Selective Training and Service Act.

Regarding the first issue, Judge Black reviewed the articles of incorporation of the Pacific Coast League and stated that these clearly indicated the league was a for-profit enterprise. He added that the Selective Training and Service Act made no concessions for not-for-profit organizations or for any other type of employer, so really the issue was irrelevant. As for Niemiec's skill and ability to perform the job of baseball player:

> The law says [Niemiec] is entitled to his position for a year. The veteran
> must be qualified to perform the duties of his position. The evidence shows

he was. The employer may adopt fair and reasonable standards of qualification for work performance. Under the evidence there was no qualification or standard at all. In substance the most Mr. Skiff said was that he had the idea that Mr. Niemiec would not be able to complete the season. He had no right to anticipate Mr. Niemiec's inability until it occurred. The employer may discharge at any time for cause, but that cause must be something other than prediction or hunch of a manager.[15]

The contract issue was dealt with as a matter of contract law. The employer in this case wrote the contract, and the employee was not allowed any input or modification — he had to take it or leave it as written. In fact, the evidence showed that the management of the Rainiers, as officers of a member club of the National Association, could no more modify the standard contract than could Niemiec. As the employer had complete control over the wording of the contract, it had a duty to write the contract in clear and unambiguous language, which, according to Judge Black, it did not. "Any player reading this contract, I am satisfied, would believe his rights were protected. Personally, after I have read it, I think his rights are protected."[16]

Judge Black reserved more pointed criticism for the behavior of the game as a whole toward its returning veterans.

> Baseball is an American institution. Professional baseball is a great American institution. Compared with many professional sports and entertainments it holds a very high regard of the people of the nation. I cannot escape the view, however, that the argument of the respondent analyzed completely means just this, that if the baseball player be older when he comes back from service than when he entered it, his baseball club employer is given the right in its discretion to repeal the Act of Congress.[17]

Black then took the argument a step further, recognizing the contributions veterans made to protecting American society:

> I recognize the seriousness to baseball of having the judge dictate as to its players. But since it has been argued — and correctly — that baseball is the American game, certainly, then baseball ought to bear its share of any burden in being fair to service men. There are few institutions in American life which ought to feel a greater obligation. If Mr. Niemiec and all the others had failed in their job, there would be no American manager of any baseball if such should be played at the stadium this year. If the Nazis permitted baseball, it would not be an exhibition that any of us liked.[18]

Though Black ruled in Niemiec's favor, he was clear that his ruling did not require the Rainiers to actually play Niemiec and wrote "that as I see it the respondent need not play Mr. Niemiec but had to pay him,"[19] while later noting that "you cannot compel in a competitive sport the manager to play any player."[20] In fact, so long as the Rainiers paid him a full season's salary, minus any earnings he made in any other occupation (including non-baseball occupations), the club had no other responsibilities. The ruling satisfied Niemiec, who sent word to Providence that he was not returning, and on July 1 he began a new job as a beer salesman — working for a brewery owned by Emil Sick. Niemiec returned to baseball briefly as general manager for the Great Falls Electrics (a Rainiers farm team) of the Pioneer League in 1948 before leaving the game for good.

The ruling did not sit well with baseball's executives. Chandler sent a telegram to the club about appealing the decision. "The Niemiec case should be appealed through the higher courts. Organized baseball will help bear the expense of the appeal."[21] Chandler attended a special meeting of the Pacific Coast League board of directors on July 22–23, and the parties agreed to pursue an appeal with the expenses underwritten by the majors and the National Association, an agreement that applied not only to the Niemiec case but to any others that arose. Per the meeting minutes:

> Following discussion of the Al Niemiec case, Director Starr moved that the Pacific Coast League concur in the arrangement whereby the Major Leagues and the National Association will take care of half of the survey and further legal involvement in the Niemiec case as well as any other National Defense Player situation that may arise. Duly seconded, and carried unanimously.[22]

The potential ramifications were significant — *The Sporting News* estimated that the ruling might impact as many as 143 former major leaguers, another 900 players at the AAA level, and even more at the lower levels. However, players had to file a complaint in order to pursue their benefits, and many decided it was not worth the trouble. Others encountered roadblocks erected by the very people who were supposed to help them. Bob Harris, for example, was pressured by his local district attorney to settle amicably his case for back pay against the Philadelphia Athletics.[23]

Discussion regarding a possible appeal of Judge Black's ruling continued through the summer, but at the close of the PCL season the Rainiers were ready to step aside. A judgment in the amount of $2,884.50 (unpaid contract value of $3,552.00, minus $75.00 Niemiec earned playing for Providence, and minus $592.50 he earned as a salesman) was entered against the Rainiers on September 18, and they were prepared to pay. Ironically the judgment was reduced by the amount that Niemiec earned as a beer salesman working for Emil Sick. By October, correspondence between the Rainiers and baseball officials focused on determining the costs owed by each party, with no further talk of appeals. By that time the majors and National Association understood how profitable the 1946 season had been and were ready to put this issue behind them. The Rainiers finally satisfied the judgment on November 1 with a payment of $2,905.36 (including post-judgment interest), though the satisfaction of judgment was not filed with the court until December 21, a time specifically chosen to fall after the winter baseball meetings to reduce the likelihood of questions about it from the press.[24]

In the end, the immediate cost of the Niemiec case was $1,718.28 in legal expenses each to the majors and the National Association, while the Rainiers incurred the cost of the judgment. The costs to professional baseball as a whole are much more difficult to measure. At least two other Rainiers players received payments as a result of Judge Black's ruling — John Yelovic ($1,000.00) and Larry Guay ($1,100.00).[25] Another veteran, Bruce Campbell, who was released by the Washington Senators and then subsequently by the minor league Buffalo Bisons of the International League, reached an out of court settlement with Senators owner Clark Griffith in the wake of the Niemiec decision. Griffith attempted to spin the situation as an example of his own generosity in paying off the roughly $5,000 still owed to Campbell, who played 13 seasons in the majors prior to being called to the service and spending 38 months with the Army Air Corps. "The fact that I was willing to settle the Bruce Campbell case should not be looked upon as setting a precedent for future cases of this sort, for I was prompted in making this settlement by my friendship and good feeling toward Campbell for what he has meant to baseball in the past," said Griffith. The owner went on to discuss how the Senators had given Campbell the opportunity to get into shape, and that Griffith had personally made calls on Campbell's behalf in an effort to secure him a spot with a minor league club. Though Griffith believed that "had this case gone to trial, I feel sure that my equity in it would have been recognized," he still opted to cut a check to Campbell, a strong indication that he was influenced by the Niemiec ruling.[26]

Not all vets were as fortunate as Niemiec and Campbell. Steve Sundra was a pitcher beginning his eighth major league season when he was drafted on May 9, 1944. He was released from the service in February 1946, and re-signed with his former team, the St. Louis Browns, for the same $8,000 salary he contracted for in 1944. Despite starting the 1946 season with a 2–0 record and a 1.42 ERA, Sundra was released on May 29, with the Browns stating that he was no longer able to pitch effectively at the major league level. Like Niemiec, Sundra took his case to court, though it was not heard until mid–1949 by the United States District Court for the Eastern District of Missouri.

Major League Baseball engaged in some gamesmanship during the trial. One of the witnesses the plaintiffs wanted to call on the behalf of Sundra was his 1946 Browns teammate Al Holingsworth, who in 1949 was the manager of the Allentown Cardinals of the Class B Interstate League. The Cardinals organization, however, would not permit Holingsworth time off from his duties to attend the trial despite having been subpoenaed, and since the court did not have reach to the state where Holingsworth was located, he could not be compelled to attend. According to Allan Goodloe, the district attorney representing Sundra, "the Cardinals informed us that, since they are themselves involved in court proceedings with the Browns over the rental of Sportsman's Park, they didn't care to do anything detrimental or embarrassing to their neighbors, the Browns."[27] That didn't stop Goodloe from presenting subpoenas to three members of the Boston Red Sox who arrived in St. Louis for a series against the Browns, so Sundra received support from Jack Kramer, Vern Stephens, and Al Zarilla, all of whom agreed that the Browns did not give Sundra a fair chance to succeed. A number of other players, coaches, and managers were called to testify for the two sides. Perhaps the most surprising expert witness was J. G. Taylor Spink of *The Sporting News*, who told the court that any good pitcher could have found work in 1946, despite the fact that Spink's own publication reported that same year that over 1,000 professional players with Major League or AAA level experience were returning from the service. The same 16 teams made up the majors in 1946 that fielded teams in 1945, so there were not more major league pitching positions available in 1946, and given the influx of vets attempting to return to their playing careers it should have been obvious that Spink's testimony was patently false. In fact, at the start of the 1946 season *The Sporting News* indicated that the St. Louis Browns' pitching staff "continues as one of the team's strongest departments, with Galehouse and Sundra back from service."[28] However, just a week later the paper reported that Sundra was injured with "two maimed knees,"[29] though it is unclear if this was a baseball-related injury or the result of his military service. Were the Browns simply trying to get rid of an injured ballplayer? It is unclear if these issues were discussed during the proceedings. Given that *The Sporting News* was a publication entirely devoted to professional baseball, one can easily see Spink's motivation in supporting the game that provided his livelihood.

Unlike Judge Black in *Niemiec*, Judge Harper ruled in *Sundra* that professional baseball was not like other jobs.

> The status of a professional baseball player is unlike that of employees in virtually every other employment. Baseball is not only a business, but a sport and source of entertainment. The position of each player is constantly subject to personal competition. The public demands the highest in skill and ability, and the will of the public is supreme, for it is the result of their patronage that professional baseball is the popular American past time [*sic*]. This is probably why the players' contracts provide that they may be terminated or assigned at any time.[30]

Harper went on to discuss how various managers, coaches, and players testified that Sundra was not an effective pitcher in 1946 despite being given the opportunity by the Browns to get back into shape, conveniently ignoring his winning record and low ERA at the start of the 1946 season, and the testimony of Kramer, Stephens, and Zarilla. Harper took the opinions of Sundra's detractors a step further by including his own ideas about pitching when he noted, "Sundra was a fast ball pitcher, and while the records do not disclose, I think the court is fully justified in concluding that the pitching life of fast ball pitchers is less in most instances than that of other pitchers."[31]

In almost every way possible, the court's ruling in *Sundra* differs from Judge Black's stance in the *Niemiec* decision, even though *Niemiec* was cited in *Sundra*. Harper ultimately concluded:

> The basis of respondent's action was such as a fair-minded person might act upon and was not a mere excuse or an arbitrary action to avoid the provisions of the statute. Sundra lacked the skill and ability to pitch in the major leagues in 1946 and he was given his unconditional release for just cause within the meaning of the act.[32]

Harper's interpretation of the Act was that the alleged diminished skills on Sundra's part was sufficient "just cause" to allowing the Browns to release the pitcher. The district attorney disagreed, saying, "If he reported in physical shape, and that means that he was capable of throwing the ball from the mound to the catcher's box, Sundra was entitled to his job. Skill had nothing to do with it."[33]

It is interesting that following the *Niemiec* ruling, owners still took different approaches to handling returning veterans. In some circumstances, such as that of Bruce Campbell, the owner opted to buy out the contract of the player. In others, such as Sundra, they continued to hold firm, even as that case dragged on for three years. A variety of factors may have contributed to these divergent decisions, including the financial status of the club involved (the Browns were in chronically poor financial shape), the number of other players potentially impacted by the club's decision, or simply the team's belief in its ability to prevail in court. Regardless, the precedent that was seemingly set in *Niemiec* was not universally followed by other jurisdictions within the federal court system. Had *Sundra* been heard first, one could reasonably assume that players like Niemiec and Campbell would never have been paid the full value of their contracts by their teams. After all, even in the months immediately following *Niemiec*, the owners still thought that their handling of the returning veterans was both fair and reasonable. Chandler "pointed out that hundreds of ex–GIs whom he contacted among the players were well satisfied with conditions after returning from the war,"[34] and the owners reiterated the fairness of their system in the 1946 *Steering Committee Report*. Writing just two months after Judge Black's ruling, the committee noted that "During the past year baseball got a bad press on the returned G.I. problem in spite of the fact that no business has done a better job for its returning service men, or for the service people while they were in uniform."[35] This belief was completely unsupported and patently false, though the owners chose to believe it anyway.

To say that the owners had extremely high opinions about their handling of the returning players is an understatement. This despite the fact that they unilaterally decided that the federal laws enacted to guarantee veterans the right to return to their old jobs simply didn't apply to baseball, and instead came up with their own set of rules. Offering a player 30 days of training and 15 days of full pay is a far cry from guaranteeing him his job for one year, but the owners were used to calling their own shots. They had crushed unions, weathered the threats from rival leagues, gained a surprising antitrust exemption by the Supreme Court, and used the reserve clause to maintain their unilateral position of power over the players for decades. The owners were used to getting their way with almost no interference from forces outside their elite group, and the ways they ran their business reflected that attitude. Judge Black's ruling, though not affirmed in other jurisdictions, was the one of the first cracks in the façade of Major League Baseball. More cracks would soon follow.

Lost Years, Lost Careers

World War II baseball historian Gary Bedingfield estimates that over 4,000 minor leaguers and close to 500 major leaguers served in the military during the war.[36] Most served with the United States, though a few served with the Canadian forces. Of those men, 143 minor leaguers and two major leaguers lost their lives while in the military.[37] Regardless of whether they died in combat, accidents, or from illnesses, all made the ultimate sacrifice to help keep American and Canadian societies free.

The stories of the two major leaguers who died in the service during World War II, Elmer Gedeon and Harry O'Neill, are well known. Much less publicity surrounds the minor leaguers who died during the war, though Bedingfield has done a tremendous amount of work to honor them and bring their stories to light. Most of them, had they survived the war, probably would have had typical minor league careers, with perhaps a select few making it to the big leagues for a cup of coffee. Probably. But was there a future Stan Musial or Whitey Ford among their ranks? No one will ever know for sure.

When historians discuss the impact of World War II on the majors, one of the primary areas of focus is the "what ifs" associated with the years players lost to the war. A number of Hall of Famers served in the military, and as a result missed the opportunity to reach some major statistical milestones. The most notable was Ted Williams, who spent three full seasons (1943–1945) with the Marines (as well as parts of the 1952 and 1953 seasons when he was recalled to serve in the Korean War) as a pilot and instructor, and finished his baseball career with 521 home runs and 2,654 hits. Had Williams played during the 1943–1945 period, which was early in his career, he almost certainly would have reached the 600 home run plateau and joined the 3,000 hit club. Fellow slugger Hank Greenberg missed over four seasons' worth of games to military service (he appeared in nineteen games in 1941, and 78 games in 1945, missing all of 1942–1944), prior to which he averaged 43 home runs per season between 1937 and 1940. Given that Greenberg clouted 44 round-trippers in his first full season back in the majors in 1946, it's not unreasonable to think he would have maintained this average throughout the war years. Greenberg finished his career with 331 home runs, and he would have become a member of the 500 home run club had he averaged just over 42 homers per season during those years of service. Stan Musial also finished his career just shy of the magical 500 home run total, though given his power numbers immediately before and after his lost season of 1945 it is unlikely he would have hit the 25 homers needed to reach that milestone.

Pitchers too were affected by the war, and one would expect the impact to have been even greater on that position as hurlers not only lost the arm strength and conditioning, but also years of refining their craft and learning how to pitch, not just throw. Bob Feller joined the Navy on December 8, 1941, the day after Pearl Harbor, and insisted on combat duty. The Navy obliged, and Feller spent nearly four years as a gunner on the U.S.S. *Alabama*. He finished his major league career with 266 wins and 2,581 strikeouts, and certainly would have eclipsed both the 300 win and 3,000 strikeout marks had he even spent two of those four wartime seasons on the diamond instead of serving in the Pacific. Ted Lyons and Red Ruffing also missed out on chances to reach the 300-win mark. Warren Spahn, who saw combat in the Battle of the Bulge, could possibly have reached the 400 win plateau had he not lost three seasons at the very beginning of his career.[38]

Of course it wasn't just the superstars and future Hall of Famers who served, as major leaguers of every skill level gave up seasons in the sun for seasons in khaki. Some resumed their careers where they left off; others never got another shot at the big leagues and moved on with their lives. The same was true of minor leaguers, and more than a few promising baseball careers came to an end on the battlefields of Asia and Europe. Art Keller played a number of seasons in the minors, and in 1943 he was one of the last players sent down from the St. Louis Browns' spring training camp. He made it as far as the American Association before entering the Army in late 1943, and less than a year later he was killed in action in France. Hank Nowak was a promising pitcher in the St. Louis Cardinals organization and a six-year veteran of the minors before he joined the Army in early 1942, serving for almost three years before being killed during the Battle of the Bulge.[39]

Not all the stories had unhappy endings, as the war also provided examples of perseverance and courage. Perhaps the most famous story involving a minor leaguer is that of Bert Shepard, a ballplayer and fighter pilot who was shot down and captured by the Germans. Shepard lost part of right leg and his foot, but he still had dreams of one day pitching again and taught himself to pitch on a prosthetic leg while a prisoner of war. Upon his return to the states, his story caught the attention of Clark Griffith, who gave Shepard the chance to live his dream by coming out of the bullpen to pitch just over five innings with the Washington Senators during a game in 1945.

Shepard wasn't the only wounded minor leaguer to make it to the big leagues. Elmer "Red" Durrett played D league ball prior to joining the Marines, where the 21-year-old took part in the Guadalcanal campaign. The brutal jungle fighting left Durrett with a host of ailments, including an infected foot, dysentery, malaria, and "shell shock," that left him hospitalized for 18 months and eventually resulted in his discharge. The Brooklyn Dodgers took him to camp in 1944, and even though the sounds of the artillery pieces from West Point, located near the Dodgers' training base, caused him to dive for cover, he was able to get back into sufficient physical and mental condition to resume his career.[40] Solid seasons with Montreal in the International League earned him call-ups to the Dodgers in both 1944 and 1945, where he appeared in 19 games with the parent club, and his minor league career continued until 1950.

Less discussed, but also very significant, was the financial sacrifice made by ballplayers, especially major leaguers, who missed out on some lucrative years in what was a limited earnings window. Ted Williams received a $35,000 salary (equivalent to over half a million dollars in 2011) from the Boston Red Sox in 1942, his last season prior to entering the service, and likely lost out on a minimum of $105,000 in salary alone due to the war. Hank Greenberg gave up even more salary than Williams, leaving behind a $55,000 annual contract (nearly $850,000 in 2011 dollars) when he re-enlisted following Pearl Harbor. In many cases the impact was even greater, as successful players could expect their salaries to increase annually. In the cases of Hall of Famers like Williams and Greenberg, both would likely have received multiple pay raises during the years they lost to the service, though it is impossible to gauge the impact as we cannot know how any given player or team would have performed had the war not taken place. More difficult to estimate is the lost endorsement earnings, which for star players could exceed their actual baseball salaries. Even for players who gave up much lower salaries, the war still had a financial impact. While many major leaguers, particularly those making near the league minimum of $3,500, had to work in the off-season to make extra money to support their families, the loss of their baseball salaries for a number of years still hurt them financially, both in lost earnings and in future earning potential.

Professional baseball players were not unique, as workers in other professions who left their jobs to join the military also suffered financial hardships. Professional athletes were unusual, however, in that their peak earning years fell within what was generally a relatively short period. Even a long career by baseball standards might have lasted roughly 15 years, significantly shorter than that of the average person in the workforce. Players also had to face the prospect of looking for an entirely new career later in life when their playing days were over, one for which they had limited or no experience. Though many professional ballplayers held down non-baseball jobs in the off-season, it would have been difficult to improve their abilities in these professions when they only worked at them for three or four months each year during their baseball careers. They had to take advantage of their prime baseball earning years.

* * *

Despite the complaints from the owners about the impact of the war on their businesses, all 16 teams weathered the storm and survived to see unprecedented attendance and earnings increases in 1946. During the war years they consistently fielded teams, albeit of diminished quality, and the lower attendance during the war was offset by the reduced salary costs due to the highest priced stars serving in the military. Most of the players on major league rosters at the outset of the war, however, gained nothing. Certainly the war created opportunities for some to make it to the majors when they would not have been able to do so otherwise, and while this was a gain for those individuals, it was not a gain for the game as a whole. As for the players who were good enough to play professionally prior to the war, most lost years off their careers and some lost their careers entirely. Prime earning years disappeared, never to be regained. Skills eroded. Some men returned from the service no longer able to perform well enough to continue as professional baseball players. Some never returned at all, making the ultimate sacrifice for their country.

The business of baseball came through the war and emerged into its own golden age of stability and financial success. The owners touted the wartime contributions of the players when it suited their interests, but casually cast aside those men who went off to war and came home just a little bit older, a little bit slower, and with a little bit less on the ball. The players made the sacrifices, and the owners reaped the lion's share of the benefits.

CHAPTER 8

The Boom — Baseball
Following World War II

In the early hours of December 16, 1944, the Germans launched the Ardennes Offensive, a last-ditch offensive in Belgium and France that they hoped would put the Allies back on their heels on the Western Front. The attack caught the Allies off-guard with their men hunkered down in the dead of a frigid winter, and the Germans quickly sliced through the front to create the deep bulge in the Allied line that later gave this battle its more well-known name, the Battle of the Bulge. Over 20,000 Allied soldiers lost their lives in the battle that raged in the snow, including a number of former professional baseball players. Among the very first casualties resulting from the initial German artillery barrages that opened the offensive was a 32-year-old private named Ernie Holbrook, who had played in the minors between 1935 and 1937 in the Piedmont and Mid-Atlantic leagues.[1] At least a half-dozen other minor leaguers were killed over the course of the roughly six weeks it took to contain and repulse the German advance, including black professional player John Aubrey Stewart.[2] The Germans committed significant resources to this desperate attempt to turn the tide of the war in the West, and the staggering losses they suffered all but assured an eventual Allied victory in Europe in either 1945 or at the very latest 1946. The war also reached a tipping point in the Pacific as 1944 came to a close, with the Japanese navy depleted and the Allied island-hopping campaign securing strongholds in the Pacific that were used for both supply and air bases, allowing long-range American bombers to reach the Japanese home islands.

American casualties remained high on both fronts as Axis desperation forced the German and Japanese forces into riskier strategies and more rigid defenses now that their backs were at the borders of their own homelands. However, by the start of 1945 ultimate Allied victory appeared fairly certain given the ever-growing industrial output and massive mobilization efforts.

While the prospect for a successful end of the war was favorable, there was still considerable apprehension as no one expected the Germans and Japanese to capitulate without the total destruction of their respective armed forces, and that meant more American wives and parents receiving telegrams or visits to inform them of the loss of their husbands and sons in battles fought thousands of miles away.

Fortunately the Germans did not hold out long following the failure of the Ardennes Offensive, and less than four months later they formally signed surrender documents on May 7, 1945. Though the Germans were now out of the war, America still faced the daunting prospect of landing troops on the Japanese home islands, and restrictions on the home front remained in effect, one of the results of which was the cancellation of the 1945 All-Star Game as the nation geared up for its final military push in the Pacific. The bombing campaign against Japan intensified, culminating in the infamous atomic bombings of Hiroshima and Nagasaki in early August that contributed to the Japanese decision to surrender on August 15, saving their country from total destruction and saving countless lives on both sides.

Baseball's owners and political leaders had talked of canceling the World Series in the face of the likely invasion of Japan, but with the end of the war coming just as playoff races heated up, Americans could now look forward to enjoying the World Series without being under the specter of war for the first time in four years. It was the start of a popularity boom the likes of which the game had never before experienced.

The Business of Professional Baseball Following World War II

Major League Baseball made it through World War II completely intact, both financially and ideologically. The owners survived the lean years of 1942 and 1943, and only four of the 16 teams registered financial losses over the course of the four-year war era. By way of comparison, six teams failed to be profitable over the four-year period that immediately preceded the war (1938–1941), and one has to go back to the 1920s to find a period of four consecutive years in which fewer than four teams lost money (1925–1928).[3] In 1945 attendance not only surpassed that of 1941 by over a million fans, it also set a new all-time high at 10.8 million.[4] No teams folded or relocated, though there were some ownership changes and the league was forced to prop up the Phillies for a period of time. Ideologically the game did not compromise on its stance regarding integration, and it successfully maintained the sanctity of its contracts and the reserve clause in the face of potential governmental meddling.

There was also a new commissioner whom the owners anticipated they could control and direct more successfully than they had the very independent Landis. In all, the owners came out of the war years not only unscathed, but also facing a very promising economic future.

The Steering Committee Report

The mood was not entirely optimistic, however, and the owners recognized that they faced a number of challenges in the immediate post-war years. Their thoughts were outlined in the 1946 *Steering Committee Report*, particularly in the much longer first draft that addressed issues ultimately excluded from the final version. The draft outlined six main areas that the committee believed warranted consideration:

1. The relationship with the minor leagues
2. Challenges to the game's monopoly status
3. Relationships with the players including contract revisions, representation, and the pension fund
4. Public relations
5. Race and integration
6. Operational problems around bonuses, schedules, and ticket pricing[5]

The final approved version of the *Steering Committee Report* completely omitted the sections on monopoly status, public relations, and race.[6] These omissions are telling not because they indicate the owners did not believe these issues were legitimate areas for concern, but that they were wary of having any discussion of them appear in print where they could be discoverable later, which is exactly what happened when two different versions of the *Steering Committee Report* surfaced during the House Hearings in 1951.

The attempt to oust William Bramham as president of the National Association in 1943 served notice to the owners that there was a growing tide of dissatisfaction in the minors, specifically with regards to their relationship with the majors. The rapid expansion of the minors following the war further burdened the system, with the number of leagues opening the 1946 season more than triple that of 1945,[7] which created organization problems and inconsistency as the newly formed and re-established leagues attempted to stock their rosters and catch up on how the game had changed during the war. The owners sought a firmer grip on the relationship between the majors and minors, though they recognized that they could not do so without the participation and ultimately approval of the minors. The *Steering Committee Report* noted, "In considering any revision of the over-all [*sic*] administrative set-up for Baseball, your Committee recognizes that changes in Major-Minor relations can not be effected without the concurrence of the Minor Leagues,"[8] though it also indicated that such changes were necessary. "Your Committee is, however, of the opinion that this matter should be discussed with authorized representatives of the Minor Leagues."[9]

The committee proposed the creation of an Executive Council comprised of the commissioner, the presidents of the two major leagues, and two representatives from the minor leagues (with a note that for issues specifically related to player relations, two player representatives would also participate). This structure would give the minors some input into the global operation of baseball as a business, while still retaining the majority of the power in the hands of major league representatives. Even with council approval, however, changes that impacted the majors would still need to be put before a vote of the major league owners — they were not prepared to relinquish the final say over any issues that could affect their businesses, even if approved by their own representatives.

As early as 1946 the owners were able to anticipate the coming challenges to baseball's monopoly status that later came to a head during the 1951 House Hearings, even titling the section of the *Steering Committee Report* that dealt with this topic "Legality of Structure." The real concern was not about the role monopoly status played in preventing competition from outside leagues, but instead focused on the need to ensure the continuation of the reserve clause, which the committee recognized was open to legal challenge because it gave all the power in negotiations to the owners. Arbitration of salary disputes was considered "impractical," and the focus was not on leveling the negotiating field between owner and player but instead limiting the amount an owner could cut a player's salary without his agreement. The committee believed this would sufficiently resolve the appearance of unilateral determination of salaries by the owners, even though this was still the reality, with the only caveat that the new salary could not result in a reduction of more than 25 percent of the previous salary nor fall below the major league minimum.[10] These were not significant concessions, and once again show the importance the owners placed on holding as much of the power over the game as possible.

The committee actually met with player representatives during the summer of 1946 as they worked on the *Steering Committee Report*, particularly on the areas covered in the "Player Relationships" section that dealt with recommendations for an increase in the minimum salary, contract improvements, spring training money, and a player pension fund. On the surface this appeared to be a tremendous effort of good will in improving player involvement in the business from which both the owners and players earned their living. However, in reality it was in direct response to two situations that arose in

1946 — the attempt to unionize the Pittsburgh Pirates and the player raids conducted by the Mexican League.

Robert Murphy had an extensive background in labor relations work, and in 1946 he set his sights on baseball. Murphy recognized that the business structure of the game put all the power in the hands of the owners, and that the reserve clause made it impossible for players to effectively negotiate their pay. He established the American Baseball Guild and focused his energy on Pittsburgh, a traditionally strong union city that would likely support his efforts to unionize baseball players. Murphy found considerable support on the Pirates roster, and the unwillingness of the Pirates owners to recognize the union forced a strike vote on June 7. After initially ignoring the threat Murphy posed, Chandler and Pirates owner William Benswanger appealed to the loyalty of the players to thwart the strike.[11] As Chandler later recounted at the House Hearings in 1951,

> You remember we ran into trouble, shortly after I came in, in Pittsburgh over a union. The owners didn't know what happened to the union. I know what happened to it. We used one man from my office, who was a former pitcher for the American Association, and Rip Sewell and Jimmie Brown, and they beat the union. Every boy has got a right to join in this country, Mr. Congressman, anything he wants to and stay in as long as he wants to, except something that is against this country, trying to destroy it. In anything else, American institutions, he has got a right to join, pay dues, and quit when he gets ready.
>
> But they had a union virtually organized there. A man named Murphy came around to organize the players into a union.
>
> We questioned the wisdom of it and the owners were disturbed, and at their request I wired the managers, and they had a meeting and elected a player representative for the first time on each of the clubs, and then those player representatives in turn elected league representatives, and they are now Mr. Hutchinson, pitcher for Detroit, who represents the American League players, and Ralph Kiner of Pittsburgh, who represents the National League players.[12]

By promising to address many of the issues Murphy raised when trying to convince players of the need to unionize, the owners dodged a bullet and put the union issue onto the back burner, where it remained for years. They gave the players a voice, but no real say, in the business of the game. The *Steering Committee Report* was clear in how seriously the owners took this threat, describing it as "our most pressing problem" and warning how close the union had come to being a reality. "Mr. Murphy would have been successful, in our opinion, if he had started with Minor League players. In that event we would probably have awakened to what is known as a 'fait accompli.'"[13]

The Mexican League presented a different type of challenge to baseball's hegemony. In 1946 the league's primary financial backer, Jorge Pasquel, sought to improve the caliber of play in Mexico by convincing established professional ball players to jump their contracts to play for more money in Mexico. While the *Steering Committee Report* only mentioned the Mexican League raids in passing, they were an important topic at the time, as 18 major leaguers jumped to Mexico. In response Chandler placed them all on baseball's ineligible list for a period of five years.[14] Though those players who sought to return to Organized Baseball were allowed to come back in less than five years, in part due to lawsuits filed by some of the banned players, the swift action on the part of Chandler ensured that players thought long and hard about the consequences of contract jumping.

On the public relations front, the committee recognized that baseball suffered some adverse press tied to the "returned G.I. problem," Murphy's attempt to unionize players, and the players who jumped to the Mexican League. The lack of an official spokesperson with a public relations background left the game at the mercy of the press and "statements of individual Club owners whose individual opinions do not represent the views of the majority." As such the committee recommended that the proposed executive committee should take steps to ensure that baseball developed an effective and consistent public relations mechanism.[15]

The *Steering Committee Report* devoted 2.5 pages to race, but did so without providing any recommendations other than noting that the topic required further review. "Your Committee believes that the relationship of the Negro player and/or the existing Negro Leagues to professional Baseball is a real problem — one that affects all Baseball — and one that should have serious consideration by an Executive Council,"[16] it concluded. The views it expressed on race, which were discussed in detail in a previous chapter, clearly indicated the importance of the topic, and its exclusion from the final draft speaks volumes as to the owners' recognition that it was a significant danger to both the status quo and to baseball's public image. Jackie Robinson's appearance in the majors in 1947 effectively made all the concerns outlined moot, but it is very telling that even with Robinson in the high minors in 1946 and poised to break into the majors in 1947, the owners were still not prepared simply to accept racial integration as inevitable or even desirable.

The so-called "Operational Problems" were really a catch-all for miscellaneous issues. The section provided recommendations about player relationships that included limiting bonuses, establishing a new major league minimum salary of $5,000, and calling for teams to select player representatives. It also included some business recommendations such as the increase of the schedule from 154 to 168 games and the establishment of new, higher minimum ticket prices to help offset the increased expenses teams faced.

The draft version of the *Steering Committee Report* is a significant document that clearly outlines the main issues facing the game as perceived by the owners at that time. The end of the war eliminated a host of distractions and obstacles, and the owners were prepared re-consolidate their hold over the game as they moved forward into what was expected to be a new period of prosperity.

Attendance

The post-war increases in baseball attendance were nothing short of staggering, though not unprecedented. Active American involvement in World War I was much shorter than its involvement in World War II, with the nation declaring war on April 6, 1917, and participating as a belligerent until the cessation of hostilities on November 11, 1918 (though some American soldiers also served in ongoing conflicts in Russia immediately following World War I). Major league attendance dropped significantly during this period, from a pre-war level of 6.5 million in 1916, to 5.2 million in 1917, and all the way down to just under 3.1 million in 1918, which was the lowest attendance recorded since 1900. Immediately following the war the majors drew 6.5 million fans in 1919, more than doubling the 1918 level, and recorded a further 40 percent jump to 9.1 million in 1920, shattering the previous record by almost two million fans. While impressive at first glance, the increase from 1918 to 1919 was driven in part by an increase in the number of games. The 1918 season was shortened due to wartime travel restrictions, resulting in only 1,006 major league games played, while in 1919 the league returned to the standard 154-game schedule (though some teams played fewer games due to rainouts that were not made up), playing 1,113 games. If we consider the average number of fans per game, in 1918 the majors drew 3,062 fans per contest; in 1919 this increased to 5,869 fans, good for a 91 percent increase in attendance per game. This record-setting turnout established a new baseline for the majors, and attendance steadily increased throughout the 1920s.

A very similar trend occurred during and after World War II. The majors suffered through decreases during the first two years of the war just like they had in World War I. World War II was, of course, considerably longer (for the United States) than the earlier war, and attendance rebounded in the third and fourth years of the conflict. In the first post-war season attendance nearly doubled from 10.8 million in 1945 to 18.5 million in 1946, similar to the result following World War I. Once again baseball's post-war attendance established a new baseline that became the norm and lasted until America's next war in

Korea. The Korean War brought with it another decrease in attendance that, while not as dramatic as those experienced in the two previous wars, was longer in duration, as the majors saw fan support drop every year from 1950 to 1953. Another post-war increase followed, but this only served to get the majors to back where they had been during the seasons between World War II and Korea.

Table 10—Major League Attendance, Comparing Last Year of War to First Year of Peace[17]

		Total Attendance	Total Games	Avg Attendance
World War I	1918	3,080,126	1,006	3,062
	1919	6,532,439	1,113	5,869
	Increase	112.08%	10.64%	91.69%
World War II	1945	10,841,123	1,212	8,945
	1946	18,523,288	1,233	15,023
	Increase	70.86%	1.73%	67.95%
Korean War	1953	14,383,797	1,229	11,704
	1954	15,935,883	1,232	12,935
	Increase	10.79%	0.24%	10.52%

The majors were very stable during this period from 1917 to 1954, and during all three wars the same 16 major league clubs operated in the same cities, making comparisons more meaningful. There were some stadium changes between the two world wars, plus the previously mentioned shortened schedule in 1918, though these do not account for the significant increases that occurred immediately following each conflict. War has many impacts on societies, whether it occurs within their territory or outside of it. It generates a level of social tension that can make recreational activities feel unimportant and unproductive, and in the case of sports war also removes a significant number of people from the population who fall within the target fan (and participant) demographic. Those called to serve are not at home living their normal lives and attending events, while those who remain feel less comfortable in enjoying leisure activities during a time of war, and all three wars saw decreased fan turnout during their first two years. The post-war increases can be partly attributed to the return from the service of significant numbers of potential fans, along with society's attempt to return to normalcy by embracing recreational activities, especially those such as sports that also have the effect of tying the individual to the community.

To some extent the pattern can be thought to have held true during the much longer Vietnam War. American involvement in this war was more gradual than in the three previous conflicts, and this may account for the lack of a noticeable period of decline. In fact major league attendance increased fairly steadily during Vietnam. We do again see evidence of a post-war spike in fan turnout, though in this case it occurred in 1977, two years after the troops came home. That was also an expansion year when the majors added franchises in Toronto and Seattle, but even when backing out the figures for those two clubs the overall attendance increased from 31.3 million in 1976 to 35.7 million the following year.[18]

Baseball attendance following World War II had other drivers that boosted it as well. There were changes in demographics during the war years, with many people moving from rural to urban areas to work in war industries, and this benefited the major league cities, which were generally industrial and transportation hubs. The industrial work also paid good wages, giving workers more disposable income that could be spent on recreation. The G.I. Bill provided both money and opportunities for millions of returning veterans, putting many of them on stable financial footing. All in all, people sought to return to a level of normalcy in the post-war years, and more people had the economic means and proximity necessary to enjoy major league baseball.

Radio and Television

Baseball owners tended to be very conservative, and they were pessimistic when considering the potential impact of new ideas or technologies on their business. Just as they believed night baseball would be bad for attendance, many if not most of the owners felt the same way about radio and later television. The reason for their resistance was a simple one. They believed (wrongly, it turned out) that if fans could hear the games for free on the radio, they would stop coming to the ballpark, and attendance was the primary revenue generator for professional clubs at every level of the game.[19] Putting road games on radio made sense, since the local fans could not attend those games anyway, though early on teams and radio stations did not send announcers to the away games but instead had them recreate the contests in a studio using a telegraph tickertape to provide the basic facts. Radio in those situations was not only theater of the mind for the fans, but for the announcers, too, as they were forced to make up all the details and occasionally figure out how to react to huge gaps in the information. Announcer Red Barber described an incident that occurred during the 1939 preseason when he was recreating a game being sent to him via telegraph from South Carolina during which the person operating the telegraph on the other side did not know how much detail to provide Barber, leaving out even the most essential information. In the top of the first inning Barber had the bases loaded and nobody out. "Then, stunningly, came the startling announcement that the other team's first batter was up," recounted Barber. "I had the bases loaded and nobody out and wondering whether the man on third had scored or not, and now, suddenly, I've got a different team at bat."[20] Once the owners saw that radio actually benefited attendance by keeping more people connected and emotionally invested in the drama of the game and players, more than newspapers ever could, they quickly embraced it. By 1939 every major league team had a radio contract, the smallest of which was $27,500 for the Cincinnati Reds and the largest the $110,000 deals that both the Giants and Yankees had in New York.[21] The commissioner's office held radio contracts for the World Series and All-Star Game.

The lessons learned from radio had to be re-learned again when television began to move to the forefront. To be fair, early television suffered from serious limitations that made broadcasting sporting events difficult and expensive, and the cost of television sets was considerably more than that of radios, limiting the audience. The first televised major league game took place on August 26, 1939, and while the war certainly limited the availability of television sets, games continued to be televised periodically, often for the benefit of soldiers convalescing in stateside hospitals. Interest exploded immediately following the war, and by 1949 every major league team except the Pirates had at least some games on television, and most games were shot with multiple cameras as producers learned the best angles for capturing the action. The owners recognized that television rights generated revenues, but the medium still appeared to be an even greater threat to the gate than radio had in its infancy, since it allowed the viewer to experience the game visually.[22] As the broadcast rights fees continued to rise alongside attendance, these concerns quickly faded, and broadcast rights began to make up larger portions of baseball's revenues.

Broadcast rights became an important part of each team's economic model in the years following the war. While broadcast revenues remained fairly stable between 1939 and 1946, they increased sharply over the next four years.

Table 11— Major League Radio and Television Revenue as Percentage of Overall Revenues[23]

Major League Teams (Excluding World Series and All-Star Game)				
1933	*1939*	*1943*	*1946*	*1950*
Radio/Television $18,000	$884,500	$725,200	$838,212	$3,365,468
Pct — Radio/Television 0.30%	7.30%	6.70%	3.00%	10.50%

On the surface, the decrease in the percentage contribution of broadcast rights to overall revenues in 1946 seems surprising given that the actual gross dollars increased by more than 10 percent. However, this was the result if the enormous spike in attendance revenues experienced by the majors in 1946, and it took time for the value of broadcasting contracts to catch up. In fact the increase in the percentage of overall revenues generated by radio and television between 1946 and 1950 accounts for most of the 8.4 percent decrease in the percentage of revenues accounted for by attendance (an increase in 0.5 percent of overall revenues by concessions sales was another contributor).[24] Baseball was learning to reach its fans even when they were not at the stadium, and doing so in ways that still generated income while also making them want to come out to the ballpark even more to share in the experience and excitement. The post-war boom in television ownership and growing number of television stations were strong contributors to baseball's post-war leap in popularity, extending the game's reach well beyond the home city for each team.

Profits

With attendance up dramatically and broadcast revenues quadrupling from 1946 to 1950, the profitability of Major League Baseball reached new levels, at least in terms of dollars. Baseball, however, faced rising expenses due to player salary increases, ballpark renovation, the addition of lighting systems, new stadium construction, and a host of other costs. Historically attendance accounted for 85 percent or more of team revenues, but by 1950 that figure had decreased to 74.1 percent as broadcast rights and concessions took on growing importance.

In the first two years following the war the majors generated double-digit profit margins for the first time since 1930. In 1946 the profit margin was a staggering 17.7 percent, with an overall net income of just under $4.9 million. While the margin was far from record-setting, the net income more than doubled the previous high set in 1926. The following year was just as good, with 1947 recording a 16.2 percent profit margin on $4.9 million in net income. *Each* of those first two post-war seasons were more than double the entire combined net income of the league during the four war years ($2.3 million combined from 1942 to 1945). The 1940s closed out with two more excellent years, both of which resulted in profit margins just under 10 percent (9.6 percent in 1948 and 9.8 percent in 1949) and net incomes in excess of $3.2 million.[25]

At the team level the results were equally impressive. During the four years of the war 12 of 16 major league teams were profitable; over the four-year period immediately following the war (1946–1949), *every* team in the majors was profitable. The last time that had happened was in the early 1920s, as generally at any given period at least a few teams struggled financially. Perhaps even more impressive is that when one considers each of the 64 possible team/season combinations during that period (16 teams, four seasons each), only seven times did a team fail to turn a profit, with the Boston Red Sox (two seasons) and New York Giants (three seasons) accounting for the majority of the seasons in the red. The St. Louis Cardinals posted the best results in the immediate post-war era, generating $2,796,287 in profits, followed closely by the $2,518,885 posted by the New York Yankees. At the other end of the spectrum, the consistently woeful Philadelphia Phillies just scraped by with a small $37,597 surplus, making them the only club that failed to generate at least $100,000 in profits in the immediate post-war era.[26]

The attendance drop experienced by the majors in 1950 with the start of the Korean War took a deep bite out of the bottom line. The overall profit margin dropped to World War II era levels, falling to 2.2 percent on a net income of $689,000, and seven clubs registered financial losses, though the Indians and Yankees were highly successful and posted profits of over $450,000 each.[27] The period of immediate post-war prosperity had been extremely profitable, albeit short-lived. It did, however, get many teams back on solid financial footing, and proved that baseball could indeed be a very profitable business once again.

The Minor Leagues

The post-war surge in popularity and profitability extended down to the minors as well. A total of 43 minor leagues opened the 1946 baseball season, almost four times the number that operated during the last year of the war, and two more than played in 1941. The number of leagues increased each year for the remainder of the decade, reaching a peak of 59 in 1949. Of the 446 minor league teams that season, over half (235) were considered major league farm clubs, and the parent clubs made their affiliations known more overtly than in previous years. For example, ten of the 25 teams affiliated with Brooklyn were named the Dodgers, a naming trend exhibited by other major league clubs as well. This was especially true in the low minors, which included many new leagues that were created by the majors to operate exclusively as farm leagues. In 1949 there were 11 minor leagues comprised exclusively of clubs tied to a major league franchise, while only nine leagues did not include a single major league farm club. By the end of the Korean War in 1953, however, the total number of minor leagues dwindled to 38 as baseball's post-war popularity waned.[28]

Overall attendance at minor league ballparks skyrocketed after the war, though this would be expected given the rapid expansion of the minors from 1946 through 1949. However, the figures were impressive even when compared to those from before the war. In 1939, at the peak of their popularity, the 41 minor leagues set a record by drawing approximately 18.6 million fans; in

1946 the 43 minor leagues brought 32.7 million fans through the turn stiles. By 1949 total minor league attendance peaked at almost 41.9 million, before dropping sharply at the start of the 1950s, falling to 27.5 million by 1951.[29] Trends in the highest classification of the minors mirrored those of the majors. There were three AAA leagues in operation from 1946 to 1949, the American Association, the International League, and the Pacific Coast League. All three experienced huge increases in attendance in 1946 and maintained those levels through 1948. The American Association and International League dropped off in 1949, just like the majors, though the Pacific Coast League held on for one more year and did not to start to see its attendance decrease until 1950. The drop in the Pacific Coast League was even more telling as its schedule was lengthened from 188 to 200 games for 1950, and even with the extra games league attendance still dropped by over 15 percent.[30]

The House Committee examined minor league financial data as part of its investigation of Organized Baseball, and while results are not provided for specific teams and the House Committee did not have data for every league, the analysis is telling. The teams comprising the AA and AAA level minor leagues, all of which were included in the *Hearings*, were as a whole profitable from 1946 through 1949, with the 39 teams in the five leagues at these classifications topping out at a combined net profit of $1,665,459 in 1948. While a far cry from the dollars the majors generated with fewer than half the number of teams, this was an impressive result given the level of baseball and the size of the cities involved. By 1950, just two years later, the AAA leagues fell on hard times, registering a combined loss of more than $1.4 million for the season (19 of 24 teams in these leagues were farm clubs with some level of major league affiliation), while the two AA leagues hung on and turned a modest profit of $120,410. At the lower classifications the picture was even grimmer. Drawing from an admittedly small sample, the *Hearings* indicate that all classifications between A and D were profitable in 1946, but after that things fell apart. The teams surveyed in two of the four classifications remained profitable in 1947, but from 1948 through 1950 all the classifications operated at a loss, with the exception of A level, which still turned a profit in 1949. These lower classification leagues were often comprised heavily of farm teams, and major league teams were willing to operate them at a loss in order to have a place to train and store talent. These losses most certainly contributed in part to the diminished profits seen by the major league clubs starting in 1948. The first major dip in post-war major league profits was in 1950, and that year the 185 minor league teams surveyed in the *Hearings* combined to lose almost $3.3 million, a huge reversal from the nearly $1.65 million in profit turned in 1947 by the 124 teams that provided financial data.[31]

Overall the experience of the high minors (AA and AAA) was similar to that of the majors in the immediate post-war era. Spikes in attendance and overall profitability lasted for roughly four years before experiencing a fairly sharp downturn, and the impact was greater on the minors, which always suffered from a higher level of volatility than their major league counterparts. The surge aided the low minors as well (A through D), though the realities of the farm system meant that the primary purposes of many teams was not to turn a profit, but instead develop talent and minimize the expenses or losses required to run them. One thing is for certain — the rapid expansion of the minors spread professional baseball throughout the country, reaching beyond cities and into more rural locations. Even if many teams and leagues that operated in these smaller towns eventually folded, they contributed to the growth in popularity of the game at just the right time as far as the majors were concerned, with the increased quality and availability of radio and television broadcasts ensuring that major league games would be there to fill the void left by the minors.

Legal Challenges

The *Steering Committee Report* clearly recognized that baseball faced increased legal challenges to its business model. The game's status as a protected monopoly was derived from the questionable Supreme Court decision in 1922 that determined that baseball was not interstate commerce, a tenuous conclusion. At least some of the owners also recognized that the reserve clause they believed to be so essential to the professional game was on shaky ground. Baseball had already suffered a loss in the courts in the 1946 *Niemiec* case, and there was legitimate reason for concern.

Organized Baseball faced another significant legal challenge before the close of the decade, one related to the raids by the outlaw Mexican League and the subsequent five-year suspensions of 18 players who allegedly jumped their contracts to play in Mexico. While some players did in fact disregard their signed contracts to head south, others had not yet come to terms with their clubs, and were instead violating the reserve clause that bound them to their teams even in the absence of their acceptance of a new one-year contract. Regardless, Chandler still deemed them as contract jumpers and placed them on baseball's ineligible list for five years, not distinguishing between those who had signed their contracts and those who had not. The Mexican League experience quickly fell apart as the league struggled financially, and many of the players found it difficult to get used to the foreign living and playing conditions, leaving most wanting to return to Organized Baseball. Some appealed directly to the commissioner, while others took legal action.[32] The first of these legal challenges to make it to trial was the suit by New York Giants outfielder Danny Gardella in 1949.

Gardella's legal team based their suit in large part on the blacklisting of their client, which they argued was purely monopolistic because it effectively prevented him from playing professional baseball anywhere in the United States. The initial hearing in federal court was dismissed based on the reasoning that the Supreme Court *Federal Baseball* decision gave the federal courts no jurisdiction, since baseball was not interstate commerce. Gardella appealed the jurisdictional issue, and the United States Court of Appeals for the Second Circuit heard the case. The three-judge panel rendered a split decision, with two judges in favor of remanding back to the lower court for trial. Even in so doing, however, the judges could not agree on specifically which issues were and were not valid for consideration.

All three judges wrote opinions in the *Gardella* ruling. Judge Chase believed that even with the changes that had taken place in the business model of baseball, most notably radio and television broadcasts, it remained in essence the same business that the Supreme Court evaluated previously, and therefore *Federal Baseball* remained controlling. According to Chase, "Congress did not intend the antitrust acts to cover restraints upon employment," and as such Gardella's assertion that the reserve clause operated in restraint of trade was unfounded. Chase did not believe the federal courts had jurisdiction to hear the case.

The other two judges disagreed, but for differing reasons. Judge Hand took the middle ground, pointing to the rise of radio and television as factors that were not considered in *Federal Baseball* because they were not part of the business of baseball at the time of that ruling, but which now warranted a reconsideration to determine whether or not those mediums constituted interstate commerce. Hand also disagreed with Chase regarding Gardella's right to work. "Be that as it may, whatever other conduct the [antitrust] Acts may forbid, they certainly forbid all restraints of trade which were unlawful at common-law, and one of the oldest and best established of these is a contract which unreasonably forbids any one to practice his calling," he wrote. This was a direct challenge to the reserve clause.

Judge Frank offered the longest and most strongly worded opinion, opening by referring to the *Federal Baseball* ruling as an "impotent zombi [*sic*]." Frank believed that radio and television both differed from the telegraph technology previously used to transmit game accounts across state lines. "In that earlier case, persons in other states received, via the telegraph, mere accounts of the games as told by others, while here we have the very substantially different fact of instant and direct interstate transmission, via television, of the games as they are being played, so that audiences in other states have the experience of being virtually present at these games," he wrote. In Frank's opinion this constituted interstate commerce in a way that one team traveling across state lines to play another did not. This alone was reason enough to remand to the lower court for a trial, but Frank was not finished. He saved his most harsh criticisms of baseball for his discussion of the reserve clause. In differentiating *Gardella* from other non-baseball cases he wrote:

> I think it should be so distinguished, if possible, because (assuming, as we must, at this stage of the litigation, the truth of statements in the complaint) we have here a monopoly which, in its effect on ball-players like the plaintiff, possesses characteristics shockingly repugnant to moral principles that, at least since the War Between the States, have been basic in America, as shown by the *Thirteenth Amendment to the Constitution*, condemning "involuntary servitude," and by subsequent Congressional enactments on the subject. For the "reserve clause" as has been observed, results in something resembling peonage of the baseball player [emphasis in original].

Frank went on to discuss the details of the reserve clause, with emphasis on the fact that the team held all the power in the contracting relationship, thereby forcing the player to accept the proffered contract if he wanted to engage in his occupation of baseball. He later also noted that the fact that ballplayers were often well paid was irrelevant. "I may add that, if the players be regarded as quasi-peons, it is of no moment that they are well paid; only the totalitarian-minded will believe that high pay excuses virtual slavery."[33]

The *Gardella* appeal put baseball in a difficult position. The case was remanded back to federal court for trial with strongly worded opinions that struck at the core of baseball's business model. Chandler had one ace in the hole, however, in that what Gardella really wanted was an opportunity to play again before age eroded his skills to the point that he could no longer perform in the majors. The sides quietly agreed to an out of court settlement (as did two other claimants in separate cases) that provided undisclosed financial compensation along with reinstatement of the players.[34] Chandler smartly stayed out of the actual settlement, which allowed him to respond honestly that he did not know its terms and "purposely avoided knowing," when questioned about it during the House Hearings. He also made sure that the players were not retaliated against and found them homes on major league rosters, even going so far as to arrange for the Giants to release Gardella and the Cardinals to pick him up. But Chandler made it clear to the House Committee that the owners took the threat of the Gardella litigation seriously. "I do not think [the baseball lawyers] were enthusiastic about the prospects of winning the Gardella case," he testified. "I think they got some real old-fashioned religion, some of them."[35] Baseball dodged a bullet, but the situation gained enough attention to contribute directly to the initiation of the House Hearings held two years later, as Congress revisited baseball's antitrust exemption and the reserve clause.

Professional Baseball and American Society

Professional baseball long operated in a way that was very familiar to Americans, a reflection on their society. From a business standpoint, in the early decades of the 20th century teams were ruled by individual men, much as was true in American business culture. Over time this single owner model diminished and more and more frequently teams were owned by groups of shareholders and run as corporations, similar to what was happening on the national business scene. Regardless of whether the business was operated by one man or a board of directors, the owners exerted tremendous power and influence over labor. While labor unions had certainly made inroads in American society, especially in blue-collar industries, there was an ongoing undercurrent of distrust between labor and management, both in baseball and in society at large. The professional game also took on some of the less desirable characteristics of society, particularly in its exclusionary policies based on gender and race.

Gender

Baseball was always a male-dominated game, and early women's teams, while they existed, were treated at best as novelties and at worst as poor influences, unbecoming and inappropriate given women's roles in society. Much of society was also exclusionary with regards to women. There were career paths that were more or less closed to them, and talented women were funneled into a limited number of professions that were deemed appropriate for them such as nursing, teaching children, domestic service, and secretarial work. While certainly a generalization of a topic that could easily fill volumes in its own right, men held a dominant role with regards to the best paying jobs in the American workforce prior to World War II.

The war changed women's roles in the workforce. Drafting and enlisting 14 million men into the military was a tremendous blow to industry, and women who previously had limited professional opportunities were there to fill the voids. Not only did they take jobs on the factory floors, building bombers and making munitions, but they also filled more slots in colleges, where they hoped to gain an education that would open additional prospects to them. Like society, baseball also changed its relationship with women during the war with the establishment of the All-American Girls Softball League (later the All-American Girls Professional Baseball League) in 1943, though unlike their male counterparts the women athletes were still expected to conform to societal behavior expectations based on their gender.

The end of the war proved to be a difficult time for many American women when their professional and educational opportunities vanished. Military veterans were guaranteed the right to return to their pre-war jobs, which many of them did, displacing women workers. Furthermore, the G.I. Bill stripped away many educational opportunities for women, as colleges were required to give admissions preference to veterans. For example, Cornell set aside half of its open spots for the incoming 1946 freshman class for veterans, effectively forcing women to compete with non-veteran men for the remaining spots. To make things worse, the school actually set a hard cap on the number of women who would be admitted to certain programs, further limiting their opportunities.[36]

On the baseball diamond, the AAGPBL was more or less abandoned by Wrigley and the majors as the war moved into its final year, and it became obvious that its niche was soon to disappear. To Wrigley's credit, however, he did not fold the league, but instead allowed it to be taken over and run by others. The AAGBPL successfully rode the wave of baseball popularity in the immediate post-war era and remained a profitable venture for a number of years before folding in 1954. Women's roles changed during the war years, both in the workforce and on the field, but the end of the war and the return of the men from service took back many of the advances they had made.

Race

Racial segregation was a fact of life in pre–World War II society. Black Americans were discriminated against in the workplace, in education, and in society at large. They responded in part by forming their own communities, which often took on their own characteristics that differed from that of mainstream America. This was also true in baseball, as the door to participation alongside white players had been closed before the turn of the century. As a result, black ballplayers created their own teams and leagues, and like other unique aspects of their communities, so was the baseball played in the various Negro Leagues different to some extent from that found in white professional baseball, resulting in a version of the game that relied more heavily on finesse and speed.

World War II opened opportunities for black Americans, but they still faced an uphill struggle. Roosevelt's Executive Order 8802 technically made discrimination in war industries illegal, but this was not always easy to enforce. Even within a military that was in constant need for manpower, blacks found it difficult to enlist. According to historians Glenn Altschuler and Stuart Blumin:

> To begin with, African Americans were underrepresented in the armed
> forces. A higher percentage of blacks than whites were rejected for enlist-

ment and draft boards on grounds of physical health, literacy, and aptitude. About half of blacks and three-quarters of whites in their twenties and thirties served in the military during World War II. Blacks who served had substantially less education than whites. The average black GI had not completed eighth grade. About 17 percent (compared to 41 percent of whites) had graduated from high school.[37]

In baseball they were completely shut out of the majors and minors, though the war years are generally viewed as the economic high point of the Negro Leagues and black baseball. While many wanted to see integration on the diamond, some within the black community preferred to keep their game separate, viewing it as an integral part of their community identity (as well as a source of profits for black owners and promoters).[38]

Jackie Robinson's signing to a minor league contract with the Brooklyn Dodgers on November 1, 1945, was a bombshell that took the baseball world by surprise. It also happened to be the day that Happy Chandler's resignation from the United States Senate took effect, marking the start of his full-time stint as baseball's commissioner. Some in the black community had been concerned about Chandler's selection. The Kentuckian's record on racial issues was mixed, and there was no evidence that he was particularly supportive of baseball integration.[39] However, neither Chandler, the league presidents, nor the owners took any actions to void the signing, and Robinson went to Florida with the Dodgers for spring training in 1946 along with another black ballplayer, pitcher Johnny Wright. Both played with the Montreal Royals of the AAA International League that season, though Wright failed to last and was eventually demoted. Robinson, however, exceeded everyone's expectations by leading the league in batting with a .349 average, setting the stage for his promotion to the majors in 1947.

While Branch Rickey's signing of Robinson and assigning him to the minors had not generated any formal opposition, with the prospect of Robinson breaking into the majors in 1947, Rickey faced considerable resistance. Things came to a head at the August 1946 meeting at which the original *Steering Committee Report* was presented to the owners. As mentioned previously, the original draft of the report included a discussion about race and integration, though it failed to reach any conclusions or provide recommendations other than to note that the race issue was "an overall problem that vitally affects each and every one of us,"[40] and that a unified approach was the best option. According to Rickey, and later Chandler, there was heated discussion of the topic of race during that meeting. They alleged that there was actually a vote taken on the issue of allowing blacks to play in the majors, with Rickey casting the only vote in favor and all 15 other clubs in opposition. It should be noted that of the men present at that fateful meeting, only Rickey and

Chandler ever mentioned the vote, and Chandler himself never brought it up or discussed it publicly until 1972, 26 years after the meeting took place.[41]

Despite the opposition from the other 15 clubs, the Dodgers brought Robinson north with them after spring training in 1947, and he was a starter for the club. During his initial season in the majors Robinson faced particularly harsh treatment from opposing players, fans, and even some of his own teammates. However, both Chandler and National League president Ford Frick stepped in at times to support him, issuing warnings to teams that taunted Robinson outrageously with racial slurs and quelling a proposed strike by the St. Louis Cardinals, some of who did not want to take the field against a black player. Robinson's success that first season, both in his playing skills and in not overtly reacting to the harsh treatment he at times received, paved the way for other black ballplayers. Many teams quickly took advantage of this new pool of talent, creating a rush to sign the best black players and starting the demise of the Negro Leagues, which could not hope to compete for the top players. Even with the obvious benefits in the win column that came from signing the best talent, some teams continued to resist integration; it was not until 1959, 12 years after Robinson broke the color barrier, that the Boston Red Sox finally had a black player appear on their roster, the last major league team to integrate. The Negro American League folded four years after that in 1963, marking the end of segregated black baseball.

Baseball was not necessarily at the forefront of sports racial integration, but it certainly helped set the trend in North American team sports. While the National Football League had included a very small number of black players from its inception, that league also had its own unofficial agreement among owners not to sign black players that lasted from 1933 to 1946, before it too became permanently desegregated in 1947. Like baseball, there were individual NFL teams that resisted signing blacks, most notably the Washington Redskins, who did not have any black players until 1962. The National Basketball Association quickly followed the lead of baseball and the NFL, integrating in 1950, while the National Hockey League rounded out the major team sports in 1958.[42] Many individual sports such as boxing and track and field were integrated long before baseball, though athletes in those sports also struggled to earn the right to participate, and often continued to face opposition and racial slurs long after breaking down the racial barriers.

Regardless of the exact year that each sport integrated, the meritocracy of sports, where winning was paramount, ensured that once the barrier was broken most teams would be quick to take advantage by signing the best available players. According to sociologist John Wilson, "When the Civil Rights Act was passed in 1964, professional sports leagues, despite their history of race segregation, had become one of the most integrated of all American social institutions. The breakdown of caste barriers thus preceded the political mandate to do so. *Competitive resources* seem to have been more efficacious in the history of sport than pressure resources" (emphasis in original).[43] Baseball was arguably the most popular professional team sport in America at the time and at the forefront of this change. However, it had to be dragged into desegregation, kicking and screaming, primarily due to the efforts of one man who did not agree with discrimination and, perhaps just as importantly, wanted to win.

* * *

Baseball not only survived World War II, it emerged from the war more popular and profitable than ever before. With the near-total collapse of the minors during the war years, the majors took on even greater importance on the national stage. The commissioners and owners successfully navigated the sometimes rough waters of public opinion, and though professional baseball often found itself in the crosshairs of public and political debate (both justified and unjustified) regarding its purpose and contributions, the game survived intact and on a solid financial footing. The return to civilian life of American servicemen brought home millions of men, many looking to resume their baseball careers with new-found appreciation for their jobs, and most simply seeking to return to some sense of normalcy and stability in their lives. Baseball, the "National Pastime," had been a part of many of their lives growing up and prior to going to war, so it was only natural that the game was one of the anchors many used to reintegrate themselves back into peacetime life.

The immediate post-war era was also the swan song of baseball's business model. The game faced legal challenges that eventually took it back to the Supreme Court in the infamous *Flood v. Kuhn* ruling of 1972. The power of the owners slowly eroded as they were forced to treat the players more and more as business partners instead of simply labor. Baseball lost its innocence in the eyes of society, though what it in fact lost was not innocence but simply the veneer of it. While the game itself may have been pure, the business never was, instead being fraught with a massively disproportionate power relationship between owners and players along with the undercurrent of racial discrimination. Baseball was never innocent, as became clear when the layers were forcibly peeled back in the years and decades following World War II.

Conclusion

The story of professional baseball during World War II is one with many characters. It was much more than simply the players who served in the military and the game played on the field. It was also the machinations of the owners who sought to protect their businesses, the demands of a government trying to balance domestic affairs and an international conflict, a military facing the demands of a two-front war, and a population at home trying to cope with the impact of millions of its sons, brothers, and husbands serving at home and abroad. In some ways it seems foolish even to talk about the impact the war had on baseball, considering the toll it took on hundreds of millions if not billions of lives across the globe. However, baseball was a part of American society, a part of the national social fabric that received considerable attention, and an examination of how it functioned as a business, recreation, and symbol of the nation during a time of war is warranted as a way of examining the impact of war on society. Ultimately it is a story of six groups and how they interacted with one another: baseball's commissioners, the government, the players, the military, society, and the owners.

The Commissioners

While baseball's wartime experience started with the Selective Training and Service Act of 1940, the first proactive step was Commissioner Landis' letter to President Roosevelt on January 14, 1942, less than two months after Pearl Harbor forced America into World War II. Roosevelt's response to Landis' query about the future of baseball became known as the "Green Light Letter," and it set the stage for the continuation of baseball during the war. Writing to the president, whom he had criticized previously, required Landis to swallow his pride, and acquiescing to Roosevelt's suggestion of more night games was also a bitter pill, but Landis complied despite his own opposition to night baseball. The commissioner became the public face of baseball's role in the war effort until his passing in late 1944, acting as the point of contact with government officials and leading some of the early war charity initiatives. Based on the available evidence it appears that Landis was legitimately concerned about the war from a national perspective and recognized that it tran-

Ford Frick (left) and Gillette executive Boone Gross discuss a television advertising deal. Frick served as the President of the National League from 1934 to 1951 before replacing Happy Chandler as baseball's third Commissioner. His testimony in front of the House of Representatives in 1951 was heavily biased in support of Major League Baseball's business practices (Transcendental Graphics).

scended baseball. While he continued to be involved in the business of baseball, he generally gave proper consideration to the needs and requests of the
government and the military. However, he retained his dictatorial and often
ruthless streak, making decisions without consulting the owners and continuing to stymie any attempts at racial integration, despite the fact that the
government was attempting to eliminate segregation in war industries and
blacks were serving in the military. For Landis this is one of his unfortunate,
though earned, legacies.

By the time Happy Chandler was selected as baseball's new commissioner
in 1945, a military victory was already a foregone conclusion, though his selection was important as it provided a glimpse into the thinking of the owners.
The previous decades under Landis' iron rule and the lessons learned from
the war heavily influenced the selection process. The owners sought to limit
the powers of the commissioner, retaining more of the decision-making within
their own group. They recognized the importance of a commissioner who was
politically connected, someone who had *entre* into the halls of government
and could use his influence to the benefit of the game and their businesses.
Chandler was an excellent choice in this regard, though he proved much more
difficult to manage than the owners expected, and as a result served only one
term as commissioner before being replaced with a baseball insider, National
League President Ford Frick, in 1951. The owners' business interests remained
their paramount concern.

The Government

The "Green Light Letter" left the door open for baseball to continue
during the war, so long as it complied with government and military requests
and regulations. That meant War Manpower Commission Chairman Paul V.
McNutt took on an increasingly important role in the baseball world, as it
was McNutt who had to be convinced that the players on the field were somehow contributing to the war effort in meaningful ways instead of working in
a war industry. As the war progressed, Office of War Mobilization Director
James F. Byrnes became another important figure, and the commissioner and
owners found themselves in the unaccustomed position of having the weaker
negotiating position while they attempted to secure enough players of satisfactory ability to continue with baseball. Roosevelt's statements in support of
the game in early 1945 helped pave the way for the final wartime season, even
in the face of increasing demands by Byrnes.

The government had more important things to worry about during the
war years, and it was primarily concerned with baseball when it came to

resource management and allocation. Landis adroitly self-imposed spring training travel restrictions on the majors, and the national limitations on wartime travel were one of the factors that contributed to the demise of many of the minor leagues. The players represented a resource in the eyes of the government, but also a distraction when it faced questions and sometimes criticisms about the fact that men who were healthy enough to play professional sports were not able to serve in the military, or at the very least in a war industry. Throughout the conflict the owners lived in constant fear that the players, their product, would be taken from them and the game shut down. Fortunately, with the shutdown of roughly 75 percent of the minor leagues professional baseball's manpower demands were really quite small, and since the majors were able to make do with men who did not qualify for military service due to age, health conditions, etc, it remained possible to work within the guidelines and manpower demands of the government while continuing to put an acceptable product on the field.

The Players

The most visible group in the story of wartime baseball was the players. They were the ones out there on the field and in the press, both due to their play and their service. They also suffered the most criticisms, often unfairly. Those whose service was deferred by their local draft boards were questioned, even though they operated within the guidelines set forth by the government and the military. So too were the 4-Fs, who were excluded from military service because of medical conditions that limited their usefulness or required too many resources to manage in the military, and who had to suffer the indignity of being re-evaluated late in the war in the face of political and popular backlash for something that was not their fault. The same was true for those who served in the military but were kept away from the front, often so they could play on service baseball teams. Certainly they could have requested combat roles, and some did, but ultimately they served where the military placed them and had little or no say in the matter.

The players, like most of society, followed the laws of the land and sought out those opportunities that made the most sense to them. Many volunteered for the military following Pearl Harbor. Others waited to be drafted. Those who remained on the home front and outside the service made decisions about what type of work to pursue, whether it was professional baseball, war industry labor, or something else. However, they had the unfortunate distinction of being much more visible than the average man because of the public nature of their profession, which left them open to criticism and judgment by others.

Regardless, they, like the rest of society, served as best they could. Thousands entered the service, and more than a hundred never returned. Whether at home or overseas, they did their duty, and did it without public complaint.

The Military

The military maintained a relationship with professional baseball both at home and overseas. Professional teams provided free tickets to soldiers in uniform and often played exhibition games at military bases for the benefit of the troops. Groups of coaches and players toured the world in the off-season to provide some relief and boost the morale of troops overseas, often covering vast distances and sometimes finding themselves uncomfortably close to the fighting. The Ball and Bat Fund provided equipment to troops so they could at least try to play some rudimentary baseball wherever they were stationed, while the majors also worked with the military to distribute films of important games and arranged for radio broadcasts that could be beamed to those serving overseas. The military recognized that baseball was important to many servicemen, and that giving them access to it provided them with something familiar, a piece of home.

Many ballplayers, of course, also found themselves in the military during the war. How they were utilized often depended on where they reported for their initial training, as many large bases skimmed off top talent to put on their camp or service baseball teams. While certainly the exhibitions played by these teams served a morale purpose, the service teams prompted some legitimate questions about why these men were permitted to stay at home and play baseball while others were shipped overseas to fight. An examination of the data shows that major leaguers were far less likely to be killed while in the service than the average soldier, while minor leaguers were actually *more* likely to die. Clearly professional baseball players were above average physically, which resulted in minor leaguers being routed more frequently to combat roles. The major leaguers were obviously protected for various reasons, some reasonable, others not. Often though it was due to the egos of commanding officers, who believed that the success of their base or service branch baseball teams was somehow a positive reflection on them. This is a criticism best laid at the feet of the military, and not the players.

Society

Society retained strong ties to baseball during the war. While attendance in the majors and the remaining minor leagues certainly dropped during the conflict's first two years, the decreases were far from disastrous. People still needed avenues for relaxation, and one of those avenues was baseball. To fill the void left by the collapse of so many minor leagues, companies often banded together to form industrial leagues that served as recreation for their workers (both as players and spectators) and generated positive publicity. Baseball also served as a conduit for public support of the war effort. War bond and material drives were held at major and minor league parks, and the games themselves sometimes raised money for war charities. Players were involved off the field as well, often visiting factories and shipyards to meet workers, further promoting war bonds and charitable donations. The games themselves became patriotic events, with the regular singing of the national anthem, military precision drills, and induction ceremonies. Baseball clearly tied itself to the country and the military in very public ways.

Socially, baseball mirrored some of the other things that were happening in society. As women found their roles in the workforce and society increasing in importance, baseball responded with the creation of the first professional women's baseball league, spearheaded and funded by the owner of the Chicago Cubs, Philip Wrigley. Unfortunately baseball's stance on race was also similar to that of society. Roosevelt attempted to use an executive order to eliminate segregation and discrimination in war industries, but in reality many companies found ways to skirt the law with no repercussions. Even the military remained segregated, keeping black soldiers in their own units and usually placing them in non-combat, labor roles. The nation experienced race riots during the war years as black workers protested their treatment. Like society, professional baseball continued its unofficial policy of segregation until after the conclusion of the war. Ironically, even the man who eventually broke baseball's color barrier, Jackie Robinson, experienced considerable discrimination while serving as an officer in the Army, including a court martial in the aftermath of refusing to move to the back of a bus. In many ways baseball and society moved in parallel to each other during the war years with regards to social issues.

The Owners

Baseball had its commissioner, league presidents, and an overarching organization in the form of the National Association, but the people who really controlled the game were the owners of the 16 major league franchises. At times Landis was able to force them to do things they did not want to do, and during the war they certainly had to answer to the demands of the various government and military organizations, but ultimately they exerted tremendous control over the entire professional game at all levels. Individuals owned many teams, and even those owned by multiple shareholders generally had one dominant voice who controlled the team, so in essence 16 men ran the entire business of baseball. Like any such group, it was comprised of the competent and those of questionable ability, by progressives and conservatives, and perhaps most importantly by the rich and not rich. Even within the exclusive club of major league owners there existed a smaller elite group that held the most sway, those with the most money.

The owners were businessmen, and baseball was their business. While some of baseball's leaders took an active approach to supporting the war effort, many were primarily concerned about their own financial futures. Despite Landis' edict that he alone would be the point of contact between the game and the government, the evidence shows that many owners worked behind the scenes using their own connections when they believed it was in their individual or collective best interests. They generally sought to maintain the status quo, as was evidenced by the continued resistance to night baseball and the policy of racial discrimination, and above all they wanted to retain the powers provided by the game's antitrust exemption and the reserve clause. Their actions and words, both public and private, support this view.

Conclusion

Major League Baseball's contributions to the war effort were those expected of a non-essential, entertainment industry seeking to remain in operation during a time of war. Its owners and leaders took steps to publicize both the game's importance to society and its contributions to the war effort. However, these efforts were limited in scope and had a minimal impact on the overall war effort. The real contributions came from the players, both those who served and those who played. The true importance of baseball was as a symbol of America.

Major League Baseball was capable of doing much more in support of the war effort, both financially and socially, but instead it retained its conservative nature in an effort to maintain the status quo and the control of the owners. In the end, the owners behaved just as one would expect of businessmen who were used to getting their way, making the minimum possible sacrifice to ensure the protection of their investments.

Chapter Notes

Chapter 1

1. John Thorn, *Baseball in the Garden of Eden: The Secret History of the Early Game* (New York: Simon & Schuster, 2011), 4.

2. Mark Lamster, *Spalding's World Tour: The Epic Adventure That Took Baseball Around the Globe and Made It America's Game* (New York: PublicAffairs, 2006), 215–16.

3. Thorn, *Baseball in the Garden of Eden*, 1–6.

4. David Block, *Baseball Before We Knew It: A Search for the Roots of the Game* (Lincoln: University of Nebraska Press, 2005), 50–55; Thorn, *Baseball in the Garden of Eden*, 278–79.

5. George B. Kirsch, *Baseball in Blue and Gray: The National Pastime During the Civil War* (Princeton: Princeton University Press, 2003), 47.

6. Ibid., 132.

7. Wanda Ellen Wakefield, *Playing to Win: Sports and the American Military, 1898–1945* (Albany: State University of New York Press, 1997), 4–5.

8. Ibid., 9.

9. John Keegan, *The First World War* (New York: Vintage, 1998), 295, 372.

10. John Thorn, ed., *Total Baseball: The Ultimate Baseball Encyclopedia*, 8th ed. (Toronto: SPORT Media, 2004), 2420.

11. "Military Idea Games's Savior Since Declaration of War," *The Sporting News*, April 12, 1917, 1.

12. Lloyd Johnson and Miles Wolff, ed., *The Encyclopedia of Minor League Baseball*, 2d ed. (Durham: Baseball America, 1997), 205–11.

13. "Do Your Bit for the Boys in Khaki," *The Sporting News*, April 26, 1917, 5.

14. "Johnson Reasoning with Tax Assessors," *The Sporting News*, May 19, 1917, 3.

15. *The Sporting News*, August 19, 1917, 4.

16. *The Sporting News*, August 23, 1917, 4.

17. David Quentin Voigt, *American Baseball,*

Volume II: From the Commissioners to Continental Expansion (University Park: Pennsylvania State University Press, 1983), 121.

18. "Johnson Makes His Idea on Draft Plan," *The Sporting News*, November 29, 1917, 2.

19. Ralph S. Davis, "Reason for Protest on Johnson's Plan," *The Sporting News*, November 29, 1917, 5.

20. Burt Whitman, "Exemption Plea a Mistake," *The Sporting News*, February 14, 1918, 1.

21. Voigt, *American Baseball, Volume II*, 121.

22. "Dallas Club Fixed Against Draft Loss," *The Sporting News*, February 14, 1918, 6.

23. "Decision on War Prices Most Important Work by Majors," *The Sporting News*, February 21, 1918, 3.

24. "Holdout Antics of Players Incite Wrath of Joe Vila," *The Sporting News*, February 28, 1918, 1.

25. *The Sporting News*, June 13, 1918, 4.

26. "Baker Refuses to Modify 'Work' Rule for Baseball," *The Sporting News*, July 25, 1918, 2.

27. Geoffrey C. Ward and Ken Burns, *Baseball: An Illustrated History* (New York: Alfred A. Knopf, 1994), 131–32.

Chapter 2

1. David Pietrusza, *Judge and Jury: The Life and Times of Judge Kenesaw Mountain Landis* (South Bend: Diamond Communications, 1998), 157.

2. Ibid.

3. Voigt, *American Baseball, Volume II*, 118–19.

4. Pietrusza, *Judge and Jury*, 177–87.

5. "Baseball Leaders Won't Let White Sox Return to the Game," *New York Times*, August 4, 1921.

6. House Subcommittee on Study of Monopoly Power of the Committee on the Judiciary, *Report of the House Subcommittee on Study of*

Monopoly Power of the Committee on the Judiciary, Organized Baseball, 82nd Cong., 2nd sess., 1952, H. Rep. 2002, 60–61.

7. *Federal Baseball Club of Baltimore, Inc. v. National League of Professional Baseball Clubs, et al.,* 259 U.S. 200 (United States Supreme Court, 1922).

8. G. Edward White, *Creating the National Pastime: Baseball Transforms Itself 1903–1953* (Princeton: Princeton University Press, 1996), 115–16.

9. House Subcommittee on Study of Monopoly Power of the Committee on the Judiciary, *Report of the House Subcommittee on Study of Monopoly Power of the Committee on the Judiciary, Organized Baseball,* 90.

10. Ibid., 86.

11. Ibid., 75.

12. White, *Creating the National Pastime,* 116.

13. *The Sporting News,* November 2, 1933, 4.

14. House Subcommittee on Study of Monopoly Power of the Committee on the Judiciary, *Report of the House Subcommittee on Study of Monopoly Power of the Committee on the Judiciary, Organized Baseball,* 90.

15. Ibid.

16. Dick Clark and Larry Lester, eds., *The Negro League Book* (Cleveland: The Society for American Baseball Research, 1994), 15–19.

17. Denman Thompson, "Football Kicks Up Annual Griff Worry," *The Sporting News,* September 5, 1940, 5.

18. Dan Daniel, "High Prices Lowering Giants' Trade Hopes," *The Sporting News,* October 24, 1940, 2.

19. Stoney McLinn, "Mulcahy's Number 2231st from Bowl," *The Sporting News,* November 7, 1940, 9.

20. Edgar G. Brands, "Few Leading Players Included in Early Draft Numbers Drawn," *The Sporting News,* November 7, 1940, 10.

21. Dan Daniel, "'Smile and Take It' Policy on U.S. Draft," *The Sporting News,* November 14, 1940, 6.

22. Daniel M. Daniel, "U.S. Likely to Keep Draft from Heavy Inroads on Majors," *The Sporting News,* April 24, 1941, 1.

23. Richard Goldstein, *Spartan Seasons: How Baseball Survived the Second World War* (New York: Macmillan, 1980), 6–8.

24. "Greenberg and Briggs Do Their Bit," *The Sporting News,* May 1, 1941, 4.

25. John P. Carmichael, "Carmichael Visits Hank at Camp Custer," *The Sporting News,* May 15, 1940, 4.

26. Delbert C. Miller, "The Measurement of National Morale," *American Sociological Review* 6, no. 4 (August 1941): 491, 493.

27. House Subcommittee on Study of Monopoly Power of the Committee on the Judiciary, *Report of the House Subcommittee on Study of Monopoly Power of the Committee on the Judiciary, Organized Baseball,* 76.

28. John Drebinger, "Ott Pays $50,000 for First Baseman," *New York Times,* December 12, 1941.

29. "Service Men to Get Bat and Ball Kits," *New York Times,* December 31, 1941.

30. J. G. Taylor Spink, "O.B. Ready to Spark War Morale Again," *The Sporting News,* December 11, 1941, 1.

31. Pietrusza, *Judge and Jury,* 1–2, 109–115.

32. J. G. Taylor Spink, *Judge Landis and 25 Years of Baseball* (St. Louis: The Sporting News, 1974), 211.

33. Richard Crepeau, *America's Diamond Mind* (Lincoln: University of Nebraska Press, 1980), 209.

34. "Martin, House Minority Leader, Sees Curbs in War as 'Foolish'— Wadsworth Among Other Ex-Players Lauding Game," *New York Times,* January 9, 1942.

35. Letter, Kenesaw M. Landis to Franklin D. Roosevelt, January 14, 1941; Franklin D. Roosevelt Library, Hyde Park, New York.

36. Bill Gilbert, *They Also Served: Baseball and the Home Front, 1941–1945* (New York: Crown, 1992), 42.

37. Letter, Franklin D. Roosevelt to Kenesaw M. Landis, January 15, 1941; Franklin D. Roosevelt Library, Hyde Park, New York.

38. John Drebinger, "The Increase in Major League Night Baseball," *Baseball Magazine,* April 1942, 497.

Chapter 3

1. James M. Gould, "The President Says 'Play Ball,'" *Baseball Magazine,* March 1942, 435.

2. Dan Daniel, "Gotham Would Run F.D.R. for President," *The Sporting News,* January 22, 1942, 3.

3. Ibid.

4. J. G. Taylor Spink, "Stirring Wartime Pledges Mark Fun-Filled N.Y. Writers' Frolic," *The Sporting News,* February 5, 1942, 2.

5. James M. Gould, "War and Baseball," *Baseball Magazine,* February 1942, 389.

6. Eduard C. Lindeman, "Recreation and Morale," *American Journal of Sociology* 47, no. 3 (November 1941): 403.

7. Ibid., 399.

8. Ward and Burns, *Baseball: An Illustrated History,* 242.

9. Goldstein, *Spartan Seasons,* 124.

10. "Off-Hour Contests Favored by M'Nutt," *New York Times,* May 13, 1943.

11. "Baseball May Ask Government Help," *New York Times,* February 4, 1945.

12. "Brooklyn Ball Club Announces All-Out Program in Support of War Effort," *New York Times*, February 18, 1942.

13. Arthur Daley, "Sports of the Times: In the Wake of the Baseball Meetings," *New York Times*, December 15, 1944.

14. "Troops Will Hear Games," *New York Times*, April 13, 1944.

15. George Gallup, "Pro Sports for Duration of War Heavily Favored in Poll of Public," *New York Times*, April 15, 1942.

16. "Sanctioning of Spectator Sports by Congress Asked to Aid Morale," *New York Times*, March 3, 1943.

17. "Favor Baseball in Poll," *New York Times*, March 25, 1943.

18. Letter, John C. Wood to the National Baseball Hall of Fame, April 6, 2001; World War II File, National Baseball Hall of Fame and Museum, Cooperstown, New York.

19. Letter, Louis A. Repetto to the National Baseball Hall of Fame, September 30, 1994, World War II File, National Baseball Hall of Fame and Museum, Cooperstown, New York.

20. Letter, Major Gordon Jones to Will Harridge, January 5, 1945, World War II File, National Baseball Hall of Fame and Museum, Cooperstown, New York.

21. Daniel M. Daniel, "Baseball's War Effort Seeks Vast Sums for Vital Causes," *Baseball Magazine*, June 1942, 291–92.

22. John Drebinger, "Dodgers Defeat Giants in Twilight Game Raising $59,859 for Navy Relief," *New York Times*, May 9, 1942.

23. "Baseball's 1942 War-Aid Showing," *Baseball Magazine*, March 1943, 468.

24. "Further World Series Aid to U.S.," *The Sporting News*, November 26, 1942.

25. "Landis in Warning on Bogus War Aid," *New York Times*, June 5, 1942.

26. John Drebinger, "Sports Thrived During 1942 as Part of War Effort," *New York Times*, December 20, 1942.

27. Lauren Rebecca Sklaroff, "G.I. Joe Louis: Cultural Solutions to the 'Negro Problem' during World War II," *Journal of American History* 89, no. 3 (December 2002): 958–83.

28. Harry Cross, "Auctioning of Yankee, Dodger, and Giant Players Nets $123,850,000 in War-Bond Pledges," *New York Herald-Tribune*, June 9, 1943.

29. Goldstein, *Spartan Seasons*, 89.

30. "War Relief Figures Given," *New York Times*, February 8, 1945.

31. House Subcommittee on Study of Monopoly Power of the Committee on the Judiciary, *Hearings Before the Subcommittee on Study of Monopoly Power of the Committee on the Judiciary, Organized Baseball*, Serial No. 1, Part 6, 82nd Cong., 1st sess., 1951, 41.

32. Harold Parrott, "Many Notables Make Stirring Talks for Sport," *The Sporting News*, February 11, 1943, 1–2.

33. Daniel M. Daniel, "Major Leagues Tack on Service Stars as Players Answer Call of Uncle Sam," *Baseball Magazine*, May 1942, 534.

34. L. H. Addington, "Important Meeting," *Baseball Magazine*, December 1942, 325.

35. These figures were derived using various pages and lists on Gary Bedingfield's extraordinary website "Baseball in Wartime" (http://www.baseballinwartime.com).

36. J. G. Taylor Spink, "It's Not the Same Game in Japan," *The Sporting News*, December 18, 1941, 4.

37. Arthur O. W. Anderson, "What Do the Fans Prefer?" *Baseball Magazine*, June 1942, 315.

38. John Drebinger, "Majors Set Plans to Pick New Head," *New York Times*, December 13, 1944.

39. Ward and Burns, *Baseball: An Illustrated History*, 220–21.

40. Voigt, *American Baseball, Volume II*, 251.

41. The 1943 and 1944 World Series attendance and financial figures came from J.G. Taylor Spink, *Sporting News Baseball Guide and Record Book, 1944* (St. Louis: Charles C. Spink & Son, 1944), 143, and J.G. Taylor Spink, *Sporting News Baseball Guide and Record Book, 1945* (St. Louis: Charles C. Spink & Son, 1945), 168.

42. Figures based on the actual percentages for the 1939 season per the *Report of the House Subcommittee on Study of Monopoly Power of the Committee on the Judiciary, Organized Baseball*, 5–6.

43. John Kieran, "Sports of the Times: A Bad Play for Baseball," *New York Times*, May 21, 1942.

44. "Baseball Raised $329,555," *New York Times*, November 1, 1944.

45. House Subcommittee on Study of Monopoly Power, *Report of the House Subcommittee on Study of Monopoly Power of the Committee on the Judiciary, Organized Baseball*, 94.

46. Dan Daniel, "Drafting of Fathers Builds Major Manpower Problems for Big Leagues," *Baseball Magazine*, December 1943, 247.

47. "Preparing for Baseball Season Up to Clubs, McNutt Says," *New York Times*, February 16, 1943.

48. House Subcommittee on Study of Monopoly Power of the Committee on the Judiciary, *Hearings Before the Subcommittee on Study of Monopoly Power of the Committee on the Judiciary, Organized Baseball*, 41.

49. Ibid., 1636.

50. Daniel, "U.S. Likely to Keep Draft from Heavy Inroads on Majors," 1.

51. Figures based on the actual percentages for the 1939 season per the *Report of the House*

Subcommittee on Study of Monopoly Power of the Committee on the Judiciary, Organized Baseball, 6.

52. Daniel M. Daniel, "Drafting of Fathers Builds Major Manpower Problem for Big Leagues," *Baseball Magazine,* December 1943, 222.

53. Wilbur Jennings, "'Players Joining Shipyard Clubs Contract Jumpers'— Bramham," *The Sporting News,* July 1, 1943, 4.

54. "Baseball May Ask Government Help," *New York Times,* February 4, 1945.

55. "Baseball a 'Must,' Writers Are Told," *New York Times,* February 5, 1945.

56. "Griff Visits Roosevelt," *The Sporting News,* March 15, 1945, 12.

57. George Zielke, "Game Okayed by FDR in 'Pinch-Hitter' Form," *The Sporting News,* March 22, 1945, 8.

Chapter 4

1. William B. Mead, *Baseball Goes to War: Stars Don Khaki, 4-Fs Vie for Pennant* (Washington, DC: A Broadcast Interview Source, 1998), 42–43.

2. http://www.baseball-reference.com/leagues.

3. Daniel M. Daniel, "Nearly 100 New Players Set Rookie Record for the Major Leagues," *Baseball Magazine,* June 1942, 343.

4. James M. Gould, "They Also Serve," *Baseball Magazine,* June 1942, 306.

5. L. H. Addington, "Important Meeting," 325.

6. Letter, M. B. E. to the Sports Editor of the *New York Times,* dated May 18, 1942, published in *New York Times,* May 23, 1942.

7. Richard Ben Cramer, *Joe DiMaggio: The Hero's Life* (New York: Simon & Schuster, 2000), 200–203, 207.

8. Goldstein, *Spartan Seasons,* 24.

9. John Drebinger, "This Changing Baseball World," *Baseball Magazine,* February 1943, 388.

10. "M'Nutt Clarifies Baseball Status," *New York Times,* January 7, 1943.

11. "Players Seen Free to Quit War Jobs," *New York Times,* January 9, 1943.

12. Daniel M. Daniel, "Manpower Problems? Sure! But Baseball Will Carry On," *Baseball Magazine,* March 1943, 480.

13. Dick Farrington, "Drafting of Papas Would Hit 22 Cards," *Sporting News,* February 18, 1943, 5.

14. Daniel, "Drafting of Fathers Builds Major Manpower Problem for Big Leagues," 222.

15. It should be noted that Nuxhall was not simply some type of novelty brought into a game

simply because he was young. He was a very able pitcher and spent 15 more seasons in the majors from 1952 to 1966.

16. Arthur Mann, "Baseball's Peace-Time 4-F's," *Baseball Magazine,* May 1944, 419–20.

17. Goldstein, *Spartan Seasons,* 197.

18. James M. Gould, "What's Happened to the Ball?" *Baseball Magazine,* September 1942, 435.

19. Herbert Simons, "Cork-Balata Center for Duration Baseball," *Baseball Magazine,* May 1943, 523.

20. Gould, "What's Happened to the Ball?" 435.

21. Arthur Mann, "Baseball's Unseen Sacrifices," *Baseball Magazine,* June 1944, 221–22.

22. "Baseball's Role Praised," *New York Times,* January 11, 1945.

23. "Baseball Should be Ruled Out with Racing, Says Military Affairs Committee Chairman," *New York Times,* January 19, 1945.

24. Arthur Daley, "Sports of the Times: Baseball Learns the Score," *New York Times,* January 25, 1945.

25. "WMC Decision Lets Baseball Players Leave War Plants," *New York Times,* March 22, 1945.

26. "ODT Asks 25% Cut in Baseball Travel," *New York Times,* February 22, 1945.

27. Herbert Simons, "The Road Ahead," *Baseball Magazine,* October 1945, 363.

28. Johnson and Wolff, ed., *The Encyclopedia of Minor League Baseball,* 322–28.

29. Mead, *Baseball Goes to War,* 27.

30. Ibid., 29.

31. L. H. Addington, "Let's Go!" *Baseball Magazine,* March 1942, 456.

32. Johnson and Wolff, eds., *The Encyclopedia of Minor League Baseball,* 331–36.

33. L. H. Addington, "War Effort," *Baseball Magazine,* September 1942, 469.

34. L. H. Addington, "Important Meeting," 325.

35. Johnson and Wolff, eds., *The Encyclopedia of Minor League Baseball,* 337–38.

36. L. H. Addington, "The Minor League Picture," *Baseball Magazine,* May 1945, 425.

37. Carlos Bauer, *The Early Coast League Statistical Record, 1903–1957* (San Diego: Baseball Press Books, 2004), 308–309.

38. "Minors' Outlook Rests Upon Manpower Action," *The Sporting News,* March 15, 1945, 5.

39. Simons, "The Road Ahead," 364.

40. Neil Lanctot, *Negro League Baseball: The Rise and Ruin of a Black Institution* (Philadelphia: University of Pennsylvania Press, 2004), 67.

41. Ibid., 97, 147.

42. Ibid., vii, 139.

43. Ward and Burns, *Baseball: An Illustrated History,* 18–19.

44. Merrie A. Fidler, *The Origins and History of the All-American Girls Professional Baseball League* (Jefferson, NC: McFarland, 2006), 25.

45. Patricia Vignola, "The Patriotic Pinch Hitter: The AAGBL and How the American Woman Earned a Permanent Spot on the Roster," *NINE* 12, no. 2 (2004): 102.

46. Fidler, *The Origins and History of the All-American Girls Professional Baseball League*, 34.

47. Ibid., 36. Quoting from "All-American Girls Softball League," ca. 1943, Meyerhoff Files, Drawer 19, 1945 Management Corporation Softball Enterprise folder.

48. Ibid., 52.

49. Ibid., 46, 68.

Chapter 5

1. Wakefield, *Playing to Win*, 60–61.

2. Quoted in Wakefield, *Playing to Win*, 61; quote originated from General Douglas MacArthur in *A Soldier Speaks: Public Papers and Speeches of General of the Army Douglas MacArthur*, Major Vorin E. Whan, Jr., ed. (New York: Frederick A. Praeger, 1965), 21–22.

3. Donald J. Mrozek, "The Interplay of Metaphor and Practice in the U.S. Defense Establishment's Use of Sport, 1940–1950," *Journal of American Culture* 7, no. 1 (Spring/Summer 1984): 55.

4. Bullock, *Playing for Their Nation*, 11.

5. Mrozek, "The Interplay of Metaphor and Practice in the U.S. Defense Establishment's Use of Sport, 1940–1950," 56.

6. John J. McGrath, *The Other End of the Spear: The Tooth-to-Tail Ratio (T3R) in Modern Military Operations*, (Fort Leavenworth, KS: Combat Studies Institute Press, 2007), 20.

7. Gary Bedingfield, "In Memoriam—World War II," Baseball in Wartime, http://www.baseballinwartime.com/in_memoriam/in_memoriam.htm; number does not include those signed to contracts or on major league rosters but who did not appear in a major league game.

8. Player ages derived from the individual team pages linked from "1941 Major League Baseball Team Statistics and Standings," Baseball-Reference.com, http://www.baseball-reference.com/leagues/MLB/1941.shtml.

9. AA American Association (26.8 years), AA International League (27.4 years), AA Pacific Coast League (28.2 years), A Eastern League (25.3 years).

10. Based on the Piedmont League (24.2 years), Interstate League (24.2 years), Western International League (24.5 years), and South Atlantic League (24.0 years).

11. Based on the Pioneer League (22.9 years), Western Association (23.0 years), Middle At-

lantic League (23.2 years), and Canadian-American League (24.5 years).

12. Based on the Florida State League (22.3 years), Appalachian League (21.9 years), Coastal Plains League (23.1 years), and Pennsylvania State Association (20.7 years).

13. R. Ernest Dupuy and Trevor N. Dupuy, eds., *The Harper Encyclopedia of Military History*, 4th ed. (New York: Harper Collins, 1993), 1309.

14. Gary Bedingfield, "Elmer Gedeon," Baseball in Wartime, http://www.baseballinwartime.com/player_biographies/gedeon_elmer.htm.

15. Gary Bedingfield, "Harry O'Neill," Baseball in Wartime, http://www.baseballinwartime.com/player_biographies/oneill_harry.htm.

16. Dick Thompson, "Baseball's Greatest Hero," *Baseball Research Journal* 30 (2001): 3–10.

17. Gary Bedingfield, "Jack Lummus," Baseball's Greatest Sacrifice, http://www.baseballsgreatestsacrifice.com/biographies/lummus_jack.html.

18. Bullock, *Playing for Their Nation*, 97.

19. "Baseball Should be Ruled Out with Racing, Says Military Affairs Committee Chairman," *New York Times*, January 19, 1945.

20. Bullock, *Playing for Their Nation*, 98–99.

21. Arthur Daley, "Sports of the Times," *New York Times*, January 9, 1945.

22. Gary Bedingfield, "Negro Leaguers Who Served with the Armed Forces in WWII," Baseball in Wartime, http://www.baseballinwartime.com/negro.htm.

23. Jimmy Scott interview with Monte Irvin, http://www.jimmyscottshighandtight.com/node/1010.

24. Dan Yount, "Battle of Bulge Massacre Cover-up: 'They Were Just 11 Black Soldiers,'" *Cincinnati Herald*, December 18, 2010.

25. Bullock, *Playing for Their Nation*, 76–77.

26. Clifford Bloodgood, "All-Star Double Feature," *Baseball Magazine*, September 1942, 461.

27. Bill Bryson, "The Navy Goes for Baseball," *Baseball Magazine*, August 1943, 313.

28. Bullock, *Playing for Their Nation*, 76–87.

29. Jerry Malloy, "Black Bluejackets," *The National Pastime* (Winter 1985): 72–77.

30. Bullock, *Playing for Their Nation*, 60.

31. Ibid., 50–56.

32. Sgt. Harold Winerip, "Of Baseball and Soldiers," *Baseball Magazine*, December 1944, 222.

33. Herbert Simmons, "Lieut. Mickey Cochrane, U.S.N.," *Baseball Magazine*, March 1943, 459–60.

34. Mead, *Baseball Goes to War*, 197.

35. John Drohan, "Cronin Changes Uniforms," *Baseball Magazine*, May 1943, 522.

36. "Editorial Comment," *Baseball Magazine*, February 1945, 289.

37. Fred G. Lieb, "Baseball Trips to War Theaters," *Baseball Guide and Record Book, 1945* (St. Louis: Charles C. Spink & Son, 1945), 180–83.

38. Bob Feller quote from William B. Mead, "Shooting Ended and the Baseball War Resumed," *Boston Globe*, April 29, 1978.

Chapter 6

1. House Subcommittee on Study of Monopoly Power of the Committee on the Judiciary, *Hearings Before the Subcommittee on Study of Monopoly Power of the Committee on the Judiciary, Organized Baseball*, 3.

2. Major League Steering Committee, "Report of Major League Steering Committee for Submission to the National and American Leagues at Their Meetings in Chicago," August 27, 1946, 1.

3. House Subcommittee on Study of Monopoly Power of the Committee on the Judiciary, *Hearings Before the Subcommittee on Study of Monopoly Power of the Committee on the Judiciary, Organized Baseball*, 471–507.

4. Ibid.

5. Ibid., 474–88, 497–505.

6. David Quentin Voigt, *American Baseball, Volume I: From the Gentleman's Sport to the Commissioner System* (University Park: University of Pennsylvania Press, 1983), 73–4.

7. Roger I. Abrams, *Legal Bases: Baseball and the Law* (Philadelphia: Temple University Press, 1998), 15.

8. *1904 Reach Baseball Guide*, 115–23.

9. Leo Lowenfish and Tony Lupien, *The Imperfect Diamond* (New York: Stein and Day, 1980), 85–90.

10. *Federal Baseball Club of Baltimore, Inc. v. National League of Professional Baseball Clubs, et al.*, 259 U.S. 200 (Supreme Court of the United States, 1922).

11. Ibid.

12. House Subcommittee on Study of Monopoly Power of the Committee on the Judiciary, *Hearings Before the Subcommittee on Study of Monopoly Power of the Committee on the Judiciary, Organized Baseball*, 30.

13. Ibid., 49–50.

14. Major League Steering Committee, "Report of Major League Steering Committee for Submission to the National and American Leagues at Their Meetings in Chicago," 2.

15. Ibid., 10.

16. Ibid., 11.

17. House Subcommittee on Study of Monopoly Power of the Committee on the Judiciary, *Hearings Before the Subcommittee on Study of Monopoly Power of the Committee on the Judiciary, Organized Baseball*, 16.

18. Ibid., 853.

19. Ibid., 74.

20. Ibid., 733.

21. Ibid., 345.

22. Happy Chandler and Vance Trimble, *Heroes, Plain Folks, and Skunks: The Life and Times of Happy Chandler* (Chicago: Bonus, 1989), 178.

23. Ibid., 75–76.

24. Ibid., 1610.

25. The *Hearings* report provides attendance data, but in some instances the sum of the individual teams does not match the total shown for the league. As a result I relied upon Thorn et al., *Total Baseball*, 2421. The annual totals of *Total Baseball* match those of *Hearings*.

26. House Subcommittee on Study of Monopoly Power of the Committee on the Judiciary, *Hearings Before the Subcommittee on Study of Monopoly Power of the Committee on the Judiciary, Organized Baseball*, 1595–98.

27. Ibid., 1594.

28. Philip J. Lowry, *Green Cathedrals: The Ultimate Celebration of Major League and Negro League Ballparks* (New York: Walker & Company, 2006), 39, 154, 160, 202.

29. Drebinger, "The Increase in Major League Night Baseball," 524.

30. Shirley Povich, "Defiant Griff Turns to 'Twi-Night' Ball," *The Sporting News*, July 16, 1942, 1; Dan Daniel, "Keyed Up Yankees Put Lock on Slump," *The Sporting News*, July 16, 1942, 17.

31. J. G. Taylor Spink, *Sporting News Baseball Guide and Record Book, 1943* (St. Louis: Charles C. Spink & Son, 1943), 167.

32. Spink, *Sporting News Baseball Guide and Record Book, 1944*, 112–15.

33. House Subcommittee on Study of Monopoly Power of the Committee on the Judiciary, *Hearings Before the Subcommittee on Study of Monopoly Power of the Committee on the Judiciary, Organized Baseball*, 1603.

34. Spink, *Sporting News Baseball Guide and Record Book, 1945*, 199.

35. J. G. Taylor Spink, *Sporting News Baseball Guide and Record Book, 1946* (St. Louis: Charles C. Spink & Son, 1946), 190.

36. Daniel, "Drafting of Fathers Builds Major Manpower Problem for Big Leagues," 222.

37. House Subcommittee on Study of Monopoly Power of the Committee on the Judiciary, *Hearings Before the Subcommittee on Study of Monopoly Power of the Committee on the Judiciary, Organized Baseball*, 1603, 1607.

38. Ibid.

39. "War Relief Figures Given," *New York Times*, February 8, 1945.

40. House Subcommittee on Study of Monopoly Power of the Committee on the Judiciary, *Hearings Before the Subcommittee on Study of*

Monopoly Power of the Committee on the Judiciary, Organized Baseball, 41.

41. Spink, *Sporting News Baseball Guide and Record Book, 1946*, 166.

42. House Subcommittee on Study of Monopoly Power of the Committee on the Judiciary, *Hearings Before the Subcommittee on Study of Monopoly Power of the Committee on the Judiciary, Organized Baseball*, 41.

43. John Drebinger, "Sports of the Times: Will Baseball Go Spartan Again?" *New York Times*, August 9, 1944.

44. House Subcommittee on Study of Monopoly Power of the Committee on the Judiciary, *Hearings Before the Subcommittee on Study of Monopoly Power of the Committee on the Judiciary, Organized Baseball*, 1610–11.

45. Ibid., 41.

46. "War Effort Comes First," *New York Times*, November 17, 1942.

47. House Subcommittee on Study of Monopoly Power of the Committee on the Judiciary, *Hearings Before the Subcommittee on Study of Monopoly Power of the Committee on the Judiciary, Organized Baseball*, 1615.

48. Ibid., 1599–1601.

49. Ibid. Note that there is an error in the *Hearings* table. The Boston Red Sox show an amount of 312, 41 for 1943, which is obviously incorrect. To derive the Boston figure used here I made an assumption that the American League total and the amounts shown for the other seven American League teams for 1943 were correct.

50. Ibid., 1600–1601.

51. "Preparing for Baseball Season Up to Clubs, McNutt Says," *New York Times*, February 16, 1943.

52. John Rossi, "The Nugent Era: Phillies Phlounder in Phutility," *National Pastime* 25 (2005), 16.

53. David M. Jordan, Larry R. Gerlach, and John P. Rossi, "A Baseball Myth Exploded: Bill Veeck and the 1943 Sale of the Phillies," *National Pastime* 18 (1998), 3–5.

54. Pietrusza, *Judge and Jury*, 437–40.

55. J. G. Taylor Spink, "A Declaration of Policy," *The Sporting News*, February 17, 1944, 8.

56. Letter to President Franklin Delano Roosevelt dated January 28, 1944, from J. G. Taylor Spink, as quoted in Edgar G. Brands, "Manpower Regulations Will Govern," *The Sporting News*, February 10, 1944, 2.

57. Letter to J. G. Taylor Spink dated February 1, 1944, from Stephen Early, as quoted in Edgar G. Brands, "Manpower Regulations Will Govern," *The Sporting News*, February 10, 1944, 2.

58. "No Questions on Players' Draft Status," *The Sporting News*, February 17, 1944, 8.

59. Letter to General Lewis B. Hershey dated December 23, 1943, from Kenesaw Mountain Landis, as quoted in "Landis Disclaims Plea for Baseball," *New York Times*, February 12, 1944.

60. Drebinger, "Sports of the Times: Will Baseball Go Spartan Again?"

61. James P. Dawson, "Brooklyn Ball Club Announces All-Out Program in Support of War Effort," *New York Times*, February 18, 1942.

62. "Judge Landis Dies; Baseball Czar, 78," *New York Times*, November 26, 1944.

63. John Drebinger, "Majors Set Plans to Pick New Head," *New York Times*, December 13, 1944.

64. "Baseball May Ask Government Help," *New York Times*, February 4, 1945.

65. House Subcommittee on Study of Monopoly Power of the Committee on the Judiciary, *Hearings Before the Subcommittee on Study of Monopoly Power of the Committee on the Judiciary, Organized Baseball*, 255–56.

66. "Landis on Negro Players," *The Sporting News*, July 23, 1942, 11.

67. Edgar G. Brands, "Political Slugfest Marks Minors' Meet," *The Sporting News*, December 9, 1943, 7.

68. All quotes from this editorial are from J.G. Taylor Spink, "No Good From Raising Race Issue," *The Sporting News*, August 6, 1942, 4.

69. Dan W. Dodson, "The Integration of Negroes in Baseball," *Journal of Educational Sociology* 28, No. 2 (October 1954), 74–5.

70. All quotes regarding the Race Question section of the *Steering Committee Report* are from Major League Steering Committee, "Report of Major League Steering Committee for Submission to the National and American Leagues at Their Meetings in Chicago," August 27, 1946, 18–20.

71. Bill Veeck and Ed Linn, *Veeck as in Wreck* (Chicago: University of Chicago Press, 1962), 173. Quote taken from the 2001 edition.

72. Jordan, Gerlach, and Rossi, "A Baseball Myth Exploded: Bill Veeck and the 1943 Sale of the Phillies," 3–13.

73. Dodson, "The Integration of Negroes in Baseball," 82.

74. House Subcommittee on Study of Monopoly Power of the Committee on the Judiciary, *Hearings Before the Subcommittee on Study of Monopoly Power of the Committee on the Judiciary, Organized Baseball*, 747.

75. Letter to Peter S. Craig dated July 25, 1951, from A.E. Meyerhoff, as quoted in House Subcommittee on Study of Monopoly Power of the Committee on the Judiciary, *Hearings Before the Subcommittee on Study of Monopoly Power of the Committee on the Judiciary, Organized Baseball*, 750.

76. Official Uniform Player's Contract of All-American Girls Professional Ball League as

quoted in House Subcommittee on Study of Monopoly Power of the Committee on the Judiciary, *Hearings Before the Subcommittee on Study of Monopoly Power of the Committee on the Judiciary, Organized Baseball,* 748.

77. House Subcommittee on Study of Monopoly Power of the Committee on the Judiciary, *Hearings Before the Subcommittee on Study of Monopoly Power of the Committee on the Judiciary, Organized Baseball,* 1621.

78. Ibid., 800.

79. Ibid., 359.

80. Ibid., 258.

81. Ibid., 162.

82. Ibid., 197.

83. Brands, "Political Slugfest Marks Minors' Meet," 3, 6, 7.

84. Ibid., 6.

85. "'Conduct Detrimental to Baseball,' Landis Reply to Rebel Loops' Appeal," *The Sporting News,* December 9, 1943, 3.

86. J.G. Taylor Spink, "Hot Heads Make Cool Customers," *The Sporting News,* December 9, 1943, 10.

87. House Subcommittee on Study of Monopoly Power of the Committee on the Judiciary, *Hearings Before the Subcommittee on Study of Monopoly Power of the Committee on the Judiciary, Organized Baseball,* 1616.

88. "They Said It," *Sports Illustrated,* November 19, 1962, 16.

Chapter 7

1. Lowenfish and Lupien, *The Imperfect Diamond,* 129–32.

2. *Fishgold v. Sullivan Drydock & Repair Corp. et al.,* 328 U.S. 275 (Supreme Court of the United States, 1946), 7.

3. Ibid., 9.

4. "Niemiec's Case Watched," *Seattle Times,* June 25, 1946.

5. Letter addressed TO WHOM IT MAY CONCERN dated April 20, 1946, from Bill Skiff and R. C. Torrance, *Seattle Rainier Baseball Club Records Collection,* Washington State Historical Society.

6. Letter to Emil Sick dated April 24, 1946, from Lt. B. V. Vercuski, *Seattle Rainier Baseball Club Records Collection,* Washington State Historical Society.

7. Letter to Victor Ford Collins dated May 17, 1946, from Stephen Chadwick, *Seattle Rainier Baseball Club Records Collection,* Washington State Historical Society.

8. Dan Raley, *Pitchers of Beer: The Story of the Seattle Rainiers* (Lincoln: University of Nebraska Press, 2011), 12–22, 98.

9. Bullock, *Playing for Their Nation,* 56.

10. Letter to Roscoe C. Torrance dated June 2, 1946, from Albert B. Chandler, *Seattle Rainier Baseball Club Records Collection,* Washington State Historical Society.

11. Letter to A. B. "Happy" Chandler dated April 27, 1946, from R. C. Torrance, *Seattle Rainier Baseball Club Records Collection,* Washington State Historical Society.

12. Minutes of Special Meeting, Board of Directors, Seattle Rainiers Baseball Club, Inc. dated Monday, June 10, 1946, *Seattle Rainier Baseball Club Records Collection,* Washington State Historical Society.

13. Royal Brougham, "Niemiec Hearing Closes, Judge Takes Case Under Advisement," *The Sporting News,* June 26, 1946, 10.

14. *Niemiec v. Seattle Rainier Baseball Club, Inc.,* 67 F. Supp. 705 (U.S. Dist. Ct. 1946).

15. Ibid.

16. Ibid.

17. Ibid.

18. Ibid.

19. Ibid.

20. Ibid.

21. Western Union telegram to Roscoe Torrance dated June 25, 1946, from Albert B. Chandler, *Seattle Rainier Baseball Club Records Collection,* Washington State Historical Society.

22. Minutes of a Special Meeting of the Board of Directors of the Pacific Coast Baseball League, July 22 and 22 [sic], 1946, *Seattle Rainier Baseball Club Records Collection,* Washington State Historical Society.

23. Lowenfish and Lupien, *The Imperfect Diamond,* 137.

24. Letter to Joseph C. Hostetler dated November 7, 1946, from S. F. Chadwick, *Seattle Rainier Baseball Club Records Collection,* Washington State Historical Society.

25. Notes from Special Meeting, Board of Directors, Seattle Rainier Baseball Club, Inc., November 25, 1946, *Seattle Rainier Baseball Club Records Collection,* Washington State Historical Society.

26. George Zielke, "Settlement of Campbell's GI Case 'No Precedent,' Declares Griffith," *The Sporting News,* August 14, 1942, 13.

27. Oscar K. Ruhl, "Court Hears Sundra Case vs. Browns," *The Sporting News,* June 15, 1949, 4.

28. J. G. Taylor Spink, "Cardinals Favored on Pitching, Yankees on Power," *The Sporting News,* April 18, 1946, 5.

29. Frederick G. Lieb, "Cards Live Up to Blue-Ribbon Billing; Browns Back in 'Hitless Wonder' Ways," *The Sporting News,* April 25, 1946, 6.

30. *Sundra v. St. Louis American League Baseball Club,* 87 F. Supp. 471 (U.S. Dist. Ct., 1949).

31. Ibid.

32. Ibid.

33. Ruhl, "Court Hears Sundra Case vs. Browns," 4.

34. "Happy Urges One-City Headquarters for Game," *The Sporting News*, July 31, 1946, 2.

35. Major League Steering Committee, "Report of Major League Steering Committee for Submission to the National and American Leagues at Their Meetings in Chicago," 17.

36. Gary Bedingfield, *Baseball's Dead of World War II: A Roster of Professional Players Who Died in Service* (Jefferson, NC: McFarland, 2010), 3.

37. Gary Bedingfield, "In Memoriam — World War II," *Baseball in Wartime*, http://www.baseballinwartime.com/in_memoriam/in_memoriam.htm, last accessed August 21, 2011.

38. Bullock, *Playing for Their Nation*, 126–36.

39. Bedingfield, *Baseball's Dead of World War II*, 64–67, 81–83.

40. Arthur Mann, "Gamest of the Game," *Baseball Magazine*, August 1945, 297.

Chapter 8

1. Gary Bedingfield, "Ernie Holbrook," http://www.baseballinwartime.com/in_memoriam/holbrook_ernie.htm.

2. Names culled from biographies appear on Gary Bedingfield's "Baseball in Wartime" website. Other minor leaguers killed include Bill Hanson, Ernie Hrovatic, Hank Nowak, Paul Melllblom, George Meyer, and Elmer Wachtler.

3. House Subcommittee on Study of Monopoly Power of the Committee on the Judiciary, *Hearings Before the Subcommittee on Study of Monopoly Power of the Committee on the Judiciary, Organized Baseball*, 1599–1601.

4. Thorn, *Total Baseball*, 2420–2421.

5. Major League Steering Committee, "Report of Major League Steering Committee for Submission to the National and American Leagues at Their Meetings in Chicago," August 27, 1946, unnumbered "Synopsis" page.

6. House Subcommittee on Study of Monopoly Power of the Committee on the Judiciary, *Hearings Before the Subcommittee on Study of Monopoly Power of the Committee on the Judiciary, Organized Baseball*, 497–505.

7. Twelve minor league teams opened the 1945 baseball season, excluding the independent Mexican League; in 1946 there were 43 minor leagues in operation. Johnson and Wolff, eds., *The Encyclopedia of Minor League Baseball*, 2d ed., 343–54.

8. Major League Steering Committee, "Report of Major League Steering Committee for Submission to the National and American

Leagues at Their Meetings in Chicago," August 27, 1946, 5.

9. Ibid.

10. Ibid., 10–12.

11. Lowenfish and Lupien, *The Imperfect Diamond*, 139–53.

12. House Subcommittee on Study of Monopoly Power of the Committee on the Judiciary, *Hearings Before the Subcommittee on Study of Monopoly Power of the Committee on the Judiciary, Organized Baseball*, 258–59.

13. Major League Steering Committee, "Report of Major League Steering Committee for Submission to the National and American Leagues at Their Meetings in Chicago," August 27, 1946, 12.

14. Those players were Ace T. Adams (New York Giants), Alejandro Carrasquel (Chicago White Sox), Roberto Estallela (Philadelphia Athletics), Harry Feldman (New York Giants), Murray Franklin (Detroit Tigers), Roland Gladu (Brooklyn Dodgers), Daniel Gardella (New York Giants), George Hausmann (New York Giants), Louis Klein (St. Louis Cardinals), Max Lanier (St. Louis Cardinals), Sal Maglie (New York Giants), Rene Monteagudo (Philadelphia Phillies), Fred Martin (St. Louis Cardinals), Mickey Owen (Brooklyn Dodgers), Louis Olmo (Brooklyn Dodgers), Napoleon Reyes (New York Giants), Adrian Zabala (New York Giants), and Roy Zimmerman (New York Giants). House Subcommittee on Study of Monopoly Power of the Committee on the Judiciary, *Hearings Before the Subcommittee on Study of Monopoly Power of the Committee on the Judiciary, Organized Baseball*, 1303.

15. Major League Steering Committee, "Report of Major League Steering Committee for Submission to the National and American Leagues at Their Meetings in Chicago," August 27, 1946, 17.

16. Ibid., 20.

17. All data for attendance and games played derived from Thorn, *Total Baseball*.

18. All attendance figures in the preceding paragraphs are from Thorn, *Total Baseball*, 2420–2423.

19. Voigt, *American Baseball, Volume II*, 230–33.

20. Red Barber and Robert Creamer, *Rhubarb in the Catbird Seat* (Lincoln: University of Nebraska Press, 1968), 34.

21. House Subcommittee on Study of Monopoly Power of the Committee on the Judiciary, *Hearings Before the Subcommittee on Study of Monopoly Power of the Committee on the Judiciary, Organized Baseball*, 1603, 1607.

22. Walker and Bellamy, "Baseball on Television," 5–13.

23. House Subcommittee on Study of Mo-

nopoly Power of the Committee on the Judiciary, *Hearings Before the Subcommittee on Study of Monopoly Power of the Committee on the Judiciary, Organized Baseball*, 1602–1610.

24. Ibid., 1610.

25. Ibid., 1615.

26. Ibid., 1599–1600.

27. Ibid., 1599, 1600, 1615.

28. Johnson and Wolff, eds., *The Encyclopedia of Minor League Baseball*, 348–87, 421–27.

29. House Subcommittee on Study of Monopoly Power of the Committee on the Judiciary, *Hearings Before the Subcommittee on Study of Monopoly Power of the Committee on the Judiciary, Organized Baseball*, 1616.

30. Ibid., 1621.

31. Ibid., 1625.

32. Daniel Gardella, Max Lanier, and Fred Martin all filed lawsuits against various entities and individuals that were part of Organized Baseball.

33. All quotes from this case taken from *Gardella v. Chandler*, 172 F.2d 402 (United States Court of Appeals Second Circuit).

34. White, *Creating the National Pastime*, 294–96.

35. House Subcommittee on Study of Monopoly Power of the Committee on the Judiciary, *Hearings Before the Subcommittee on Study of Monopoly Power of the Committee on the Judiciary, Organized Baseball*, 289–90.

36. Glenn C. Altschuler and Stuart M. Blumin, *The G.I. Bill: A New Deal for Veterans* (New York: Oxford University Press, 2009), 126.

37. Ibid., 129.

38. Lanctot, *Negro League Baseball*, x.

39. John Paul Hill, "Commissioner A. B. 'Happy' Chandler and the Integration of Major League Baseball: A Reassessment," *NINE* 19, no. 1 (Fall 2010): 32–39.

40. Major League Steering Committee, "Report of Major League Steering Committee for Submission to the National and American Leagues at Their Meetings in Chicago," August 27, 1946, 20.

41. Hill, "Commissioner A. B. 'Happy' Chandler and the Integration of Major League Baseball: A Reassessment," 32.

42. Professional hockey at levels below that of the NHL did have some limited integration, or at least made attempts at it. For example, in 1953 the Seattle Bombers of the Western Hockey League brought in black players Alf Lewsey and Bill Geary for tryouts. Neither made the roster for the 1953–54 season, but both appeared in a pre-season exhibition game against the NHL's New York Rangers on September 27, 1953. See Jeff Obermeyer, *Hockey in Seattle* (Charleston, SC: Arcadia, 2004), 60.

43. John Wilson, *Playing by the Rules: Sport, Society, and the State* (Detroit: Wayne State University Press, 1994), 57.

Bibliography

Archives

National Baseball Hall of Fame and Museum, Cooperstown, New York. Baseball and World War II Archive Files.
Washington State Historical Society, Tacoma, Washington. Seattle Rainier Baseball Club Records Collection.

Legal Cases

Federal Baseball Club of Baltimore, Inc. v. National League of Professional Baseball Clubs, et al., 259 U.S. 400 (Supreme Court of the United States, 1922).
Fishgold v. Sullivan Drydock & Repair Corp. ET AL. 328 U.S. 275 (Supreme Court of the United States, 1946).
Gardella v. Chandler, 172 F.2d 402 (United States Court of Appeals Second Circuit, 1949).
Niemiec v. Seattle Rainier Baseball Club, Inc., 67 F. Supp. 705 (U.S. Dist. Ct., 1946).
Sundra v. St. Louis American League Baseball Club, 87 F. Supp. 471 (U.S. Dist. Ct., 1949).

Primary Sources

Addington, L.H. "Important Meeting." *Baseball Magazine*, December 1942, 325, 331.
_____. "Let's Go!" *Baseball Magazine*, March 1942, 456, 476.
_____. "The Minor League Picture." *Baseball Magazine*, May 1945, 425, 429.
_____. "War Effort." *Baseball Magazine*. September 1942, 469, 473.
Anderson, Arthur O. W. "What Do the Fans Prefer?" *Baseball Magazine*, June 1942, 315–16, 320–21.
"Baker Refuses to Modify "Work" Rule for Baseball." *The Sporting News*. July 25, 1918, 2.
"Baseball a 'Must,' Writers Are Told." *New York Times,* February 5, 1945.
"Baseball Leaders Won't Let White Sox Return to the Game." *New York Times,* August 4, 1921.
Baseball Magazine. "Baseball's 1942 War-Aid Showing." March 1943, 468.
_____. "Editorial Comment." February 1945, 289.
"Baseball May Ask for Government Help." *New York Times,* February 4, 1945.
"Baseball Raised $329,555." *New York Times,* November 1, 1944.
"Baseball's Role Praised." *New York Times,* January 11, 1945.
"Baseball Should be Ruled Out with Racing, Says Military Affairs Committee Chairman." *New York Times,* January 19, 1945.
Bloodgood, Clifford. "All-Star Double Feature." *Baseball Magazine,* September 1942, 459–61, 470.
_____. "The Long, Long Trail." *Baseball Magazine*, November 1942, 560–63, 572–73.
Brands, Edgar G. "Few Leading Players Included in Early Draft Numbers Drawn." *The Sporting News*, November 7, 1940, 10.
_____. "Manpower Regulations Will Govern." *The Sporting News*, February 10, 1944, 1–2.
_____. "Political Slugfest Marks Minors' Meet." *The Sporting News*, December 9, 1943, 3, 6, 7.
"Brooklyn Ball Club Announces All-Out Program in Support of War Effort." *New York Times,* February 18, 1942.
Brougham, Royal. "Niemiec Hearing Closes, Judge Takes Case Under Advisement." *The Sporting News*, June 26, 1946, 10.

Bryson, Bill. "The Navy Goes for Baseball." *Baseball Magazine*, August 1943, 313–14, 318.

Carmichael, John P. "Carmichael Visits Hank at Camp Custer." *The Sporting News*, May 15, 1940, 4.

Chadwick, Stephen. Letter to Victor Ford Collins, May 17, 1946. Seattle Rainier Baseball Club Records Collection, Washington State Historical Society, Tacoma, WA.

_____. Letter to Joseph C. Hostetler, November 7, 1946. Seattle Rainier Baseball Club Records Collection, Washington State Historical Society, Tacoma, WA.

Chandler, Happy. Letter to Roscoe C. Torrance, June 2, 1946. Seattle Rainier Baseball Club Records Collection, Washington State Historical Society, Tacoma, WA.

_____. Western Union Telegram to Roscoe Torrance, June 25, 1946. Seattle Rainier Baseball Club Records Collection, Washington State Historical Society, Tacoma, WA.

_____, and Vance Trimble. *Heroes, Plain Folks, and Skunks: The Life and Times of Happy Chandler*. Chicago: Bonus, 1989.

"'Conduct Detrimental to Baseball,' Landis Reply to Rebel Loops' Appeal." *The Sporting News*, December 9, 1943, 3.

Cross, Harry. "Auctioning Yankee, Dodger, and Giant Players Nets $123,850,000 in War-Bond Pledges." *New York Herald-Tribune*, June 9, 1943.

Daley, Arthur. "Sports of the Times." *New York Times*, January 9, 1945.

_____. "Sports of the Times: Baseball Learns the Score." *New York Times*, January 25, 1945.

_____. "Sports of the Times: In the Wake of the Baseball Meetings." *New York Times*, December 15, 1944.

"Dallas Club Fixed Against Draft Loss." *The Sporting News*. February 14, 1918, 6.

Daniel, Daniel. "Baseball's War Effort Seeks Vast Sums for Vital Causes." *Baseball Magazine*, June 1942, 291–92, 332.

_____. "Drafting of Fathers Builds Major Manpower Problems for Big Leagues." *Baseball Magazine*, December 1943, 221–22, 247–48.

_____. "Gotham Would Run F.D.R. for President." *The Sporting News*, January 22, 1942, 3.

_____. "High Prices Lowering Giants' Trade Hopes." *The Sporting News*, October 24, 1940.

_____. "Keyed Up Yankees Put Lock on Slump." *The Sporting News*, July 16, 1942, 17.

_____. "Major Leagues Have Proud Record in War and Relief Enterprises." *Baseball Magazine*, September 1943, 327–28, 358.

_____. "Major Leagues Tack on Service Stars as Players Answer Call of Uncle Sam." *Baseball Magazine*, May 1942, 533–44, 571–73.

_____. "Manpower Problems? Sure! But Baseball Will Carry On." *Baseball Magazine*, March 1943, 443–44, 478–79.

_____. "Nearly 100 New Players Set Rookie Record for the Major Leagues." *Baseball Magazine*, June 1942, 343–44.

_____. "Roosevelt Saved Baseball With His 1942 Letter to Judge Landis." *Baseball Magazine*, June 1945, 227–28, 249.

_____. "'Smile and Take It' Policy on U.S. Draft." *The Sporting News*, November 14, 1940, 6.

_____. "U.S. Likely to Keep Draft from Heavy Inroads on Majors." *The Sporting News*, April 24, 1941, 1.

_____. "Wartime Baseball 'Rationing' Finds Fans Tolerant, Eager for Game." *Baseball Magazine*, April 1944, 367–68, 396.

Davis, Ralph S. "Reason for Protest on Johnson's Plan." *The Sporting News*, November 29, 1917, 5.

Dawson, James P. "Brooklyn Ball Club Announces All-Out Program in Support of War Effort." *New York Times*, February 18, 1942.

"Decision on War Prices Most Important Work by Majors." *The Sporting News*, February 21, 1918, 1.

Dodson, Dan W. "The Integration of Negroes in Baseball." *Journal of Educational Sociology* 28, no. 2 (October 1954): 73–82.

Drebinger, John. "Dodgers Defeat Giants in Twilight Game Raising $59,859 for Navy Relief." *New York Times*, May 9, 1942.

_____. "The Increase in Major League Night Baseball." *Baseball Magazine*, April 1942, 497–98, 523–24.

_____. "Majors Set Plans to Pick New Head." *New York Times*, December 13, 1944.

_____. "Ott Pays $50,000 for First Baseman." *New York Times*, December 12, 1941.

_____. "Sports Thrived During 1942 as Part of War Effort." *New York Times*, December 20, 1942.

_____. "Sports of the Times: Will Baseball Go Spartan Again?" *New York Times*, August 9, 1944.

_____. "This Changing Baseball World."

Baseball Magazine, February 1943, 387–88, 426–27.

Drohan, John. "Cronin Changes Uniforms." *Baseball Magazine*, May 1943, 521–22, 550.

Farrington, Dick. "Drafting Papas Would Hit 22 Cards." *The Sporting News*, February 18, 1943, 5.

"Favor Baseball in Poll." *New York Times*, March 25, 1943.

Freeburg, Dwight. "War-Time Baseball." *Baseball Magazine*, April 1942, 509–10, 522.

"Further World Series Aid to U.S." *The Sporting News*, November 26, 1942.

Gallup, George. "Pro Sports for Duration of War Heavily Favored in Poll of Public." *New York Times*, April 15, 1942.

Gould, James M. "The President Says 'Play Ball.'" *Baseball Magazine*, March 1942, 435–36, 475.

_____. "They Also Serve." *Baseball Magazine*, June 1942, 305–6, 331.

_____. "War and Baseball." *Baseball Magazine*, February 1942, 389–90, 427.

_____. "What's Happened to the Ball?" *Baseball Magazine*, September 1942, 435–36, 475.

"Greenberg and Briggs Do Their Bit." *The Sporting News*, May 1, 1941, 4.

"Griff Visits Roosevelt." *The Sporting News*, March 15, 1945, 12.

"Happy Urges One-City Headquarters for Game." *The Sporting News*, July 31, 1946, 2.

House Subcommittee on Study of Monopoly Power of the Committee on the Judiciary. *Report of the House Subcommittee on Study of Monopoly Power of the Committee on the Judiciary, Organized Baseball*. 82nd Cong., 2nd sess., 1952, H. Rep. 2002.

House Subcommittee on Study of Monopoly Power of the Committee on the Judiciary. *Hearings Before the Subcommittee on Study of Monopoly Power of the Committee on the Judiciary, Organized Baseball*. Serial No. 1, Part 6, 82nd Cong., 1st sess., 1951.

Jennings, Wilbur. "'Players Joining Shipyard Clubs Contract Jumpers'—Bramham." *The Sporting News*, July 1, 1943, 4.

"Johnson Makes His Idea on Draft Plan." *The Sporting News*, November 29, 1917, 2.

Jones, Major Gordon. Letter to Will Harridge, January 5, 1945. World War II File, National Baseball Hall of Fame and Museum, Cooperstown, New York.

"Judge Landis Dies; Baseball Czar, 78." *New York Times*, November 26, 1944.

Kieran, John. "Sports of the Times: A Bad Play for Baseball." *New York Times*, May 21, 1942.

Landis, Kenesaw Mountain. Letter to Franklin D. Roosevelt, January 14, 1941. Franklin D. Roosevelt Library, Hyde Park, NY.

"Landis Disclaims Plea for Baseball." *New York Times*, February 12, 1944.

"Landis in Warning of Bogus War Aid." *New York Times*, June 5, 1942.

"Landis on Negro Players." *The Sporting News*, July 23, 1942, 11.

Lieb, Frederick G. "Cards Live Up to Blue-Ribbon Billing; Browns Back in 'Hitless Wonder' Ways." *The Sporting News*, April 25, 1946, 6.

Lowenfish, Leo, and Tony Lupien. *The Imperfect Diamond*. New York: Stein and Day, 1980.

Lowry, Philip J. *Green Cathedrals: The Ultimate Celebration of Major League and Negro League Ballparks*. New York: Walker & Company, 2006.

"M'Nutt Clarifies Baseball Status." *New York Times*, January 7, 1943.

Major League Steering Committee. "Report of Major League Steering Committee for Submission to the National and American Leagues at Their Meetings in Chicago." August 27, 1946.

Mann, Arthur. "Baseball's Peace-Time 4-F's." *Baseball Magazine*, May 1944, 419–20.

_____. "Baseball's Unseen Sacrifices." *Baseball Magazine*, June 1944, 221–22.

_____. "Gamest of the Game." *Baseball Magazine*, August 1945, 297–98, 319.

"Martin, House Minority Leader, Sees Curbs in War as 'Foolish'—Wadsworth Among Other Ex-Players Lauding Game." *New York Times*, January 9, 1942.

M.B.E. Letter to the Sports Editor of the *New York Times* dated May 23, 1942. *New York Times*, May 23, 1942.

McLinn, Stoney. "Mulcahy's Number 2231st from Bowl." *The Sporting News*, November 7, 1940, 9.

"Military Idea Games's Savior Since Declaration of War." *The Sporting News*. April 12, 1917, 1.

"Minors' Outlook Rests Upon Manpower Action." *The Sporting News*, March 15, 1945, 5.

"Niemiec's Case Watched." *Seattle Times*, June 25, 1946.

1904 Reach Baseball Guide.

"No Questions on Players' Draft Status." *The Sporting News*, February 17, 1944, 8, 12.

"Off-Hour Contests Favored by M'Nutt." *New York Times*, May 13, 1943.

"ODT Asks 25% Cut in Baseball Travel." *New York Times*, February 22, 1945.

Parrott, Harold. "Many Notables Make Stirring Talks for Sport." *The Sporting News*, February 11, 1943, 1–2.

"Players Seen Free to Quit War Jobs." *New York Times*, January 9, 1943.

Povich, Shirley. "Defiant Griff Turns to 'Twi-Night' Ball." *The Sporting News*, July 16, 1942, 1.

"Preparing for Baseball Season Up to Clubs, McNutt Says." *New York Times*, February 16, 1943.

Repetto, Louis A. Letter to National Baseball Hall of Fame, September 30, 1994. World War II File, National Baseball Hall of Fame and Museum, Cooperstown, NY.

Roosevelt, Franklin D. Letter to Kenesaw Mountain Landis, January 15, 1941. Franklin D. Roosevelt Library, Hyde Park, NY.

Ruhl, Oscar K. "Court Hears Sundra Case vs. Browns." *The Sporting News*, June 15, 1949, 4.

"Sanctioning of Spectator Sports by Congress Asked to Aid Morale." *New York Times*, March 3, 1943.

Seattle Rainiers Baseball Club. "Minutes of Special Meeting, Board of Directors." June 10, July 22, November 25, 1946. Seattle Rainier Baseball Club Records Collection, Washington State Historical Society, Tacoma, WA.

"Service Men to Get Bat and Ball Kits." *New York Times*, December 31, 1941.

Simmons, Herbert. "Cork-Balata Center for Duration Baseball." *Baseball Magazine*, May 1943, 523–24.

_____. "Lieut. Mickey Cochrane, U.S.N." *Baseball Magazine*, March 1943, 459–60, 473.

_____. "The Road Ahead." *Baseball Magazine*, October 1945, 363–64.

Simons, Herbert. "Cherchez La Femme." *Baseball Magazine*, March 1944, 336, 358, 360.

_____. "Cork-Balata Center for Duration Baseball." *Baseball Magazine*, May 1943, 523–24, 550.

_____. "Major League Service Stars Now Number 468." *Baseball Magazine*, January 1945, 269–70.

_____. "The Road Ahead." *Baseball Magazine*, October 1945, 363–64.

Skiff, Bill, and R.C. Torrance. Letter to TO

WHOM IT MAY CONCERN, April 20, 1946. Seattle Rainier Baseball Club Records Collection, Washington State Historical Society, Tacoma, WA.

Spink, J.G. Taylor. "Cardinals Favored on Pitching, Yankees on Power." *The Sporting News*, April 18, 1946, 5.

_____. "A Declaration of Policy." *The Sporting News*, February 17, 1944, 8.

_____. "Hot Heads Make Cool Customers." *The Sporting News*, December 9, 1943, 10.

_____. "It's Not the Same Game in Japan." *The Sporting News*, December 18, 1941, 4.

_____. "No Good From Raising Race Issue." *The Sporting News*, August 6, 1942, 4.

_____. *Sporting News Baseball Guide and Record Book 1943*. St. Louis: Charles C. Spink & Son, 1943.

_____. *Sporting News Baseball Guide and Record Book 1944*. St. Louis: Charles C. Spink & Son, 1944.

_____. *Sporting News Baseball Guide and Record Book 1945*. St. Louis: Charles C. Spink & Son, 1945.

_____. *Sporting News Baseball Guide and Record Book 1946*. St. Louis: Charles C. Spink & Son, 1946.

_____. "Stirring Wartime Pledges Mark Fun-Filled N.Y. Writers' Frolic." *The Sporting News*, February 5, 1942, 2.

The Sporting News, June 13, 1918, 4.

The Sporting News. August 19, 1917, 4.

The Sporting News. August 23, 1917, 4.

The Sporting News, November 2, 1933, 4.

Tarvin, A. H. "Baseball and the War Again." *Baseball Magazine*, January 1943, 369–70, 374–75.

Thompson, Denman. "Football Kicks Up Annual Griff Worry." *The Sporting News*, September 5, 1940, 5.

Torrance, R.C. Letter to A.B. "Happy" Chandler, April 27, 1946. Seattle Rainier Baseball Club Records Collection, Washington State Historical Society, Tacoma, WA.

"Troops Will Hear Games." *New York Times*, April 13, 1944.

"War Effort Comes First." *New York Times*, November 17, 1942.

"War Relief Figures Given." *New York Times*, February 8, 1945.

Whitman, Burt. "Exemption Plea a Mistake." *The Sporting News*, February 14, 1918, 5.

Winerip, Sgt. Harold. "Baseball in Their Hearts." *Baseball Magazine*, February, 1945, 305, 318.

_____. "Of Baseball and Soldiers." *Baseball Magazine*, December, 1944, 222.

_____. "The Tales They Tell." *Baseball Magazine*, July, 1945, 258, 283.

"WMC Decision Lets Baseball Players Leave War Plants." *New York Times*, March 22, 1945.

Wood, John C. Letter to National Baseball Hall of Fame, April 6, 2001. World War II File, National Baseball Hall of Fame and Museum, Cooperstown, New York.

Zielke, George. "Game Okayed by FDR in 'Pinch-Hitter' Form." *The Sporting News*, March 22, 1945, 8.

_____. "Settlement of Campbell's G.I. Case 'No Precedent,' Declares Griffith." *The Sporting News*, August 14, 1942, 13.

Secondary Sources

Abrams, Roger I. *Legal Bases: Baseball and the Law*. Philadelphia: Temple University Press, 1998.

Altschuler, Glenn C., and Stuart M. Blumin. *The G.I. Bill: A New Deal for Veterans*. New York: Oxford University Press, 2009.

Ardell, Jean. *Breaking Into Baseball: Women and the National Pastime*. Carbondale: Southern Illinois University Press, 2005.

Barber, Red, and Robert Creamer. *Rhubarb in the Catbird Seat*. Lincoln: University of Nebraska Press, 1968.

Bauer, Carlos. *The Early Coast League Statistical Record, 1903–1957*. San Diego: Baseball Press Books, 2004.

Bazer, Gerald, and Steven Culbertson. "Baseball During World War II: The Reaction and Encouragement of Franklin Delano Roosevelt and Others." *NINE* 10, no. 1 (2001): 114–29.

Bedingfield, Gary. *Baseball's Dead of World War II: A Roster of Professional Players Who Died in Service*. Jefferson, NC: McFarland, 2010).

Block, David. *Baseball Before We Knew It: A Search for the Roots of the Game*. Lincoln: University of Nebraska Press, 2005.

Briley, Ron. "Danny Gardella and Baseball's Reserve Clause: A Working-Class Stiff Blacklisted in Cold War America." *NINE* 19, no. 2 (Fall 2010): 52–66.

Bullock, Steven R. *Playing for Their Nation: Baseball and the American Military during World War II*. Lincoln: University of Nebraska Press, 2004.

_____. "Playing for Their Nation: The American Military and Baseball During World War II." *Journal of Sport History* 27, no. 1 (Spring 2000): 67–89.

Clark, Dick, and Larry Lester, eds. *The Negro League Book*. Cleveland: The Society for American Baseball Research, 1994.

Cramer, Richard Ben. *Joe DiMaggio: The Hero's Life*. New York: Simon & Schuster, 2000.

Crepeau, Richard. *America's Diamond Mind*. Lincoln: University of Nebraska Press, 1980.

Dupuy, R. Ernest, and Trevor N. Dupuy, eds. *The Harper Encyclopedia of Military History*, 4th ed. New York: HarperCollins, 1993.

Feldman, Jay. "Baseball Behind Barbed Wire." *National Pastime* 12 (1992): 37–41.

Fidler, Merrie A. *The Origins and History of the All-American Girls Professional Baseball League*. Jefferson, NC: McFarland, 2006.

Finoli, David. *For the Good of the Country: World War II Baseball in the Major and Minor Leagues*. Jefferson, NC: McFarland, 2002.

Gilbert, Bill. *They Also Served: Baseball and the Home Front, 1941–1945*. New York: Crown, 1992.

Goldstein, Richard. *Spartan Seasons: How Baseball Survived the Second World War*. New York: Macmillan, 1980.

Graham, Frank. "When Baseball Went to War." *Sports Illustrated* (April 17, 1967): 78–86.

Hill, John Paul. "Commissioner A.B. 'Happy' Chandler and the Integration of Major League Baseball: A Reassessment." *NINE* 19, no. 1 (Fall 2010): 28–51.

Johnson, Lloyd and Miles Wolff, eds. *The Encyclopedia of Minor League Baseball*, 2d ed. Durham: Baseball America, 1997.

Jordan, David M., Larry R. Gerlach, and John P. Rossi. "A Baseball Myth Exploded: Bill Veeck and the 1943 Sale of the Phillies." *National Pastime* 18 (1998): 3–13.

Keegan, John. *The First World War*. New York: Vintage Books, 1998.

Kirsch, George B. *Baseball in Blue and Gray: The National Pastime During the Civil War*. Princeton: Princeton University Press, 2003.

Kolbert, Jered Benjamin. "Major League Baseball During World War II." *National Pastime* 14 (1994): 102–5.

Lamster, Mark. *Spalding's World Tour: The Epic Adventure that Took Baseball Around the Globe and Made it America's Game*. New York: PublicAffairs, 2006.

Lanctot, Neil. *Negro League Baseball: The Rise and Fall of a Black Institution*. Philadelphia: University of Pennsylvania Press, 2004.

Lewis, Robert F., II. *Smart Ball: Marketing the Myth and Managing the Reality of Major League Baseball.* Jackson: University Press of Mississippi, 2010.

Lindeman, Eduard C. "Recreation and Morale." *American Journal of Sociology* 47, no. 3 (November 1941): 394–405.

Malloy, Jerry. "Black Bluejackets." *The National Pastime* (Winter 1985): 72–77.

McGrath, John J. *The Other End of the Spear: The Tooth-to-Tail Ratio (T3R) in Modern Military Operations.* Fort Leavenworth, KS: Combat Studies Institute Press, 2007.

Mead, William B. *Baseball Goes to War: Stars Don Khaki, 4-Fs Vie for Pennant.* Washington, DC: Broadcast Interview Source, 1998.

_____. "Shooting Ended and the Baseball War Resumed." *Boston Globe*, April 29, 1978.

Miller, Delbert C. "The Measurement of National Morale." *American Sociological Review* 6, no. 4 (August 1941): 487–98.

Moskowitz, Eric. "The Sporting News During World War II." *National Pastime* 23 (2003): 44–54.

Mrozek, Donald J. "The Interplay of Metaphor and Practice in the U.S. Defense Establishment's Use of Sport, 1940–1950." *Journal of American Culture* 7, no. 1 (Spring/Summer 1984): 54–59.

Noll, Roger G., ed. *Government and the Sports Business.* Washington, DC: The Brookings Institution, 1974.

Pietrusza, David. *Judge and Jury: The Life and Times of Judge Kenesaw Mountain Landis.* South Bend: Diamond Communications, 1998.

Raley, Dan. *Pitchers of Beer—The Story of the Seattle Rainiers.* Lincoln: University of Nebraska Press, 2011.

Rossi, John. "The Nugent Era: Phillies Phlounder in Phutility." *National Pastime* 25 (2005): 15–18.

Sklaroff, Lauren Rebecca. "Constructing G.I. Joe Louis: Cultural Solutions to the 'Negro Problem' during World War II." *Journal of American History* 89, no. 3 (December 2002): 958–83.

Spink, J.G. Taylor. *Judge Landis and 25 Years of Baseball.* St. Louis: The Sporting News, 1974.

"They Said It." *Sports Illustrated*, November 19, 1962, 16.

Thompson, Dick. "Baseball's Greatest Hero." *Baseball Research Journal* 30 (2001): 3–10.

Thorn, John. *Baseball in the Garden of Eden: The Secret History of the Early Game.* New York: Simon & Schuster, 2011.

_____, ed. *Total Baseball: The Ultimate Encyclopedia*, 8th ed. Toronto: SPORT Media, 2004.

Tygiel, Jules. "Revisiting Bill Veeck and the 1943 Phillies." *Baseball Research Journal* 30 (2001): 3–10.

Veeck, Bill, and Ed Linn. *Veeck as in Wreck.* Chicago: University of Chicago Press, 1962.

Vignola, Patricia. "The Patriotic Pinch Hitter: The AAGBL and How the American Woman Earned a Permanent Spot on the Roster." *NINE* 12, no. 2 (2004): 102–11.

Voigt, David Quentin. *American Baseball, Volume I: From the Gentleman's Sport to the Commissioner System.* University Park: Pennsylvania State University Press, 1983.

_____. *American Baseball, Volume II: From the Commissioners to Continental Expansion.* University Park: Pennsylvania State University Press, 1983.

Wakefield, Wanda Ellen. *Playing to Win: Sports and the American Military, 1898–1945.* Albany: State University of New York Press, 1997.

Walker, James R., and Robert V. Bellamy, Jr. "Baseball on Television." *NINE* 11, no. 2 (2003): 1–15.

Ward, Geoffrey C., and Ken Burns. *Baseball: An Illustrated History.* New York: Alfred A. Knopf, 1994.

Weaver, Bill L. "The Black Press and the Assault on Professional Baseball's 'Color Line.'" *Phylon* 40, no. 4 (4th Quarter 1979): 303–17.

White, G. Edward. *Creating the National Pastime: Baseball Transforms Itself 1903–1953.* Princeton: Princeton University Press, 1996.

Wilson, John. *Playing by the Rules: Sport, Society, and the State.* Detroit: Wayne State University Press, 1994.

Yount, Dan. "Battle of the Bulge Massacre Cover-Up: 'They Were Just 11 Black Soldiers.'" *Cincinnati Herald*, December 18, 2010.

Websites

http://www.baseball-reference.com
http://www.baseballinwartime.com
http://www.baseballsgreatestsacrifice.com
http://www.jimmyscotthighandtight.com

Index

Numbers in *bold italics* indicate pages with photographs.